Tomoo Ishida

The Royal Dynasties in Ancient Israel

Tomoo Ishida

The Royal Dynasties in Ancient Israel

A Study on the Formation and Development of Royal-Dynastic Ideology

Walter de Gruyter · Berlin · New York
1977

Beiheft zur Zeitschrift für die alttestamentliche Wissenschaft

Herausgegeben von Georg Fohrer

142

Library of Congress Cataloging in Publication Data

Ishida, Tomoo, 1931 –
The royal dynasties in ancient Israel.
(Beiheft zur Zeitschrift für die alttestamentliche Wissenschaft ; 142)
Originally presented as the author's thesis, Hebrew University of Jerusalem, 1974.
Includes indexes.
1. Jews – History – 1200-953 B. C. 2. Kings and rulers – Biblical teaching. I. Title. II. Series : Zeitschrift für die alttestamentliche Wissenschaft. Beihefte ; 142.
BS410. Z5 vol. 142 [DS121.55] 221'.08s [933'.004'924]
ISBN 3-11-006519-3 76-29049

CIP-Kurztitelaufnahme der Deutschen Bibliothek

Ishida , Tomoo
The royal dynasties in ancient Israel : a study on the formation and development of royal-dynastic ideology. – 1. Aufl. – Berlin, New York : de Gruyter, 1977.
(Zeitschrift für die alttestamentliche Wissenschaft : Beih. ; 142)
ISBN 3-11-006519-3

Printed in Germany
Satz und Druck: Rheingold-Druckerei, Mainz
Bindearbeiten: Lüderitz & Bauer, Berlin 61

To the memory of my parents
Tomoji Ishida (1881-1942)
Mitsuji Ishida (1891-1946)

Preface

The present study is the result of my doctoral dissertation which was submitted to the Faculty of Humanities and the Senate of the Hebrew University of Jerusalem in March 1974, and was approved by them in November of the same year. The work was carried out under the supervision of Professors A. Malamat and B. Mazar. Some revisions of the text and additions of the literature which appeared since that date have been introduced, but only to a limited extent.

Although I undertook the research for this study in 1968, it is clear that this is a product of my study in Jerusalem since 1963, where many prominent scholars and serious students are engaged with unparalleled enthusiasm in researches into the history, languages and other studies of ancient Israel and the ancient Near East. Without participating in these exciting academic activities in Jerusalem, I could have never produced this study. Therefore, I am much indebted to all my teachers and colleagues in Jerusalem who illuminated problems of my study directly and indirectly.

At this opportunity, I should like to express my special thanks to Professors A. Malamat and B. Mazar for their constant guidance and encouragement as the supervisors of my doctoral research and their most inspiring teaching, which I have enjoyed since the first year of my study in Jerusalem. Thanks are owed to those who took part in the seminar of the Hebrew University for the graduate students of the School of History of the Jewish People in Biblical Times, conducted by both my supervisors, where I read parts of the study and received valuable comments. I am very grateful to Professor K. Deller of Heidelberg and Professor H. Tadmor of Jerusalem, both of whom kindly showed me their unpublished manuscripts of Akkadian texts, which I could utilize in the study.

I owe thanks to the Hebrew University, the Memorial Foundation for Jewish Culture and the Ministry of Foreign Affairs of Israel for their generous grants, which enabled me to complete my ten-year study in Jerusalem.

I thank Professor G. Fohrer for his kind acceptance of my disserta tion in the series of Beihefte zur Zeitschrift für die alttestamentliche Wissenschaft. I am also obliged to Mr. M. Nurock for his help in improving my English text.

University of Tsukuba, Japan, August 1976 Tomoo Ishida

Table of Contents

Abbreviations

AfO	Archiv für Orientforschung
AHw	W. von Soden, Akkadisches Handwörterbuch, 1958–
AJSL	American Journal of Semitic Languages and Literatures
AKA	L. W. King, The Annals of the Kings of Assyria, I 1902
ANET	Ancient Near Eastern Texts relating to the Old Testament, ed. J. B. Pritchard, 1969³
AnSt	Anatolian Studies
ARAB	D. D. Luckenbill, Ancient Records of Assyria and Babylonia, I–II 1926–1927
ARI	A. K. Grayson, Assyrian Royal Inscriptions, I 1972
ARM	Archives royales de Mari, 1950–
ArOr	Archiv Orientální
ARW	Archiv für Religionswissenschaft
ASTI	Annual of the Swedish Theological Institute in Jerusalem
BA	The Biblical Archaeologist
BAR	The Biblical Archaeologist Reader
BASOR	Bulletin of the American Schools of Oriental Research
Bib	Biblica
BiOr	Bibliotheca Orientalis
Borger, Asarh.	R. Borger, Die Inschriften Asarhaddons Königs von Assyrien, 1967²
BoTU	E. Forrer, Die Boghazköi-Texte in Umschrift, I–II 1922–1926
BR	Biblical Research
BZ	Biblische Zeitschrift
BZAW	Beihefte zur Zeitschrift für die alttestamentliche Wissenschaft
CAD	The Assyrian Dictionary of the Oriental Institute of the University of Chicago, 1956–
CAH	The Cambridge Ancient History (revised edition), 1962–
CBQ	Catholic Biblical Quarterly
CH	Codex Hammurapi
CQR	Church Quarterly Review
CRAI	Comptes rendus de l'académie des inscriptions et belles-lettres
EA	J. A. Knudtzon, in collaboration with O. Weber & E. Ebeling, Die El-Amarna-Tafeln, I–II 1915
EI	Eretz-Israel
EncBib	Encyclopaedia Biblica, 1950– (Hebrew)
ET	English Translation
EThL	Ephemerides Theologicae Lovanienses
FuF	Forschungen und Fortschritte
HAB	F. Sommer & A. Falkenstein, Die hethitisch-akkadische Bilingue des Hattušili I (Labarna II), 1938

HThR	Harvard Theological Review
HUCA	Hebrew Union College Annual
IAK	E. Ebeling, B. Meissner & E. F. Weidner, Die Inschriften der altassyrischen Könige, 1926
IEJ	Israel Exploration Journal
JANES	The Journal of the Ancient Near Eastern Society of Columbia University
JAOS	Journal of the American Oriental Society
JBL	Journal of Biblical Literature
JCS	Journal of Cuneiform Studies
JEA	Journal of Egyptian Archaeology
JESHO	Journal of Economic and Social History of the Orient
JHS	Journal of Hellenic Studies
JNES	Journal of Near Eastern Studies
JNSL	Journal of Northwest Semitic Languages
JPOS	Journal of the Palestine Oriental Society
JQR	Jewish Quarterly Review
JSS	Journal of Semitic Studies
JThS	Journal of Theological Studies
JWH	Journal of World History (= Cahiers d'histoire mondiale)
KAH	Keilschrifttexte aus Assur historischen Inhalts, I–II 1911–1922
KAI	H. Donner & W. Röllig, Kanaanäische und aramäische Inschriften, I–III 1966^2–1969^2
KBo	Keilschrifttexte aus Boghazköi, 1916–
KUB	Keilschrifturkunden aus Boghazköi, 1921–
MDOG	Mitteilungen der deutschen Orient-Gesellschaft
MIO	Mitteilungen des Instituts für Orientforschung, Berlin
NBKI	S. Langdon, Die neubabylonischen Königsinschriften, 1911
Noth, ÜSt	M. Noth, Überlieferungsgeschichtliche Studien, 1957^2
NRTh	Nouvelle revue théologique
OLZ	Orientalische Literaturzeitung
Or	Orientalia
OrAnt	Oriens Antiquus
OTS	Oudtestamentische Studiën
PEQ	Palestine Exploration Quarterly
PRU	Le palais royal d'Ugarit, 1955–
R	H. Rawlinson, The Cuneiform Inscriptions of Western Asia, I–IV 1861–1891
RA	Revue d'assyriologie et d'archéologie orientale
RB	Revue biblique
RHPhR	Revue d'histoire et de philosophie religieuses
RHR	Revue de l'histoire des religions
RLA	Reallexikon der Assyriologie, 1932–
SEÅ	Svensk Exegetisk Årsbok
Streck, Asb.	M. Streck, Assurbanipal und die letzten assyrischen Könige bis zum Untergang, 1916
Sturtevant, Chrest.	E. H. Sturtevant & G. Bechtel, Hittite Chrestomathy, 1935

SVT	Supplements to Vetus Testamentum
ThLZ	Theologische Literaturzeitung
ThR	Theologische Rundschau
ThS	Theological Studies
ThZ	Theologische Zeitschrift
UF	Ugarit-Forschungen
UT	C. H. Gordon, Ugaritic Textbook, 1965
VT	Vetus Testamentum
Weidner, Tn.	E. Weidner, Die Inschriften Tukulti-Ninurtas I. und seiner Nachfolger, 1959
WHJP	The World History of the Jewish People. First Series: Ancient Times, 1964–
WO	Die Welt des Orients
WZ Leipzig	Wissenschaftliche Zeitschrift der Karl-Marx-Universität Leipzig
ZA	Zeitschrift für Assyriologie
ZÄS	Zeitschrift für ägyptische Sprache und Altertumskunde
ZAW	Zeitschrift für die alttestamentliche Wissenschaft
ZDMG	Zeitschrift der deutschen morgenländischen Gesellschaft
ZDPV	Zeitschrift des deutschen Palästina-Vereins
ZThK	Zeitschrift für Theologie und Kirche

Chapter 1: Introductory

A. THE PROBLEMS

The men of Israel proposed to Gideon, who returned triumphant from the campaign against the Midianites: "Rule over us, you and your son and your grandson also; for you have delivered us out of the hand of Midian." According to the chronology of the biblical historiographer, this was the first attempt to found a hereditary rulership in Israel. But the proposal was declined by Gideon, who replied: "I will not rule over you, and my son will not rule over you; Yahweh will rule over you" (Judg 8 22–23).

Scholars have puzzled over the implications of this episode. Was the rulership which was offered to Gideon a kingship? If so, what was the nature of the kingship? Did he really espouse the idea of theocracy? If his reply is historically genuine, from where did he get the idea? But if its historicity is doubtful, in what historical *milieu* did the episode originate? Was it associated with Gideon only secondarily at a later time? Or does a historical reality lie behind it? All these and many other questions have been posed, and various answers have been propounded. In the present study, these problems will be dealt with only after investigation of various aspects of the royal dynasties, the embodiment of hereditary rulership in Israel. We think that an isolated event like the Gideon episode – there is no parallel in the pre-monarchical period – can be elucidated only in the broad context of the stream of tradition in ancient Israel.

Whatever its historical value, the episode doubtless preserves the basic problem of the origin of kingship in Israel. According to the story, when a victorious campaign gave proof of the divine designation of Gideon as the war-leader, his elevation to the ruler was suggested by the people. The same development took place after Saul returned from his brilliant triumph over the Ammonites. But he, unlike Gideon, accepted the people's proposal. Thus was the first Israelite monarchy founded – according to one of the narratives on the beginning of the kingship in Israel (I Sam 11). Analysing this process, Albrecht Alt[1] suggested that the Israelite monarchy came into existence when the

[1] Die Staatenbildung der Israeliten in Palästina (1930), in: Kleine Schriften, II 1953,

acclamation of the people was added to Yahweh's designation of the charismatic leader, and he called it a "charismatic monarchy". Developing this theory further, he came to the conclusion that the original and distinctive features of Israelite kingship can be found in the institution of the "charismatic monarchy", which, by its very nature, was inconsistent with the hereditary principle, while a hereditary monarchy developed only as a deviation from the genuine Israelite tradition. This thesis has influenced modern scholarship to no small extent[2].

Obviously, however, the rulership offered to Gideon was a hereditary office from the onset. Clearly, what the men of Israel asked of their charismatic leader was to establish a dynastic rule over them. How was this possible, if the charismatic rulership was never consistent with the hereditary principle? This leads us to another question. As is well known, charismatic war-leaders called *šop̄eṭîm* ruled over the tribes of Israel in the pre-monarchical period, and one of the basic features of their regime was its non-dynastic nature[3]. Now, when the people tried to elevate Gideon to ruler or Saul to king, they must have had the intention of changing the current political institution, which they felt to be inadequate to cope with critical situations. If the new regime was, indeed, non-dynastic, what could have been the innovation? We can put the question in another way. Did an institution such as a non-dynastic monarchy exist? This question will be dealt with in Chapters 2 and 3 of our study. To begin with, we shall survey briefly the monarchies in the neighbouring countries, since, according to a biblical tradition, the Israelite monarchy was established when the people of Israel decided to become "like all the nations" (I Sam 8 5. 20). Then we shall examine the situation of the first monarchy in Israel.

Chapters 4 to 6 will be devoted to the problem of the dynasty of David. The main question will be how the House of David succeeded in transforming a Judaean monarchy into the most distinguished royal

---

1–65 (ET The Formation of the Israelite State in Palestine, in: Essays on Old Testament History and Religion, 1966, 171–237); idem, Das Königtum in den Reichen Israel und Juda (1951), in: Kleine Schriften, II 116–134 (ET The Monarchy in the Kingdom of Israel and Judah, in: Essays, 239–259).

[2] For instance, M. Noth, Geschichte Israels, 1954², 162f. 168f. 208f. (ET The History of Israel, 1960², 176. 183. 228f.); R. de Vaux, Les institutions de l'Ancien Testament, I 1958, 145ff. (ET Ancient Israel, 1961, 94ff.); J. Bright, A History of Israel, 1972², 191. 234f.

[3] About the regime of the *šop̄eṭîm*, see A. Malamat, The Period of the Judges, in: WHJP, III 1971, 129ff.; idem, The Deliverer-Judge as the Leader in the Period of the Judges, in: Types of Leadership in the Biblical Period, 1971, 11–25 (Hebrew); T. Ishida, The Leaders of the Tribal Leagues "Israel" in the Pre-Monarchic Period, RB 80 (1973), 514–530; idem, in: EncBib, VII 1976, 577–583 (Hebrew).

dynasty in the history of Israel. The question will include many vexed problems such as the origin of the "house of Judah", the relation of the monarchy of David to the kingship of Saul, the formation and development of the royal-dynastic ideology and the meaning of Jerusalem as the dynastic seat. In the course of this investigation, it will become clear whether the House of David deviated from the Israelite tradition or developed it, when it attempted to establish dynastic rule over Israel.

In Chapter 7, we will inevitably come again to grips with the theory of Alt. He contended that the frequent changes of dynasties in the Northern Kingdom resulted from the ideology of the charismatic monarchy, while the kingdom of Judah enjoyed dynastic stability owing to the adoption of hereditary monarchy. Rather than endorse such a theoretical dichotomy, we will inquire into various factors which acted on the determining of succession to the throne in Judah and usurpation in the Northern Kingdom. A comparison of these factors will show the source of the difference between the two monarchies.

B. SOURCES AND APPROACH

The main source materials of our study are the biblical traditions preserved in the Books of Samuel, Kings and Chronicles. It is generally assumed that the Books of Samuel and Kings are either a part of the Deuteronomic Work of History redacted in the post-exilic period[4], or the Deuteronomic editions and compilations of older materials in the pre-exilic as well as in the post-exilic period[5]. It is also accepted that the Books of Chronicles are part of the Work of the Chronicler compiled in Jerusalem after the time of Ezra and Nehemiah[6]. Few can dispute the view that these historical works were made up of traditions transmitted in diverse forms through many generations until they were finally redacted into the present versions. That is to say, we cannot regard these biblical traditions as firsthand information on historical events which they recollect. Our question is how to extract historical data from them.

---

[4] Noth, ÜSt, 3ff.

[5] O. Eissfeldt, Einleitung in das Alte Testament, 1964³, 321ff. 357ff. 376ff. (ET The Old Testament. An Introduction, 1965, 241ff. 268ff. 281ff.); E. Sellin – G. Fohrer, Einleitung in das Alte Testament, 1965, 212. 233ff. 246ff. (ET Introduction to the Old Testament, 1968, 195. 215ff. 227ff.); H. Weippert, Die „deuteronomistischen" Beurteilungen der Könige von Israel und Juda und das Problem der Redaktion der Königsbücher, Bib 53 (1972), 301–339; F. M. Cross, Canaanite Myth and Hebrew Epic, 1973, 274ff.

[6] Noth, ÜSt, 110ff.; Eissfeldt, Einleitung, 718ff. (ET 530ff.); Sellin–Fohrer, Einleitung, 259ff. (ET 240ff.).

To begin with, we must take into account that the final redactors' outlook contributed to a great extent to shaping the final form. Undoubtedly, they selected certain traditions out of numerous source materials at their disposal, and then arranged and rewrote them. To what degree did they add their own compositions during this process? This is a matter of debate. Before discussing each problem, we shall postulate our assumption that the redactors' free additions must have been limited, as a rule, to editorial work, such as references to omitted sources and some modifications of the original. But we are reluctant to assume that they made free compositions stemming from their purely ideological point of view. In fact, if we start assuming without decisive evidence that this or that could be regarded as "late inventions" added to original traditions, our judgement of the historicity of each tradition will become arbitrary. Therefore, in attributing traditions to late redactors our approach will be minimalist.

It is a well known fact that biblical traditions occasionally include repetitions and contradictions in recording the same historical event. In general, scholars have tried to solve this problem by surmising either a combination of parallel narrative strands or the compilation of independent narrative units. We shall deal with these literary-critical problems each time they arise. In our opinion, however, it is more likely that the repetitions and contradictions reflect a situation in which the same event was reported by more than one reporter, whose opinions, interests and attitudes towards the event differed. Accordingly, it is natural that the same event produced a number of dissimilar reports. It is generally believed that different traditions concerning the same event originated from different places and periods and were combined by a redactor afterwards. But if our thesis is correct, they could come from a number of contemporaneous reporters. Moreover, it is also possible to suppose that disparate contemporaneous reports with varied nuances could mirror the ideological development of a relatively short space of time. This sort of development definitely took place in a rapidly changing society such as in the period of the early monarchies.

Thus, it becomes clear that each tradition was not composed as an unbiassed report on an event but was influenced by certain opinions, interests and attitudes towards it. This tendentious character of biblical traditions becomes clearer when they are collected as a work of historiography. There is no such work which has neither claim nor tendency. A historiography has always its own purpose – an apology, a legitimation or a polemic, that is, a specific message from the historiographer. Therefore, without first treating the historiographical problem, we cannot deal with any tradition in the right way.

To sum up, we will handle the biblical traditions under discussion as collections of historiographies composed more or less contemporaneously with the historical events which they report. Of course, we shall take into consideration that they underwent several redactions and sometimes accidental changes as well as intentional modifications before they finally took the present shape. But we are sceptical about hypothetical views that attribute a large number of traditions to narrators or redactors in later times.

As for other biblical traditions, especially those of the Pentateuch and the Psalms, we must look for their *Sitz im Leben* in a different way, since the nature of them is different from that of the historical ones. We are convinced, however, that part of Pentateuchal and most of the Psalmist traditions reflect the situations in the monarchical period.

We will also utilize non-biblical records for source material. Most are inscriptions from the ancient Near East. These texts of the neighbouring peoples can lend biblical traditions a wider historical perspective. They will be referred to, therefore, whenever they can shed light on biblical traditions or serve as comparative material. Thereby, it will be shown that ancient Israel had royal dynasties "like all the nations", but in its own distinctive way.

Chapter 2: The Dynastic Principle in the Monarchies in the Ancient Near East

A. THE DIVINE ELECTION AND THE DYNASTIC PRINCIPLE IN THE MESOPOTAMIAN AND EGYPTIAN MONARCHIES

Although there was a great difference between the Egyptians and the Mesopotamians in their conception of the nature of kingship[1], these two great civilizations in the ancient Near East were of one mind on the basic idea that a monarchy originating in the divine realm was the fundamental institution of their society. Whereas the Egyptians believed that the monarchy founded by Re, when he made the universe, was succeeded by gods and semi-divine spirits, and then by the Pharaohs[2], the Mesopotamians thought that kingship descended from heaven after men and animals were created[3].

Since kingship was of divine origin, the authority of the king was derived from divine election. Even in Egypt, where the king was a god, we are sometimes told that the throne was assured by special divine election. For instance, Thut-mose III (1490–1436) tells how the god Amon chose him when he was a young acolyte in the temple of Amon[4]. Thut-mose IV (1406–1398) likewise tells that his kingship was promised by the god of the Great Sphinx at Giza in his youth[5].

In Mesopotamia, where the king was a mere servant of the gods, every king ardently tells of his election by gods throughout all the history[6]. Some typical samples of texts read:

> "When Anu (and) Enlil had called Lipit-Ištar (1934–1924) . . . to the princeship of the land in order to establish justice in the land . . ."[7]

---

[1] See C. J. Gadd, Ideas of Divine Rule in the Ancient East, 1948, 33f.

[2] See W. Helck, Untersuchungen zu Manetho und den ägyptischen Königslisten, 1956, 4ff.; cf. A. Gardiner, Egypt of the Pharaohs, 1961, 46ff.

[3] See T. Jacobsen, The Sumerian King List, 1939, 58; ANET 265f.; cf. H. Frankfort, Kingship and the Gods, 1948, 237f.

[4] ANET 446f.

[5] ANET 449. The Egyptian kings wanted a divine legitimation for the throne only when their legitimacy was not perfect enough by birth. For the problems of the Thutmoside succession, see W. C. Hayes, Egypt: Internal Affairs from Tuthmosis I to the Death of Amenophis III, Part I, CAH II ch. IX, 1962, 5ff.

[6] Cf. P. Dhorme, La religion assyro-babylonienne, 1910, 150ff.; R. Labat, Le caractère religieux de la royauté assyro-babylonienne, 1939, 40ff.; Frankfort, Kingship and the Gods, 238ff.

[7] ANET 159.

"Ye great gods . . . who have enlarged the kingdom of Tiglath-Pileser (I) (1115–1077) . . . whom in your faithful hearts ye have chosen, and whom ye have crowned with a lofty diadem, and did solemnly appoint to be king over the land of Enlil."[8]
"For me, Nabonidus (555–539) . . . in whose heart was no thought of kingship, the gods and goddesses prayed (to Sin) and Sin called me to kingship."[9]
"He (i. e. Marduk) scanned and looked (through) all the countries, searching for a righteous ruler willing to lead him (in the annual procession). (Then) he pronounced the name of Cyrus (II) (538–530), king of Anshan, declared him to be(come) the ruler of all the world."[10]

Small wonder that divine election was practically the sole basis of the authority of usurpers like Sargon (2334–2279), founder of the dynasty of Akkad, or Nabopolassar (625–605), founder of the Chaldean dynasty. While the former recounts that he was a fatherless deserted child brought up as a gardener of one Akki before Ištar chose him as the king of Akkad[11], the latter does not hesitate to confess that he was merely a "son of nobody" (*mār lā mammānim*) before Marduk called him to be ruler over the land and the people[12].

Remarkably, some Assyrian kings apparently attached more importance to divine election than to royal lineage, even when they undoubtedly belonged to the royal house. In his prayer to Ištar, Aššurnaṣirpal I (1050–1032) narrates his unexpected election by the goddess:

"I was born in the midst of the mountains, which nobody knew;
I did not think about your rulership, nor prayed constantly;
Neither the people of Assyria were acquainted with nor turned to your godhead.
You are Ištar, the awesome mistress of the gods;
By lifting up your eyes you appointed me, and desired my rulership.
You took me out of the mountains,
and called me to be shepherd of men."[13]

It is unlikely, however, that this prayer is a proof, as H. Frankfort[14] maintains, that "even in Late Assyrian times divine election and not

---

[8] ARAB I § 217; AKA 29 f. I 15–22.
[9] ANET 562; Gadd, The Harran Inscriptions of Nabonidus, AnSt 8 (1958), 56f. I 7–11.
[10] ANET 315; F. H. Weissbach, Die Keilinschriften der Achämeniden, 1911, 2f. a 11–12.
[11] ANET 119.
[12] NBKI 66 no. 4 line 4; cf. AHw 601a.
[13] R. E. Brünnow, Assyrian Hymns, ZA 5 (1890), 67 obv. 22–27; W. von Soden, apud A. Falkenstein, Sumerische und akkadische Hymnen und Gebete, 1953, 264ff.
[14] Kingship and the Gods 239; cf. Dhorme, La religion assyro-babylonienne, 156; Labat, Le caractère religieux, 77. They mistakenly attribute this prayer to Aššurnaṣirpal II instead of I.

descent was regarded as the source of the king's authority." Admittedly, Šamši-Adad IV (1054–1051), one of the sons of Tiglath-Pileser I, had scarcely any hope of becoming king of Assyria when Aššurnaṣirpal was born to him. But he seized the throne by force and left it to his son[15]. The prayer of Aššurnaṣirpal doubtless reflects this situation[16]. Yet it should not be overlooked that he mentions his royal lineage before relating Ištar's election: "I am Aššurnaṣirpal ... the son of Šamši-Adad, the king..."[17] Obviously, his authority was derived not from divine election alone but also from his royal lineage.

One of the reasons for laying stress on divine election in Assyria can be found in the custom that the right of primogeniture was not regarded as the absolute basis for the royal succession[18]. Thus Esarhaddon (680–669) speaks of his installation as crown prince:

> "I was (indeed) the(ir) youngest (brother) among my elder brothers, (but) my own father, upon the command of Aššur, Sin, Šamaš ... has chosen me ... saying: 'This is the son to (be elevated to) the position of a successor of mine.' (Then) he put his question before Šamaš and Adad by means of an oracle and they answered him: 'He (verily) is your replacement.'"[19]

Since he was the youngest son, Esarhaddon had reason to put great emphasis on his divine election. But this does not mean that he did not try to derive his authority from his royal descent as well. On the contrary, he mentions not only his direct lineage but also, in an unusual way, his descent from a traditional founder of the Assyrian dynasty:

> "Son of Sennacherib, king of the universe, king of Assyria, son of Sargon, king of the universe, king of Assyria, viceroy of Babylon, king of Sumer and Akkad; descendant of the eternal dynasty of Bel-bani, founder of the kingdom of Assyria."[20]

---

15 Cf. von Soden, Herrscher im Alten Orient, 1954, 76f.

16 Cf. von Soden, apud Falkenstein, Sumerische und akkadische Hymnen und Gebete, 386.

17 Brünnow, ZA 5, 67 obv. 16. 21.

18 See von Soden, Der Aufstieg des Assyrerreichs als geschichtliches Problem, 1937, 29; Labat, Le caractère religieux, 70; Gadd, Ideas of Divine Rule, 46; Frankfort, Kingship and the Gods, 243. The heir-apparent was called in Assyria *mār šarri rabû ša bīt redûti* "the eldest son of the king of the *bīt redûti*". He was the first person in order of succession to the throne, but not necessarily the first-born, see M.-J. Seux, Épithètes royales akkadiennes et sumériennes, 1967, 160 n. 33. By contrast, primogeniture was established in the Hittite kingdom after Telipinu issued the Edict, see below p. 16 n. 75.

19 ANET 289; Borger, Asarh., § 27 A I 8–12.

20 Borger, Asarh., § 65 rev. 15–17. About the title "descendant of the eternal dynasty of Bel-bani", see Seux, Épithètes royales, 152 n. 30. 225 n. 100.

A. L. Oppenheim[21] maintains:

"There existed in the Assyria of the end of the second and the beginning of the first millennium B. C. two ideal ruler types, one who derived authority from the divinely guarded lineage that extended deep into the past of Assyria, and the other who saw in the very success of becoming king the approval of the gods of Assyria, who had elevated him as the man chosen for this task."

But we are somewhat sceptical about this sharp division, since almost all of the Assyrian kings mention both royal lineage and divine election as the foundation of their kingship:

"Shalmaneser (I) (1274–1245), governor of the god Enlil. . . when Aššur, the lord, faithfully chose me for his worshipper, gave me the sceptre, weapon, and staff to (rule) properly the black-headed people, and granted me the true crown of lordship . . . faithful shepherd whose name the gods Anu and Enlil called forever, I, eternal seed, one who knows the gods; son of Adad-nirari (I), governor of the god Enlil, vice-regent of Aššur; son of Arik-den-ili who was also governor of the god Enlil (and) vice-regent of Aššur."[22]
"Tukulti-Ninurta (I) (1244–1208), king of the universe, strong king, king of Assyria, chosen of Aššur . . . whose name the god Aššur and the great gods faithfully called, the one whom they gave the four quarters to administer and the one to whom they entrusted their dominion . . . and to whom authority is given . . . son of Shalmaneser (I), king of Assyria; son of Adad-nirari (I) (who was) also king of Assyria."[23]
"Aššur-reš-iši (I) (1133–1116), governor of the god Enlil, vice-regent of the god Aššur, the one whom the gods Anu, Enlil, and Ea, the great gods faithfully claimed in his mother's womb, the one whose dominion they designated for the proper administration of Assyria. . . son of Mutakkil-Nusku, vice-regent of Aššur; son of Aššur-dan (I) who was also vice-regent of Aššur."[24]
"Tiglath-Pileser (I) (1115–1077), the exalted prince, whom Aššur and Ninurta have brought unto the desire of his heart . . . the son of Aššur-reš-iši, the mighty king . . . the grandson of Mutakkil-Nusku, whom Aššur, the great lord, eagerly chose . . . the lawful descendant of Aššur-dan, who swayed a shining sceptre and ruled the men of Enlil . . . the descendant of Ninurta-apil-Ekur, the powerful king, the beloved of Aššur."[25]

"Šamaš . . . Adad . . . Ninurta . . . Nergal . . . Nusku . . . Ninlil . . . Ištar . . . Adad-nirari (II) (911–891), the exalted prince, they have duly created . . . afterward the

[21] Ancient Mesopotamia, 1964, 101.
[22] ARI I § 526. 527. 533; IAK 110ff. I 1. 22–26. 120. III 27–37; ARAB I § 113. 118.
[23] ARI I § 688; Weidner, Tn., § 1 I 1–20.
[24] ARI I § 950; Weidner, Tn., § 60 1–8.
[25] ARAB I § 255–258; AKA 92ff. VII 36–56.

great gods uttered their decree and put into my hand a sceptre, (called) 'Ruler of Peoples' ... Adad-nirari, king of Assyria, they called me. Mighty king, king of Assyria, king of the four regions (of the world), the Sun of all peoples, am I. Son of Aššur-dan ... (grand)son of Tiglath-Pileser ... illustrious offspring of Aššur-reš-iši."[26]

It is true that Tiglath-Pileser III (744–727), Sargon II (721–705) and Sennacherib (704–681) scarcely mention their lineage in their formal inscriptions. But their silence concerning their royal descent is exceptional. We must look for special reasons for it[27].

Recently, A. K. Grayson[28] has pointed out that the Assyrian monarchy was born in a true sense with the reign of Šamši-Adad I (1813–1781), and that this fact is relevant to the evolution of the format of the Assyrian King List at that time. He has further maintained that this list issued from the attempt of Šamši-Adad to make up his legitimate genealogy by combining his non-Assyrian ancestors with a genuine Assyrian lineage[29], and "with its emphasis on the continuity of the Assyrian royal line, became the pillar of the concept of hereditary monarchy in Assyria."[30] This also shows that the foundation of the Assyrian monarchy was established on the dynastic principle.

---

[26] ARAB I § 356–357; J. Seidmann, Die Inschriften Adadnirâris II, 1935, 8ff. 2–12.

[27] According to the Assyrian King List, Tiglath-Pileser III is a son of Aššur-nirari V, see I. J. Gelb, Two Assyrian King Lists, JNES 13 (1954), 229 SDAS IV 24; ANET 566. But the name Adad-nirari III is mentioned as that of his father on a brick, see KAH I no. 21 2; ARAB I § 822 1. About the problems of the genealogy of Tiglath-Pileser III, see H. Tadmor, The Inscriptions of Tiglath-Pileser III, King of Assyria, (in preparation). An inscription on an enamelled plate testifies to the fact that Sargon II was a son of Tiglath-Pileser III, see E. Unger, Sargon II. von Assyrien der Sohn Tiglatpilesers III., 1933, 16; cf. idem, Altorientalische Könige als Kulturbringer, FuF 9 (1933), 245 f.; E. Weidner, AfO 9 (1933/34), 79. But the situation of his enthronement still remains unclear, see I. Ephʿal, in: EncBib, V 1968, 1121 (Hebrew). Unger maintains that these Assyrian kings deleted their fathers' names in order either to pretend to be founders of a new era (Sargon II. von Assyrien 19) or to show their divine origin after the Babylonian fashion (FuF 9, 246). It seems, however, that their silence about the royal ancestor was motivated by political rather than philosophical considerations. About Sennacherib's case, see Tadmor, The "Sin of Sargon", EI 5 (1958), 150–163, especially 159 (Hebrew).

[28] The Early Development of Assyrian Monarchy, UF 3 (1971), 311–319, especially 317f.

[29] This thesis was first demonstrated by B. Landsberger, Assyrische Königsliste und „Dunkles Zeitalter", JCS 8 (1954), 109; cf. F. R. Kraus, Könige, die in Zelten wohnten, 1965, 11ff.

[30] UF 3, 317.

According to T. Jacobsen's analysis of the early development of political institutions in Mesopotamia[31], the ruler of the city-state was originally elected by the popular assembly either as *en*, a cult functionary, or as *lugal*, a war-leader, and his office was temporal. But as his power grew stronger, his office became permanent and his authority independent of the assembly. At that juncture the ideology of divine election was introduced as a new foundation of the ruler's authority. At the same time, the dynastic principle was established to avoid the disturbance caused by rivalry for succession to the permanent office of the ruler. This change from a rulership based on popular election to hereditary kingship had taken place by the beginning of Early Dynastic III period, that is, c. 2,500 B. C.

It seems, however, that, if Jacobsen's analysis is correct, the dynastic principle came about rather as a natural consequence of the centralization of great power in the ruler. Becoming a "great householder" (*lú gal*), presiding over a "great house" (*é gal*)[32], he must have tried to transfer his "house" to his descendants as a hereditary estate. Moreover, Jacobsen's conclusion is problematic because of the nature of the myths and epics which he utilized as the main source material for his study. Even if in a way they faithfully reflect the real situation, as he maintains, no one can regard them as historical sources in a true sense. Although we have no intention of entering into a discussion of this problem here[33], it must be mentioned that his reconstruction is limited to the "proto-historic" period, whose circumstances seem to be portrayed in these myths and epics. In other words, his theory cannot offer any evidence for the existence of elective rulership in Mesopotamia in the historic age. It is true that Jacobsen[34] also mentions the election of a certain Ipḫurkiš to kingship by the assembly of Kiš. But it is extremely difficult to deduce any conclusive argument for elective kingship in Mesopotamia from this totally isolated information[35].

Recently, W. G. Lambert[36] showed that the dynastic principle of royal legitimation arose in Mesopotamia only with the arrival of the

---

[31] Early Political Development in Mesopotamia (1957), in: Toward the Image of Tammuz and Other Essays on Mesopotamian History and Culture, 1970, 143ff.; cf. idem, Primitive Democracy in Ancient Mesopotamia (1943), in: Toward the Image of Tammuz, 157–170. 396–407.

[32] Jacobsen, Early Political Development in Mesopotamia, in: Toward the Image of Tammuz, 146.

[33] Cf. H. W. F. Saggs, The Greatness that was Babylon, 1962, 37ff.

[34] Primitive Democracy in Ancient Mesopotamia, in: Toward the Image of Tammuz, 162; about the Akkadian text, see ibid. 402 n. 35.

[35] Cf. J. A. Soggin, Das Königtum in Israel, 1967, 138f.

[36] The Seed of Kingship, in: Le palais et la royauté, ed. P. Garelli, 1974, 424–440.

Amorites early in the second millennium B. C., till when the idea was unknown to the Sumerians in the third millennium, although hereditary succession was always practised. It is worth noting, however, that the legend of Etana, one of the kings of Kiš after the Flood in the Sumerian King List, describes how Etana endeavoured to solve the problem of his childlessness in order to exercise a kingship in a right way which descended from heaven and was granted him[37]. The motif of the legend reminds us of the epic of Keret, king of Ugarit, that "poses the question how a king without heir can be truly king"[38]. It clearly shows that the dynastic principle in Mesopotamia was associated inseparably with monarchy from the very early period, if not the very beginning.

As for the relationship between the dynastic principle and divine election, it is to be observed that both ideas were closely connected with each other from the ideological point of view. The doctrine of divine election had a tendency to extend its validity to the past as well as to the future[39]. On the one hand, the king is said to have been predestined by the gods to rule over the country, while still in his childhood, in the womb of his mother, or even from more distant days[40]:

> Adad-nirari III (810–783): "... a king whom Aššur, the king of the Igigi had chosen (already) when he was a youngster."[41]
> Esarhaddon: "... whom Aššur, Šamaš, Bel and Nebo, the Ištar of Nineveh (and) the Ištar of Arbela have pronounced king of Assyria (ever) since he was a youngster."[42]
> Aššur-reš-iši I: "... the one whom the gods Anu, Enlil, and Ea, the great gods faithfully claimed in his mother's womb, the one whose dominion they designated for the proper administration of Assyria."[43]
> Nabonidus: "... whom Sin and Ningal designated to the kingship in his mother's womb."[44]
> Šamši-Adad V (823–811): "... whose name the gods have named from of old."[45]
> Aššurbanipal (668–627): "... whose name Aššur and Sin ... have named for the kingship from distant days, whom they formed in his mother's womb, for the rulership of Assyria."[46]

---

[37] ANET 114–118; cf. Oppenheim, Ancient Mesopotamia, 266.
[38] G. R. Driver, Canaanite Myths and Legends, 1956, 5.
[39] Cf. Labat, Le caractère religieux, 40ff.; J. de Fraine, L'aspect religieux de la royauté israélite, 1954, 173ff.
[40] Cf. S. M. Paul, Deutero-Isaiah and Cuneiform Royal Inscriptions, JAOS 88 (1968), 184ff.
[41] ANET 281; IR 35 no. 1 1; ARAB I § 739.
[42] ANET 289; Borger, Asarh., § 27 A I 5–7.
[43] ARI I § 950; Weidner, Tn., § 60 2–3; ARAB I § 209.
[44] NBKI 218 I 4–5.
[45] ARAB I § 714; IR 29 29–30.
[46] ARAB II § 765; Streck, Asb., 2f. I 3–5.

On the other hand, the everlasting reign and the prosperity of the king's descendants were asked for in the king's prayer:

> Tiglath-Pileser I: "Ye great gods . . . have decreed . . . that his priestly seed should have a place in Eharsagkurkurra forever."[47]
>
> Esarhaddon: "My priestly seed, may it endure, together with the foundation platform of Esagila and Babylon, for all time to come . . . May I attain a (ripe) old age, and have abundant posterity . . . May I extend my family, bring together my kin. May I spread abroad my stock, may I send forth many branches. May I keep the foundation of my priestly throne firm as a rock. May my rule be secure with heaven and earth."[48]
>
> Nebuchadnezzar II (604–562): "In Esagila and Ezida . . . may my course of life become old. I am really your faithful governor and want to carry your yoke until I will be satiated with descendants. May my name's call be called in the future. In mercy may my offspring rule the black-headed people for ever."[49]

As the divine election of the present king extended in both directions, past and future, the dynastic continuity was expressed as an "eternal royal line"[50], that is *zēru dārû* "eternal line"[51], *zērum dārium ša šarrūtim* "eternal line of kingship"[52], *zēr šarrūtim* "royal line"[53], *zēr šarrūti dārû* "eternal royal line"[54], *zēr ili dārium* "eternal divine line"[55]. Naturally, the king was eager to show his relationship to this eternal royal line as legitimizing his authority. Thus, he was not only *māru* "the son" or *aplu* "the heir"[56] of the previous king, but also *liblibbu, līpu* "the descendant"[57] or *pir'u* "the offspring"[58] of the royal ancestor.

In addition, expressions such as *kussî bīt abīja* "the throne of my father's house"[59], *šarrūti bīt abīja* "the kingship of my father's

---

[47] ARAB I § 217; AKA 29ff. I 15–27.

[48] ARAB II § 659E; Borger, Asarh., § 11 VIII 6–29.

[49] NBKI 176f. X 30–40.

[50] See the entry *zēru* in Seux, Épithètes royales, 375ff.; cf. also Lambert, The Seed of Kingship, in: Le palais et la royauté, 428ff.

[51] IAK 120 III 29 (Shalmaneser I). [52] CH V 1–2.

[53] Ibid. II 13. [54] IR 29 29 (Šamši-Adad V).

[55] E. Sollberger, Samsu-Iluna's Bilingual Inscriptions C and D, RA 63 (1969), 34 71.

[56] In the formula "RN_1 son of RN_2", *aplu* is a synonym for *māru*. The term *aplu* in this formula cannot be found in inscriptions of early kings of Assyria until Arik-den-ili (1319–1308), see IAK 54 no. 4 2. But *aplu* is dominant in the inscriptions of Tukulti-Ninurta I, see Weidner, Tn., passim. In the inscriptions of Esarhaddon the formula employs *māru* 14 times (Borger, Asarh., § 2 I 5. § 3 15. § 5 1. § 6. § 21 37. § 27A II 14. § 29 4. § 32 3. § 38. § 47 26. § 48 10. § 53 obv. 47. § 65 rev. 15. § 67 6; cf. § 108) and *aplu* nine times (§ 7 2. § 8 4. § 23 3. § 24 6. § 31 3. § 33 2. § 41 8. § 51 7. § 95 1).

[57] CAD L 180. 205; Seux, Épithètes royales, 152f.

[58] Seux, Épithètes royales, 225f.

[59] ARM IV § 20 5.

house"[60], or *palûm dūršu* "the rule is his permanent possession"[61] also show that the throne, kingship and rule were regarded as the possession of the royal family. It thus becomes clear that we have no reason to doubt that the dynastic principle was accepted in Mesopotamia both in theory and in practice[62].

In Egypt, from the start, a monarchy without the dynastic principle could not exist from the ideological point of view. According to the Memphite Theology, originating in an early phase of the Egyptian monarchy, each reigning king was Horus, the legitimate successor to his father Osiris, and, as he became Osiris when he died, the throne passed to his son Horus[63]. Accordingly, the authority of the Egyptian king was derived, in theory, solely from the king's divine ancestors. But, in practice, too, the belief in the divinity of the royal blood was so strong that the heir-apparent, if his lineage was not pure enough, sometimes had to marry his half sister who came of the legitimate line[64]. It is thus not surprising that usurpers used to marry a princess of the previous royal house to secure their legitimacy. Because of their marked inclination to keep the dynastic continuity, Egyptian official records scarcely acknowledged the changes of dynasties[65].

B. WAS THE HITTITE MONARCHY ELECTIVE?

A. Goetze[66] has maintained that the Hittite monarchy was originally elective. His argument is based on the following observations:
a) Although the reigning king designated his successor, he was required to propose the nomination to the assembly of the whole body of the noblemen and to get their acknowledgment.

---

[60] Borger, Asarh., § 27A I 58.

[61] W. L. Moran, New Evidence from Mari on the History of Prophecy, Bib 50 (1969), 41; ARM X § 51 13.

[62] Cf. Labat, Le caractère religieux, 40ff. Against Labat's assertion of the existence of a *race royal*, Frankfort argues that "the evidence shows only that rulers tended to claim that they and their families were favoured by the gods" (Kingship and the Gods 399 n. 45; cf. ibid. 406 n. 21). It is unlikely, however, that the expression "eternal royal line" only shows the ruler's claim without the popular acknowledgment of the hereditary principle of the kingship.

[63] ANET 4ff.; cf. Frankfort, Kingship and the Gods, 24ff.; H. W. Fairman, The Kingship Rituals of Egypt, in: Myth, Ritual, and Kingship, ed. S. H. Hooke, 1958, 75f. 98f.

[64] See J. A. Wilson, The Culture of Ancient Egypt, 1951, 201f.

[65] See Frankfort, Kingship and the Gods, 372 n. 1.

[66] Kleinasien, 1957², 86f.

b) The king had to respect the privilege of the noblemen in exchange for their acknowledgment of his designation. This was a sort of covenant.
c) The king was subject to the same law according to which the noblemen possessed equal rights.
d) Incessant struggles for the succession to the throne in the Old Kingdom are to be regarded as a conflict between the noblemen, who stood on their traditional rights, and the king, who made an effort to establish a hereditary monarchy.

As his main source material, Goetze utilizes chiefly the Testament of Hattusili I (c. 1650–1620)[67] and the Edict of Telipinu (c. 1525–1500)[68].

However, as F. Sommer[69] has already pointed out, it is unlikely that the assembly convened by Hattusili I was asked for its assent to the king's designation of his successor. In the Testament, the king proclaimed his decision to Mursili, his adopted son, his servants and the leading citizens, and ordered them to obey it:

> "Great King Labarna (= Hattusili I) spoke to the fighting men of the assembly and the dignitaries (saying): '... Behold, Mursili is now my son ... Till now no one of my family has obeyed my will; but you, my son Mursili, you must obey it. Keep your father's words! If you keep your father's words, you will eat bread and drink water ... Now you are my chief servants, and you must keep my words ... But if you do not keep the king's words ... you will not remain alive, you will perish."[70]

Admittedly, Hattusili mentions in the same text that in his grandfather's time the noblemen rebelled against the royal designation of the successor and set up a rival king:

> "My grandfather had proclaimed his son Labarna as heir to the throne in Sanahuitta, but afterwards his servants and the leading citizens spurned his words and set Papadilmah on the throne ... Now how many of them have escaped their fate?"[71]

But it is difficult to regard this rebellion of the noblemen as an assertion of their original right concerning the election of the king[72]. Rather, the text clearly shows that the throne was transferred from father to son by the king's designation at the very beginning of the Old Kingdom[73].

---

[67] HAB.

[68] 2 BoTU 23A; Sturtevant, Chrest., 175–200; W. Eisele, Der Telipinu-Erlass, Diss. München, 1970.

[69] OLZ 38 (1935), 279; see also HAB 209ff.

[70] O. R. Gurney, The Hittites, 1961[3], 171f.; HAB I–II 1. 37. III 26–29. 33–34. 36–37.

[71] Gurney, The Hittites, 172; HAB III 41–45.

[72] Cf. Gurney, Anatolia, c. 1750–1600 B. C., CAH II ch. VI, 1962, 28.

[73] According to the Edict of Telipinu, the history of the Old Kingdom began with Labarna I, father of Hattusili I (= Labarna II), see 2 BoTU 23A I 1–20; Sturtevant,

After Mursili I (c. 1620–1590) was assassinated by Hantili, his brother-in-law, a period of anarchy resulting from a struggle for the throne lasted for several generations. Although each usurper's relationship to the previous king in this period is not clear enough, scholarly opinion agrees that the throne was disputed by the members of one and the same royal family[74]. When Telipinu finally issued the Edict to overcome the disastrous anarchy, he regulated the precise order of succession among the members of the royal family, but no reference was made to any right of the noblemen concerning the designation of the heir-apparent:

> "Let the first-born son of the king be king. If there is no first-born son, let a son of the second place become king. If, however, there is no king's son, let them take a husband for the first-born daughter and let him become king."[75]

Moreover, both Ammuna (c. 1550–1530) and Telipinu tell in their inscriptions: "I had seated myself upon the throne of my father."[76] They legitimatized their throne by the dynastic principle. All these facts unmistakably show that the succession to the throne in the Old Kingdom was carried out according to the hereditary principle. We can find hardly any trace of the elective monarchy in it[77].

Chrest., 182f.; Eisele, Der Telipinu-Erlass, 16ff. Cf. also R. S. Hardy, The Old Hittite Kingdom. A Political History, AJSL 58 (1941), 185ff.; Gurney, CAH II ch. VI, 9ff.

[74] See Hardy, AJSL 58, 207ff.; Gurney, Anatolia, c. 1600–1380 B. C., CAH II ch. XV (a), 1966, 4ff.; K. K. Riemschneider, Die Thronfolgeordnung im althethitischen Reich, in: Beiträge zur sozialen Struktur des alten Vorderasiens, ed. H. Klengel, 1971, 81f.; cf. Goetze, Kleinasien, 86.

[75] 2 BoTU 23A II 36–39; cf. Sturtevant, Chrest., 86; Eisele, Der Telipinu-Erlass, 34. 36. Opinions are divided on the interpretation of the terms *ḫantezzi-* and *tān pedaš*, if they denote the first-born and the next son, or sons of wives of the first and second rank, respectively. The latter interpretation is advanced by many scholars, see Goetze, Kleinasien, 87; Gurney, The Hittites, 64; J. Friedrich, Hethitisches Elementarbuch, II 1967^2, 79; Eisele, Der Telipinu-Erlass, 82f. It seems, however, that the former interpretation is more logical from the practical point of view, that is, it is simply the right of primogeniture that Telipinu established in the Edict, see G. G. Giorgadze, The Order of Succession to the Throne in the Old Hittite Kingdom (On the Interpretation of § 28 in the "Decree of Telipinu"), Journal of Ancient History 110 (1969), 67–82 (Russian) (English summary on p. 83); cf. also H. Otten, Das Hethiterreich, in: Kulturgeschichte des Alten Orient, ed. H. Schmökel, 1961, 348. 366. I owe this interpretation to Mrs. G. Kellerman.

[76] For Ammuna, [I.NA ^{giš}GU.]⌜ZA⌝ A.BI.IA *e-eš-ḫa-ḫa-ti*, KUB XXXVI § 98b rev. 8'. For Telipinu, 2 BoTU 23A II 16.

[77] Cf. H. G. Güterbock, Authority and Law in the Hittite Kingdom, in: Authority and Law in the Ancient Orient, Suppl. to JAOS 17 (1954), 19; Gurney, CAH II ch. VI, 27f. Some scholars are of the opinion that the strife for the succession to the throne in

Nonetheless, it is true that the popular assembly called *panku-*[78] possessed a judicial authority to which even the royal princes and the king himself were subject[79]. Evidently, the Hittite kings in the period of the Old Kingdom were not as absolute as the Egyptian or Mesopotamian monarchs[80]. In this connection, it is also to be noted that, remarkably enough, the idea of the divine election of the king is lacking in the early Hittite monarchy[81]. Only in the period of the Empire, did the Hittite king become the representative of the Storm-god on earth:

> "The country belongs to the Storm-god; heaven and earth (and) the people belong to the Storm-god. Thus he made the Labarna, the king, his governor. He gave him the whole country of Hattusa. So let the Labarna govern the whole country with (his) hand!"[82]

At the same time, we no longer find a "democratic" assembly such as the *panku-* in the later Empire[83]. By analogy with Jacobsen's theory on the development of political ideology in early Mesopotamia (see above p. 11), both the lack of theocratic ideology and the existence of a "democratic" institution in the period of the Old Kingdom might indicate the character of the Hittite royal authority, which originally derived from the popular assembly. However, even if this is the case, a Hittite elective monarchy can be assumed to have existed only in its earliest phase in the proto-historic period, since, as we have shown, the Hittite monarchy in the historic period was always hereditary[84].

In the period of the Empire, Hittite kings mention not only their direct lineage but also their fictitious association with the kings of the

---

the Old Kingdom was due to a conflict between the systems of matrilineal and patriarchal succession, see J. G. Macqueen, Hattian Mythology and Hittite Monarchy, AnSt 9 (1959), 171–188, especially 180ff.; Riemschneider, in: Beiträge zur sozialen Struktur des alten Vorderasiens, 79–102. But this thesis seems unconvincing, see Gurney, CAH II ch. XV (a), 11f.

[78] About *panku-*, see Goetze, Kleinasien, 86ff.; Gurney, The Hittites, 68f.

[79] See 2 BoTU 23A II 46–65; Sturtevant, Chrest., 190f.; Eisele, Der Telipinu-Erlass, 36ff.

[80] Cf. Goetze, Kleinasien, 88; Gurney, CAH II ch. VI, 28f.

[81] See Gurney, Hittite Kingship, in: Myth, Ritual, and Kingship, 119.

[82] Goetze, JCS 1 (1947), 91.

[83] Cf. Güterbock, in: Suppl. to JAOS 17 (1954), 19f.; Gurney, CAH II ch. VI, 29.

[84] Cf. Gadd, Ideas of Divine Rule, 47; Otten, in: Kulturgeschichte des Alten Orient, 365. According to E. Kutsch, the rite of the royal anointing at the enthronement of the Hittite king, which is attested neither in Egypt nor in Mesopotamia, originally had the implication of the granting of the ruling power to the king by the noblemen (Salbung als Rechtsakt im Alten Testament und im Alten Orient, 1963, 36ff.). It seems unlikely, however, that such an implication was still remembered in the historic period.

Old Kingdom. For instance, Hattusili III (c. 1275–1250) begins with his lineage as follows:

> "Thus speaks Tabarna Hattusili, the great king, king of Hatti, son of Mursili, the great king, king of Hatti, grandson of Suppiluliuma, the great king, king of Hatti, descendant of Hattusili, king of Kussara."[85]

In so doing, they tried to establish the legitimacy of their throne on the ideal dynastic continuity of the Hittite monarchy.

C. THE FOUNDATION OF ROYAL AUTHORITY IN THE KINGDOMS OF SYRIA-PALESTINE

So far as source materials testify, hereditary kingship always existed in the kingdom of Ugarit. A long dynasty is attested by a list in which fourteen names of the deified kings are preserved, but, according to the estimation of scholars, at least thirty names may have been contained originally, that is, thirty reigns representing several centuries[86]. To show this ancient origin of the dynasty, the late kings of Ugarit used a dynastic seal: "Yaqarum son of Niqmaddu, king of Ugarit."[87] The legends both of Keret[88] and of Aqhat[89] deal with problems of the royal heir. According to the legend of Keret, the dynasty of Ugarit received special divine sanction from El, the chief god of the Ugaritic pantheon[90].

In reality, however, the most important source of support for the dynastic authority of the later kings of Ugarit were the Hittite overlords[91]. Similarly, the Canaanite kings in the Amarna age depended for their existence to a great extent on the Egyptian suzerains. Abdi-heba, ruler of Jerusalem, acknowledged the designation of the Egyptian king as the foundation of his royal authority:

> "It was neither my father nor my mother who set me in this place. The arm of the mighty king brought me into the house of my father."[92]

---

[85] Goetze, Hattušiliš, 1925, 6f. I 1–4; Gurney, The Hittites, 175.

[86] See C. Virolleaud, Les nouveaux textes alphabétiques de Ras-shamra, CRAI, 1963, 94f.; cf. C. F.-A. Schaeffer, Neue Entdeckungen in Ugarit (23. und 24. Kampagne, 1960–1961), AfO 20 (1963), 214f.

[87] PRU, III 1955, XLI; Ugaritica, III 1956, 66ff.; cf. G. Buccellati, Cities and Nations of Ancient Syria, 1967, 33. 67f. 74.

[88] UT Krt and § 125–128; ANET 142–149.

[89] UT Aqht and § 121–124; ANET 149–155.

[90] See UT § 128 II 11–28; ANET 146.

[91] Cf. J. Gray, Canaanite Kingship in Theory and Practice, VT 2 (1952), 198; A. F. Rainey, The Kingdom of Ugarit (1965), in: BAR 3, 1970, 81; M. S. Drower, Ugarit, CAH II ch. XXI (b), 1968, 10ff.

[92] EA § 286 9–13; cf. EA § 288 13–15; ANET 487f.

"The house of my father" (*bīt* [lú]*abīja*) is nothing but the royal dynasty ruling over Jerusalem. So, hereditary monarchy was established in the kingdom of Jerusalem. But at the same time it was the Egyptian overlord who possessed the power to designate the successor to the throne[93].

A similar situation can be found in Hittite vassal treaties, in which the Hittite king, often as the only obligation of the overlord to the vassal, guaranteed succession to the throne by the same vassal family[94]. For instance, Mursili II (c. 1353–1320) declares in the treaty with Duppi-Tešub of Amurru:

> "When I, the Sun, sought after you in accordance with your father's word and put you in your father's place, I took you in oath for the king of Hatti land, the Hatti land, and for my sons and grandsons. So honour the oath (of loyalty) to the king and the king's kin! And I, the king, will be loyal towards you, Duppi-Tešub. When you take a wife, and when you beget an heir, he shall be king in the Amurru land likewise. And just as I shall be loyal towards you, even so shall I be loyal towards your son. But you, Duppi-Tešub, remain loyal towards the king of Hatti land, the Hatti land, my sons (and) my grandsons forever!"[95]

In the Egyptian and Mesopotamian monarchies, as we have shown, the divine election ideologically guaranteed the authority of the king who succeeded to the throne of his dynasty. In the vassal kingdoms in Syria-Palestine, this divine jurisdiction over the succession was exercised by the overlords. Indeed, the Hittite and Egyptian overlords were generally addressed by their vassal kings as "my Sun-god" ([d]*Šamšija*)[96].

In the first millennium B. C. the situation did not basically change, but the overlords were no longer equated with the gods directly. The dynastic continuity in the vassal kingdom was now guaranteed by a double authority, the god and the overlord. Thus, Barrakib, king of Sam'al-Ya'dy (c. 730), says:

> "Because of the righteousness of my father and my own righteousness, I was seated by my lord Rakibel and my lord Tiglath-Pileser upon the throne of my father."[97]

In the second half of the second millennium B. C., in some cities of Syria-Palestine the popular assembly functioned at times as a self-government of the city-state either along with a local ruler or without any royal authority[98]. After the king was removed by the Hittite

---

93 Cf. below p 155.

94 Cf. D. J. McCarthy, Treaty and Covenant, 1963, 28.

95 ANET 204.

96 See EA II 1511; Seux, Épithètes royales, 283 n. 108; cf. H. T. Bossert, Meine Sonne, Or NS 26 (1957), 97–126.

97 ANET 655; KAI § 216 4–7.

98 Cf. P. Artzi, "Vox Populi" in the El-Amarna Tablets, RA 58 (1964), 159–166; H.

overlord, the inhabitants of Aleppo enjoyed autonomy[99]. On the other hand, for twenty years the people of Tunip kept on asking the Pharaoh to give them back the son of a certain Aki-Tešub, seemingly to restore the monarchy[100]. The people of Byblos expelled their ruler[101], and the kings of Irqata, Ammia and Ardata were killed by their people[102]. Thereupon, the city council and the elders established autonomy in each of these cities[103]. We can also find the people's self-government in Arwada[104], Gibeon and its neighbouring cities (Josh 9 3–10 6) and in Keilah both in the Amarna period[105] and in the time of Saul (I Sam 23 11–12). Moreover, Abimelech, the son of Jerubbaal, was made king by the lords of Shechem (Judg 9 6). This evidence shows that the popular assembly wielded strong power in these cities; at the same time it is extremely difficult to conclude from it that the popular assembly had the authority to designate the city ruler regularly[106].

On the contrary, the sources at our disposal show that the kings of city-states in Syria-Palestine in the second millennium B. C. were normally succeeded by members of the same royal family[107]. Addu-nirari king of Alalakh remembered the establishment of his dynasty by Thut-mose III in the time of his grandfather[108]. Rib-Addi of Byblos[109] and Zimriddi of Sidon[110] mentioned that their ancestors were also the loyal vassals of the previous Egyptian kings. Šum-Adda of Šamhuna (?) sought an investigation whether his fathers had made tribute of grain since the day of a certain Kuzuna, possibly the founder of his

---

Reviv, On Urban Representative Institutions and Self-Government in Syria-Palestine in the Second Half of the Second Millennium B. C., JESHO 12 (1969), 283–297.

99 Landsberger, JCS 8 (1954), 61.

100 EA § 59.

101 EA § 136–137. § 142; cf. Goetze, The Struggle for the Domination of Syria, 1400–1300 B. C., CAH II ch. XVII, 1965, 14.

102 EA § 75 26–27. 33–34. § 139 14–15. § 140 10–14.

103 EA § 140 1–2 (Byblos). § 100 1–4 (Irqata).

104 EA § 149 59.

105 EA § 280 18; ANET 487.

106 H. Reviv holds that Shechem had a system of government by which the ruling class of the city chose its ruler from abroad in times of political changes and crises (The Government of Shechem in the El-Amarna Period and in the Days of Abimelech, IEJ 16 [1966], 252–257). The thesis seems unconvincing, see Z. Kallai & H. Tadmor, Bīt Ninurta = Beth Horon – On the History of the Kingdom of Jerusalem in the Amarna Period, EI 9 (1969), 146 (Hebrew).

107 Cf. M. Liverani, La royauté syrienne de l'âge du bronze récent, in: Le palais et la royauté, 335ff.

108 EA § 51 1–9.

109 EA § 118 40–41.

110 EA § 144 32–34.

dynasty[111]. We also learn from the El-Amarna letters that Aziru king of Amurru succeeded Abdi-Aširta, his father[112], and Zatatna of Akko succeeded Zurata, his father[113]. Labaya of Shechem was also succeeded by his sons[114]. Moreover, from the inscription of Idrimi, king of Alalakh (c. 1400), we can conclude that the descendants of the royal family could claim a right to the kingship even after the family had lost its hold over the domain, and, that this claim was recognized as authentic by the ex-subjects:

> "An evil deed happened in Halab, the seat of my family, and we fled to the people of Emar, brothers of my mother, and we lived in Emar . . . They discovered that I was the son of their overlord and gathered around me . . . I went ashore and when my country heard of me they brought me cattle and sheep. And in one day, and as one man, the countries Ni', Ama'e, Mukiškhi and my city Alalakh turned to me."[115]

When the national kingdoms were established in Syria-Palestine at the end of the second and the beginning of the first millennium B. C., the regime in all of them was, so far as our sources indicate, a hereditary monarchy from the start[116]. In the eleventh to tenth centuries, dynasties are attested in Phoenician city-states, Byblos[117] and Tyre[118]. In the days of Saul, it seems that a Philistine dynasty was established in Gath (I Sam 27 2; cf. I Kings 2 39)[119]. In the days of David[120], there were

---

[111] EA § 224 10–18.

[112] EA § 107 26–27. § 147 68. § 149 35–36.

[113] EA § 8 19; cf. EA II 1027.

[114] EA § 250. § 287 30. § 289 6.

[115] ANET 557; S. Smith, The Statue of Idri-mi, 1949, p. 14 lines 3–6. 24–26. p. 16 lines 34–39.

[116] Cf. Buccellati, Cities and Nations, 125ff.

[117] ANET 27. 661; KAI § 1 1. § 5 1–2. § 6 1. § 7 1–3; cf. B. Maisler (Mazar), The Phoenician Inscriptions from Byblos and the Evolution of the Phoenician-Hebrew Alphabetical Script, Lešonenu 14 (1945/46), 166–181 (Hebrew); W. F. Albright, The Phoenician Inscriptions of the Tenth Century B. C. from Byblus, JAOS 67 (1947), 153–160.

[118] Josephus, Contra Apionem, I 116–125; cf. H. J. Katzenstein, The History of Tyre, 1973, 74. 77ff.

[119] Cf. J. Gutmann, in: EncBib, I 1950, 281f. (Hebrew); but see also S. Aḥituv, in: EncBib, VI 1971, 489 (Hebrew). G. E. Wright is of the opinion that Achish of Gath was "not one of the five Philistine lords but the client king of Gath" (Fresh Evidence for the Philistine Story, BA 29 [1966], 80ff.). It is rather difficult to accept this suggestion, since it appears that Gath was the principal city of the Philistine confederation in the time of Saul and David (II Sam 1 20), cf. B. Mazar, The Philistines and the Rise of Israel and Tyre, 1964, 5.

[120] The king of Aram-Zobah, whom David fought, was called "Hadadezer the son of Rehob" (II Sam 8 3). But the expression "son of Rehob" seems not to imply the

dynasties in Hamath (II Sam 8 9–10 I Chron 18 9–10), Ammon (II Sam 10 1 I Chron 19 1), and Edom (I Kings 11 14). In Solomon's time an Aramaean dynasty was founded in Damascus (I Kings 11 23–25 15 18)[121]. In the ninth to eighth centuries, we hear about dynasties in Moab (II Kings 3 27)[122], Sam'al-Ya'dy[123] and Arpad[124].

It has been argued that the Edomite kingship was originally elective, since the Edomite king-list (Gen 36 31–39 I Chron 1 43–51a) seems to indicate a consecutive royal succession of eight kings, who were associated with each other neither geographically nor genealogically[125]. But the argument seems too simple. Admittedly, the list raises many problems. We know practically nothing about the eight kings beyond the information in the list, nor can we with certainty identify the city-names in the list with any geographical sites except Bozrah and Teman[126]. Different sources seem to have been used by the compiler of

---

name of his dynasty but to show his native place, see M. F. Unger, Israel and the Aramaeans of Damascus, 1957, 42; A. Malamat, Aspects of the Foreign Policies of David and Solomon, JNES 22 (1963), 2; idem, The Aramaeans, in: Peoples of Old Testament Times, ed. D. J. Wiseman, 1973, 141. Therefore, the evidence for the dynastic establishment in Aram-Zobah in the time of David is inconclusive.

[121] It appears that Rezon the son of Eliada and Hezion the grandfather of Benhadad were one and the same person who founded the Aramaean dynasty of Damascus. While Maisler (Mazar) suggests that the name Rezon may be regarded as Hezion's royal title (A Study on the Personal Names in the Bible, Lešonenu 15 [1946/47], 42f. [Hebrew]), Malamat maintains that they were "two variants of the same name or title" (in: Peoples of Old Testament Times, 151f. n. 23).

[122] See also ANET 320; KAI § 181 1–3.

[123] ANET 654f.; KAI § 24 1–4. § 214 1. § 215 1. § 216 1–3; cf. Landsberger, Sam'al, 1948, 60ff.

[124] KAI § 222 A 1–3. B 1–2; cf. S. Parpola, Neo-Assyrian Toponyms, 1970, 76. It seems that the ruling dynasty in Arpad was called Bīt-Agūsi which the Assyrians knew from the days of Aššurnaṣirpal II on (ARAB I § 477), see J. A. Fitzmeyer, The Aramaic Inscriptions of Sefîre, 1967, 26. 40f.

[125] The assumption of the "elective monarchy of Edom" appeared as early as in F. Tuch's Commentar über die Genesis, 1871^2, 423; cf. J. Skinner, Genesis, 1930^2, 435. This thesis has been widely approved, see A. Alt, Die Staatenbildung der Israeliten in Palästina (1930), in: Kleine Schriften, II 1953, 29f. (ET The Formation of the Israelite State in Palestine, in: Essays on Old Testament History and Religion, 1966, 201); M. Noth, Geschichte Israels, 1954^2, 143 (ET The History of Israel, 1960^2, 154); R. de Vaux, Les institutions de l'Ancien Testament, I 1958, 142 (ET Ancient Israel, 1961, 91f.); but see also idem, Histoire ancienne d'Israël. Des origines à l'installation en Canaan, 1971, 481. On the other hand, Albright maintains that the throne was transmitted through the distaff side in the early monarchy of Edom (Archaeology and the Religion of Israel, 1956^4, 206 n. 58).

[126] Cf. J. R. Bartlett, The Edomite King-List of Genesis XXXVI 31–39 and I Chron I 43–50, JThS NS 16 (1965), 302ff.

the list. One preserved the names of the king's city (Dinhabah, Avith and Pau), the other had the names of the king's birthplace (Bozrah, the land of the Temanites, Masrekah and Rehoboth)[127]. In one the name of the king's father was mentioned (Beor, Zerah, Bedad and Achbor), in the other it was missing. Moreover, in the source for Hadar, the compiler mentions the lineage of the king's wife. To judge from the editorial note (Gen 36 31 I Chron 1 43), it is very likely that the compiler was an Israelite in the monarchical period[128]. Apparently, he was acquainted with the tradition that the Edomites had a monarchy prior to the Israelite monarchical period (Num 20 14; cf. I Sam 8 5. 20). It was he who seems to have put the several sources into the formula of the royal chronicle, that is, a king died and the other king reigned in his stead, in order to reconstruct the early Edomite monarchy according to his historical point of view. If our assumption is correct, he was responsible for the alleged continuity of the Edomite kings in the list. It appears that a similar sort of continuous succession was designed by a compiler of the list of the so-called minor judges (Judg 10 1–5 12 8–15)[129]. If the alleged continuity of the Edomite kings can be traced to the compiler's scheme, we may assume that these kings were actually local chieftains independent of each other geographically as well as chronologically. It is not unusual that tribal chieftains are called "king" (*mœlœḵ*). Thus, "the chiefs of Midian" (*n*ᵉ*śî'ê miḏyan*) (Josh 13 21) are also called "the kings of Midian" (*mălḵê miḏyan*) (Num 31 8). Likewise, the sheikhs of the nomad tribes were called *šarru* "king" in Mari documents: "seven kings (*šarrī*), fathers (*abbū*) of Hana"[130] and "the kings of Yaminites"[131]. Probably, there was no substantial difference between the Edomite kings in the list and "the chiefs of Edom" (*'ăllûpê 'ᵉḏôm*) (Ex. 15 15; cf. Gen 36 15–30. 40–43 I Chron 1 51b–54)[132].

---

[127] Cf. ibid. 302.

[128] Cf. ibid. 314.

[129] While Noth is of the opinion that the list of the minor judges reflects the historical continuity of the office of judge (Das Amt des „Richter Israels" [1950], in: Gesammelte Studien, II 1969, 71–85), W. Richter argues that this list was composed after the formula of the royal chronicles in the monarchical period (Zu den „Richtern Israels", ZAW 77 [1965], 41ff.).

[130] F. Thureau-Dangin, Iaḫdunlim, roi de Ḫana, RA 33 (1936), 51 I 15–16.

[131] ARM II § 36 11–12; cf. J.-R. Kupper, Les nomades en Mésopotamie au temps des rois de Mari, 1957, 59. Malamat has maintained that the plurality of kings of nomadic tribes both in the Mari documents and the Bible (Num 31 8 Judg 8 12 I Sam 14 47; cf. Gen 36 31ff.) refers to "subtribal rulers that collectively comprised the tribal leadership" (Mari, BA 34 [1971], 17); cf. idem, The Period of the Judges, in: WHJP, III 1971, 142.

[132] Cf. E. Meyer, Die Israeliten und ihre Nachbarstämme, 1906, 372; S. E. Loewenstamm, in: EncBib, I 1950, 102f. (Hebrew); Bartlett, JThS NS 16, 313; idem, The

The conditions of the early monarchy in the Syro-Palestinian kingdoms are directly reflected in Phoenician and Aramaic inscriptions of the tenth to eighth centuries B. C. from the same region[133]. According to these inscriptions, the royal authority in the kingdoms was based on the following three factors:
a) The royal lineage and the father's throne: "Šipitba'al king of Byblos, son of Eliba'al king of Byblos, son of Yehimilk king of Byblos."[134] "I, Kilamuwa, the son of Hayya, sat upon the throne of my father."[135]
b) The divine election: "Ba'alšamyn made me king over Hatarikka."[136]
c) The authorization of the overlord: "I was seated by my lord Tiglath-Pileser upon the throne of my father."[137]
All three elements can be found together in the inscription of Barrakib, king of Sam'al-Ya'dy (see above p. 19). Evidently, they are not mutually exclusive, but sometimes one is especially emphasized. Kilamuwa, king of Sam'al-Ya'dy (c. 830), mentions only his royal lineage and his father's throne[138]; Zakir, king of Hamath and Lu'ath (c. 780), lays emphasis exclusively on his divine election[139]. This difference doubtless arose from varied situations. Kilamuwa, who ascended the throne of his father, was so successful in establishing his rule that it was unnecessary to mention divine election to enhance his authority; Zakir seems to have been a usurper[140]. However, royal lineage and divine election are

Rise and Fall of the Kingdom of Edom, PEQ 104 (1972), 27; idem, The Moabites and Edomites, in: Peoples of Old Testament Times, 232f.; M. Weippert, Edom. Studien und Materialien zur Geschichte der Edomiter auf Grund schriftlicher und archäologischer Quellen, Diss. Tübingen, 1971, 474.

133 Cf. K. F. Euler, Königtum und Götterwelt in den altaramäischen Inschriften Nordsyriens, ZAW 56 (1938), 272–313.

134 KAI § 7 1–3.

135 ANET 654; KAI § 24 9.

136 ANET 655; KAI § 202A 3–4. H. Tawil finds the early bestowal of divine favour upon the king, bestowal of divine aid, and the king's divinely bestowed legitimacy in the opening section of the Hadad inscription, KAI § 214 1–4 (Some Literary Elements in the Opening Sections of the Hadad, Zākir, and the Nērab II Inscriptions in the Light of East and West Semitic Royal Inscriptions, Or NS 43 [1974], 40 ff.).

137 ANET 655; KAI § 216 5–7.

138 ANET 654f.; KAI § 24.

139 ANET 655f.; KAI § 202.

140 See A. Dupont-Sommer, Les Araméens, 1949, 46f.; J. Jepsen, Kleine Bemerkungen zu drei westsemitischen Inschriften, MIO 15 (1969), 1f.; J. F. Ross, Prophecy in Hamath, Israel, and Mari, HThR 63 (1970), 26f. A different opinion is held by M. Noth, La'asch und Hazrak, ZDPV 52 (1929), 129. As Tawil points out (Or NS 43, 51ff.), the expression אש ענה in Zakir A 2 seems to denote the piety of the king rather than his humble origin. Still, the inscription as a whole suggests that he was the founder of new dynasty.

usually mentioned side by side[141], and the authorization of the overlord for the vassal king is added[142].

From the foregoing survey we may conclude as follows:

a) Presumably, elective monarchy was instituted in the earliest phase of monarchy both in Mesopotamia and in Anatolia in proto-historic times.

b) Under special circumstances, the ruler of the city-state in Syria-Palestine was designated by the popular assembly in the second millennium B. C.

c) There is no evidence for an elective or non-dynastic monarchy in the ancient Near East in the historic period[143].

d) The dynastic principle, together with the divine election, and, if necessary, the authorization of the overlord, was the most important ideology for legitimation of royal authority in every monarchy in the ancient Near East.

---

141 ANET 320; KAI § 181 1–4 (Mesha); KAI § 214 1–3 (Panamuwa son of QRL).

142 ANET 655; KAI § 216 1–7 (Barrakib).

143 Cf. J. Liver, in: EncBib, IV 1962, 1094 (Hebrew).

Chapter 3: The Ideological Problems in the Establishment of the Monarchy in Israel

A. THE "SAMUEL-SAUL COMPLEX"

The so-called "Samuel-Saul complex" (I Sam 7–15) narrates the rise of the first Israelite monarchy and its development. In comparison with accounts of the origin of kingship of other peoples in the ancient Near East, the biblical narratives are strikingly free of mythological character[1]. Of course, they are hardly "historical" in a modern sense of the term owing to their peculiar theological interpretation of history[2], but no one can doubt that they reflect the historical situation at the beginning of the Israelite monarchy.

However, analysis of the complex and the historical evaluation of each narrative of which it consists are among the most vexed questions in biblical studies[3]. Although a consensus on the problem can as yet hardly be reached, it is possible to point out that, as far as literary analysis is concerned, the general trend has tended to shift from the two-source or three-source theory – which asserts the existence of parallel strata in the complex and generally regards them as some sort of continuation of the Pentateuch or Hexateuch sources – to the fragmentary theory, according to which the present form of the com-

---

[1] Cf. H. Frankfort, Kingship and the Gods, 1948, 337ff.; J. A. Soggin, Das Königtum in Israel, 1967, 3ff.

[2] In the view of the biblical narrators, it was Yahweh who guided the formation of the monarchy, and both Samuel and Saul were nothing but his instruments, see G. von Rad, Theologie des Alten Testaments, I 1957, 322ff. (ET Old Testament Theology, I 1962, 324ff.); H. W. Hertzberg, Die Samuelbücher, 1960², 49 (ET I & II Samuel, 1964, 65). According to R. P. Knierim, "the entire history of Saul is designed out of a messianic theology" (The Messianic Concept in the First Book of Samuel, in: Colwell Festschrift, 1968, 28).

[3] About the history of criticism of the "Samuel-Saul complex", see N. H. Snaith, The Historical Books, in: The Old Testament and Modern Study, ed. H. H. Rowley, 1951, 97ff.; E. Jenni, Zwei Jahrzehnte Forschung an den Büchern Josua bis Könige, ThR 27 (1961), 136ff.; O. Eissfeldt, Einleitung in das Alte Testament, 1964³, 321ff. 359ff. (ET The Old Testament. An Introduction, 1965, 241ff. 269ff.); F. Langlamet, Les récits de l'institution de la royauté (I Sam., VII–XII), RB 77 (1970), 161ff.; H. J. Stoebe, Das erste Buch Samuelis, 1973, 32ff.

plex resulted from the compilation of independent groups of traditions. The history of criticism can be summarized as follows:

J. Wellhausen[4] divided the complex into an "early pro-monarchical" source (9 1–10 16 11 1–11. 15 13–14) and a "late anti-monarchical" source (7 3–17 8 10 17–27 11 12–14), and regarded the latter as a Deuteronomistically-influenced revision of the former. These "early" and "late" sources were identified by K. Budde[5] with the J and the E source of Pentateuch, respectively. A further division of the "early" source into two narrative strands was advanced by A. Lods[6], that is, a seer-source and a Jabesh-source, while O. Eissfeldt[7] found here the L, J and E strands which run through the Heptateuch. Against the source theory, H. Gressmann[8] argued that the Books of Samuel consist of various independent narratives. I. Hylander[9] maintained that there were four stages of collection of the traditions, namely, the Benjaminite independent traditions, the Yahwistic composition, the Elohistic edition and the priestly codification. According to M. Noth[10], Wellhausen's "late" source is a composition of the Deuteronomistic historian who compiled old Saul traditions. A. Weiser[11] found two gathered groups of traditions, one from Benjaminite circles and the other from the prophetic circles, but each group has no literary unity. H. W. Hertzberg[12] held that various traditions were formed and transmitted at several sanctuaries independently. J. L. McKenzie[13] contended that the four figures of Samuel, namely, the priest, the prophet, the seer and the judge, show four different origins of traditions. On the other hand, a single continuous compilation of the complex was suggested by E. Robertson[14] and M. Buber[15]. Recently, H. Seebass[16] divided the complex again into two sources and the

[4] Die Composition des Hexateuchs und der historischen Bücher des Alten Testaments, 1899³, 239ff.; idem, Prolegomena zur Geschichte Israels, 1905⁶, 254ff. (ET Prolegomena to the History of Ancient Israel, 1885, 245ff.).

[5] Saul's Königswahl und Verwerfung, ZAW 8 (1888), 223–248; idem, Die Bücher Richter und Samuel. Ihre Quellen und ihr Aufbau, 1890, 167ff.

[6] Les sources des récits du premier livre de Samuel sur l'institution de la royauté israélite, in: Études de théologie et d'histoire, 1901, 265ff.

[7] Die Komposition der Samuelisbücher, 1931, 6ff.; idem, Einleitung, 362ff. (ET 271ff.).

[8] Die älteste Geschichtsschreibung und Prophetie Israels von Samuel bis Amos und Hosea, 1921², xiff.

[9] Der literarische Samuel-Saul-Komplex (I Sam. 1–15), 1932.

[10] ÜSt 54ff. 62 n. 1.

[11] Einleitung in das Alte Testament, 1963⁵, 150ff. (ET Introduction to the Old Testament, 1961, 162ff.); cf. idem, Samuel. Seine geschichtliche Aufgabe und religiöse Bedeutung: Traditionsgeschichtliche Untersuchungen zu 1 Samuel 7–12, 1962.

[12] Die Samuelbücher 103ff. (ET 130ff.).

[13] The Four Samuels, BR 7 (1962), 3–18.

[14] Samuel and Saul (1944), in: The Old Testament Problem, 1950, 105–136.

[15] Wie Saul König wurde (1950), in: M. Buber Werke, II 1964, 743–811 (= VT 6 [1956], 113–173).

[16] Traditionsgeschichte von I Sam 8 10 17ff. und 12, ZAW 77 (1965), 286–296; idem, I

Deuteronomistic elements, but both sources are "early", of which one is interested in the establishment of the right of the king and in Samuel's person, while the other's theme is the king as the military leader of Yahweh's war. J. A. Soggin[17] concluded that the complex consists of three different literary units – a latest anti-monarchical unit, a pro-monarchical unit and an earliest and most historical unit, but each unit is by no means homogeneous in itself.

According to Wellhausen, "the late anti-monarchical" source is totally unhistorical in contrast to the historical "early pro-monarchical" source. He maintained dogmatically: "There cannot be a word of truth in the whole narrative" in I Sam 7, which is the beginning of the late source[18]. In his view, this source is nothing but the "offspring of exilic or post-exilic Judaism"[19]. Since then, this radical and somehow naive judgement on the historical value of the sources has been considerably modified. And with the progress of the investigation into the formation of the individual traditions, Wellhausen's criterion itself has been entirely discarded for the historical evaluation of traditions. For instance, H. Wildberger[20] argues:

„Es ist ebenso sicher, daß auch die Stücke der älteren Schicht erst durch den Traditionsprozeß ihre heutige Gestalt gewonnen haben, wie andererseits die Möglichkeit durchaus besteht, daß auch die jüngeren Stücke Traditionselemente verarbeitet haben, die uns helfen können, den geschichtlichen Vorgang zu rekonstruieren."

This sort of approach seems to be accepted more and more widely[21].

Yet it must be pointed out that the two main problems still remain unsolved:

a) How to deal with Samuel's mutually contradictory attitudes towards the establishment of the monarchy.

b) How to explain Saul's triple election, once as *nagîḏ* and twice as king, in the reconstruction of the sequence of the events.

The main solutions which have been proposed are as follows:

a) Samuel was not an anti-monarchist as such. Either the last compiler changed his attitude towards the monarchy from positive to negative[22], or his criticism was directed not against the monarchy in general, but against the monarchy of "all the

---

Sam 15 als Schlüssel für das Verständnis der sogenannten Königsfreundlichen Reihe I Sam 9 1–16 11 1–15 und 13 2–14 52, ZAW 78 (1966), 133–148; idem, Die Vorgeschichte der Königserhebung Sauls, ZAW 79 (1967), 155–171.

[17] Das Königtum in Israel 29ff.

[18] Prolegomena 258 (ET 249).

[19] Ibid. 265 (ET 255).

[20] Samuel und die Entstehung des israelitischen Königtums, ThZ 13 (1957), 447.

[21] Cf. Weiser, Samuel, 26f.

[22] Wildberger, ThZ 13, 460.

nations"[23]. In contrast, in the other view, Samuel was a stubborn anti-monarchist. He did not intend to make Saul king but appointed him only as *nagîḏ*[24]. Or the person who took part in Saul's elevation to kingship was not Samuel but an anonymous man of God[25]. There is also another view, that Samuel's ambivalent attitude towards the monarchy marks a schism in the soul of Samuel himself[26].

b) Those who regard the account of Saul's enthronement at Gilgal (11 15) as the sole historical tradition generally come to the conclusion that the other two narratives of his election are either anecdotal or tendentious[27]. Another solution is suggested by placing the story of Saul's victory over the Ammonites (11 1–11) before ch. 8–10. When the elders consulted with Samuel about the appointment of a war-leader against the Philistines, Saul, hero of the Ammonite campaign, was chosen and secretly anointed (10 1 LXX), and then was made king publicly (10 14 11 15)[28]. As a modification of this view, some scholars maintain that Saul was made king only after his victory over the Philistines (ch. 13–14)[29]. According to still another theory, Saul's triple election was nothing but three successive enthronements in three different places by three different tribes[30].

To sum up, scholars have tried to solve the first problem by the elimination of one of Samuel's attitudes in one way or another, and the second by diverse interpretations and rearrangement of the narratives. But in view of unsurmounted difficulties in each solution, it seems that a new solution must be sought by a fresh approach.

First of all, it should be stressed that the establishment of the monarchy was a political matter. Admittedly, secular life and religious matters were inseparably interwoven in the way of life in ancient Israel.

---

[23] Weiser, Samuel, 42f.

[24] W. F. Albright, Samuel and the Beginning of the Prophetic Movement, 1961, 15f.; J. Dus, Die „Sufeten" Israels, ArOr 31 (1963), 463ff.

[25] H. Bardtke, Samuel und Saul. Gedanken zur Entstehung des Königtums in Israel, BiOr 25 (1968), 301f.

[26] McKenzie, BR 7, 17.

[27] W. A. Irwin, Samuel and the Rise of the Monarchy, AJSL 58 (1941), 113ff.; cf. Alt, Die Staatenbildung der Israeliten in Palästina (1930), in: Kleine Schriften, II 1953, 13ff. (ET The Formation of the Israelite State in Palestine, in: Essays on Old Testament History and Religion, 1966, 185ff.); Noth, Geschichte Israels, 1954², 156ff. (ET The History of Israel, 1960², 168ff.).

[28] Wildberger, ThZ 13, 466ff.

[29] Lods, Israël des origines au milieu du VIIIᵉ siècle, 1930, 409ff. (ET Israel from its Beginning to the Middle of the Eighth Century, 1932, 352ff.); Seebass, ZAW 79, 155ff.

[30] G. Wallis, Die Anfänge des Königtums in Israel (1963), in: Geschichte und Überlieferung, 1968, 61f.; C. E. Hauer, Does I Sam. 9:1–11:15 reflect the Extension of Saul's Dominion?, JBL 86 (1967), 306–310. J. Weingreen argues that Saul was enthroned at Mizpah by the southern tribes and at Gilgal by the northern tribes, respectively (The Theory of the Amphictyony in Pre-Monarchical Israel, in: Gaster Festschrift, JANES 5 [1973], 431f.).

Consequently, the historical events were explained in the biblical narratives "as integral parts of a God-planned and God-directed working"[31]. But no one can deny that the dynamism of politics decisively influenced the establishment of the monarchy. Therefore, although our source materials are strongly theologically-coloured narratives, we must find in them a common principle of secular politics, that is to say, a new political situation is usually created through opposition, negotiation and compromise between opposing groups which pursue their own interests in society.

Secondly, we must take into account that ancient Israel had a unique problem which introduced a complication at the establishment of the monarchy. Since the tribes of Israel had formed their fundamental traditions in the pre-monarchical period, the monarchy was unable to attain, ultimately, an indispensable position in Israelite society[32]. Under these circumstances, there must have been an ideological conflict between the monarchists and the anti-monarchists concerning the establishment of the monarchy[33]. We can assume further that, even after his elevation to the throne, the first king of Israel had to legitimatize not only his royal authority but also the monarchy itself as a new political institution. To make matters more involved, the first monarchy was short-lived and was succeeded by that of David, who was originally related neither to the royal house nor to the northern tribes which constituted the main elements of that first monarchy. It is understandable that David immediately launched out into argument for his legitimation. We should, therefore, expect from the start that conflicting opinions existed in the period of the early monarchies to which the "Samuel-Saul complex" pertains.

Thirdly, we presuppose that each narrative in the complex was composed independently in the midst of the formation of the early monarchies. In our judgment, this is the best explanation of the wide variety of viewpoints found in the narratives. It has been recognized that they are marked by sharply divergent attitudes towards the

---

[31] G. E. Wright, God who acts, 1952, 81f.

[32] Cf. Frankfort, Kingship and the Gods, 337ff.; Alt, Das Königtum in den Reichen Israel und Juda (1951), in: Kleine Schriften, II 116 (ET The Monarchy in the Kingdoms of Israel and Judah, in: Essays, 241); de Vaux, Les institutions de l'Ancien Testament, I 1958, 151ff. (ET Ancient Israel, 1961, 98f.).

[33] It has been pointed out that the recollection of the tensions and discussions in the popular assembly at the time of the establishment of the monarchy can be found in the so-called anti-monarchical traditions, see Weiser, Samuel, 31; M. Tsevat, The Biblical Narrative of the Foundation of Kingship in Israel, Tarbiz 36 (1966/67), 99–109 (Hebrew); A. D. Ritterspach, The Samuel Traditions: An Analysis of the Anti-Monarchical Source in I Samuel 1–15, Diss. Graduate Theological Union and the San Francisco Theological Seminary, 1967, 302ff.; Soggin, Das Königtum in Israel, 33.

monarchy[34], or, in the opinion of some scholars, towards Saul[35]. We agree basically that a distinction must be made between the pro-monarchical and anti-monarchical narratives, or the pro-Saul and anti-Saul narratives. But so many different nuances of this criterion can be detected in each narrative that it is by no means clear if we can divide the complex into two or three narrative groups, let alone narrative strands, on the basis of the difference in attitude towards the monarchy or Saul. Sensing this difficulty, some scholars have proposed that, before the compilation of the complex, there existed independent traditions grouped in each place with which they were associated[36]. But this explanation is also insufficient, since the narratives associated with the same place are not always of the same mind about the monarchy or about Saul. It seems more likely that the delicate shades of political opinion expressed in each narrative are a measure of the dynamic development of political and social conditions. We can hardly expect a static situation in an age of such momentous change as was the period of the formation of the early Israelite monarchies.

B. THE IDEOLOGICAL CONFLICT ON THE EVE OF THE FORMATION OF THE MONARCHY

The biblical narratives about the birth of the monarchy diverge considerably in their political opinions as well as in individual details, but they agree with each other on the fact that the monarchy was born out of the co-operation between the people and Samuel. In I Sam 8, the elders, the representatives of the people, took the initiative in replacing the *šōpeṭ*-regime by monarchy and compelled Samuel to compromise with them, while in 9 1–10 16 it was Samuel who played the leading role in the designation of a *nagîd* to meet the cry of the people afflicted by Philistine oppression. In 10 17–27 as well as in ch. 11, the election of the first king was carried out jointly by Samuel and the people. But

---

[34] This is the basic criterion of division of sources, see above p. 26 n. 3. However, Weiser does not find any fundamental rejection of the monarchy in the so-called anti-monarchical narratives (Samuel 25ff. 62ff. 79ff.). Tsevat is also of the opinion that there is no absolute opposition to a monarchy except in a late addition (I Sam 12 6–12. 16–32) to the whole complex (Tarbiz 36, 109 [Hebrew]).

[35] So Buber, Wie Saul König wurde, in: Werke, II 803ff. According to T. C. G. Thornton, the so-called anti-monarchical passages were originally a debate about the form of kingship in Saul's time, but got their present form as a result of the revision of the Davidic propaganda against Saul's monarchy (Studies in Samuel, CQR 168 [1967], 413ff.).

[36] Hertzberg, Die Samuelbücher, 104f. (ET 131f.); Weiser, Samuel, 23. 43. 68. 79. 88f.

Samuel's participation is quite active in the former, while his figure is somewhat shadowy in the latter. However, we are also told that co-operation was achieved only after hard negotiations between the two parties who had conflicting ideas about the new political organization. To understand this conflict properly, we should, to begin with, examine the nature of the two parties: Samuel, the "party in power", and the people, the "opposition party".

As for Samuel's image, the historical evaluation has undergone a great change since a few decades ago. In the opinion of scholars of the older generation, an author of the anti-monarchical version fabricated the legendary figure of Samuel as the last judge and the first king-maker, but he was actually a mere village seer and had nothing to do with the rise of the monarchy[37]. In contrast, in the opinion prevailing today, Samuel was the last of the "minor judges" whose authority in the Israelite amphictyony enabled him to make Saul king[38]. But it seems that neither earlier assertion nor modern view can explain the historical situation in which the monarchy was established. On the one hand, it is impossible to reconstruct the history of the rise of the monarchy without Samuel's contribution, embedded as it is in all the biblical traditions[39]. On the other hand, we can hardly accept the supposition that Samuel held the central office in a highly organized confederation such as an "amphictyony", as we shall show presently.

At the onset, it is important to note that, after having served as an acolyte in the presence of Eli the priest at Shiloh (I Sam 1–3), Samuel began his career as Yahweh's prophet there (3 19–4 1a). Undoubtedly, his authority was originally derived from, and was connected with, the shrine at Shiloh[40]. From I Sam 4 1b–18, we can assume that this shrine

---

[37] Gressmann, Die älteste Geschichtsschreibung, 35f.; Irwin maintained that "not a single passage relating contacts of Saul with Samuel commands respect as historically reliable" (AJSL 58, 130).

[38] Hertzberg, Die kleinen Richter, ThLZ 79 (1954), 286ff.; von Rad, Theologie, I 42 (ET 33); Wildberger, ThZ 13, 463ff.; Weiser, Samuel, 10ff.; Soggin, Das Königtum in Israel, 31; Bardtke, BiOr 25, 202. However, Noth does not assume that Samuel had any office (Geschichte 158 [ET 170]), while McKenzie holds that the tradition of Samuel as the judge-magistrate is unhistorical (BR 7, 11ff.).

[39] Cf. H. Schulte, Die Entstehung der Geschichtsschreibung im alten Israel, 1972, 106f.

[40] Noth maintains that I Sam 3 was composed by an author who wanted to show the close relation of Samuel to Shiloh (Samuel und Silo, VT 13 [1963], 390–400). On the other hand, M. Newman argues that Samuel took over the function of the covenant mediator of the amphictyony formerly exercised by Eli (The Prophetic Call of Samuel, in: Muilenburg Festschrift, 1962, 86–97), while M. A. Cohen assumes that Samuel derived his authority from his position as the Shilonite seer-priest (The Role of the Shilonite Priesthood in the United Monarchy of Ancient Israel, HUCA 36 [1965], 65ff.).

was the centre of the confederation of the Israelite tribes at that time. Apparently, it was organized by the main tribes of central Palestine, which were compelled to present a united front against ever increasing Philistine pressure that seriously threatened their very existence[41].

We have demonstrated elsewhere that the structure of the Shilonite confederation represents an important change in comparison with the tribal leagues in the preceding generations[42]. The tribal coalitions formed occasionally by a number of tribes against common enemies in the pre-monarchical period were always organized by charismatic war-leaders called *šop̄eṭîm*. They ruled over the tribal league for life on the strength of their military success, but the league dissolved on their death without hereditary succession to their authority[43]. By contrast, it is remarkable that the Shilonite confederation was neither organized nor ruled by a charismatic war-leader. It appears that the leader of it was Eli the priest (4 18b). But the elders of the tribes collectively conducted the military operations, while Eli remained at Shiloh (4 3). Evidently, Eli was a "priest-*šop̄eṭ*" whose authority over the tribal league did not stem from his charisma in military affairs. Then how did he become the *šop̄eṭ*, that is, the leader of the tribal confederation? It is very likely that he was appointed as leader by the confederation, and at the same time, his office of *šop̄eṭ* was recognized, presumably, to be as hereditary as the priesthood[44]. In our appraisal, this was an attempt to establish a stable leadership and replace the spontaneous charismatic leader by a hereditary priestly one. At that time, the Israelite tribes were compelled to organize a tribal confederation which would be more enduring than previous confederations, to cope with the most serious crisis that they had ever experienced.

After the collapse of the Shilonite confederation, Samuel made a great effort to re-establish the unity of the tribes and liberate them

---

[41] About the historical background of the war between the Israelite tribes and the Philistines, see B. Mazar, The Philistines and their War with Israel, in: WHJP, III 1971, 164–179. 324–325.

[42] T. Ishida, The Leaders of the Tribal Leagues "Israel" in the Pre-Monarchic Period, RB 80 (1973), 527f.

[43] On the charismatic leadership in the period of the Judges, see M. Weber, Gesammelte Aufsätze zur Religionssoziologie, III. Das antike Judentum, 1923², 47f. 93f.; Alt, Die Staatenbildung, in: Kleine Schriften, II 6 (ET 178); Albright, From the Stone Age to Christianity, 1957², 283f.; Malamat, The Period of the Judges, in: WHJP, III 130; idem, The Deliverer-Judge as the Leader in the Period of the Judges, in: Types of Leadership in the Biblical Period, 1971, 11–25 (Hebrew).

[44] On the hereditary priesthood, see de Vaux, Les institutions de l'Ancien Testament, II 1960, 214ff. (ET Ancient Israel, 359f.); A. Cody, A History of Old Testament Priesthood, 1969, 60.

from Philistine domination (I Sam 7)[45]. At that time, he became the "*šopeṭ* of Israel" (7 15–17). This title appears to show that he took the office of *šopeṭ* as Eli's legitimate successor by way of the reorganization of the collapsed confederation. We consider that this situation is depicted in the narratives on the sins of the sons of Eli and the oracle on the fall of Eli's house (2 11b–4 1a). The main theme of these narratives is doubtless the fall of Eli's house and the rise of Samuel, in spite of a late insertion of a Jerusalemite polemic against Shiloh (2 35–36)[46]. Samuel had reason to legitimatize his office of *šopeṭ* against the house of Eli. This offers more evidence for our supposition that the office of *šopeṭ* was recognized as hereditary at Shiloh. In any case, Samuel's league is to be regarded as a kind of continuation of the Shilonite confederation, since both organizations had the same structure. While the people of Israel waged war against the Philistines, Samuel the *šopeṭ* played the priestly role at Mizpah (7 5–11)[47]. But he himself, just like Eli, did not take command in war. We may call him the "seer-*šopeṭ*" or the "prophet-*šopeṭ*" according to his titles. Furthermore, he made clear the hereditary nature of his office by appointing his sons to be "*šopeṭîm* over Israel" (8 1)[48].

It is clear, however, that under Philistine supremacy Samuel could only organize a confederation modest both in extent and in power. The account that he moved from place to place (7 15–17) shows that he had no centre like the shrine at Shiloh. It also indicates that the extent of his confederation was limited to some parts of Ephraim and Benja-

---

[45] The historicity of I Sam 7 has been completely denied since Wellhausen, see above p. 28 n. 18; most recently Stoebe, Das erste Buch Samuelis, 170ff. However, some scholars have lately tried to find some historical recollections in it, although part of the chapter clearly reflects the situation after the victories of Saul and David over the Philistines, see Albright, Samuel and the Beginning of the Prophetic Movement, 14; Weiser, Samuel, 5ff.; Seebass, ZAW 77, 292ff.; idem, ZAW 79, 155ff.; Mazar, in: WHJP, III 177f.; cf. Langlamet, RB 77, 170.

[46] Cf. Hertzberg, Die Samuelbücher, 32 (ET 43f.); Tsevat, Studies in the Book of Samuel. I. Interpretation of I Sam 2: 27–36. The Narrative of *Kareth*, HUCA 32 (1961), 191–209; Cody, A History of Old Testament Priesthood, 68f.; J. T. Willis, An Anti-Elide Narrative Tradition from a Prophetic Circle at the Ramah Sanctuary, JBL 90 (1971), 288–308.

[47] Seebass surmises that the Israelite victory over the Philistines at Mizpah (I Sam 7 7–14a) was actually made by Saul before his elevation to the king (ZAW 79, 156). The suggestion is highly hypothetical.

[48] A note on the appointment of Samuel's sons to the *šopeṭîm* in Beersheba (I Sam 8 2) would show that the central tribes tried to form a coalition with the southern. Apparently, the name of another town in which the second son was appointed is missing, cf. D. A. McKenzie, The Judges of Israel, VT 17 (1967), 121.

min[49]. Under these circumstances, we can scarcely assume that Samuel's confederation had central authority over all the tribes of Israel. In other words, it is extremely difficult to assume that Samuel enjoyed an authority such as that of the "minor judge" recognized by the Israelite amphictyony. Had he held such an office, the elders of Jabesh-gilead would have sent the messengers directly to him, when Jabesh helplessly faced alone the attack of Nahash the Ammonite. Instead, they sent them "through all the territory of Israel" (11 3), since they knew that there was no central authority in Israel then which was capable of mobilizing reinforcements. The Israelite troop for the relief of Jabesh was organized by Saul in the manner of the charismatic war-leaders of the pre-monarchical period, but Samuel the *šopeṭ* contributed almost nothing to it (11 5–8)[50]. In fact, prior to the incident at Jabesh-gilead, having realized the impotence of the *šopeṭ*-regime, the elders of Israel began to look for a new political institution, to wit, the monarchy. This situation is plainly visible in the words of the elders to Samuel: "Behold, you are old and your sons do not walk in your ways; now appoint for us a king to govern us like all the nations" (8 5).

Now as to the "opposition party", the people of Israel, or, precisely speaking, the elders of Israel. In ancient Israel, every local community was a self-governing body ruled by the council of elders. This was the people's representative organization which exercised supreme authority in the community, especially in the pre-monarchical period[51]. The question with which we are concerned is not this well-known institution, but the concept of "Israel" as the common denominator of the local communities on the eve of the formation of the monarchy. In the story of Saul's campaign against the Ammonites (11 1–11), generally accepted as a reliable historical source, we find the expression "territo-

---

[49] "All the house of Israel" (I Sam 7 2. 3; cf. 7 5) is a later pan-Israelite expansion as in I Sam 10 17–27, see below p. 46. On the geographical position of the cities of Samuel, see Y. Aharoni, apud M. Avi-Yonah, The Macmillan Bible Atlas, 1968, no. 85.

[50] Many scholars assume that the name Samuel was inserted into ch. 11 secondarily, see Gressmann, Die älteste Geschichtsschreibung, 36. 43f.; Irwin, AJSL 58, 129; Wildberger, ThZ 13, 449. 459; Wallis, in: Geschichte und Überlieferung, 56; Soggin, Das Königtum in Israel, 44; cf. also Stoebe, Das erste Buch Samuelis, 221ff. However, some scholars regard it as original, see R. Press, Der Prophet Samuel. Eine traditionsgeschichtliche Untersuchung, ZAW 56 (1938), 203ff. 224f.; Buber in: Werke, II 786f.; Hertzberg, Die Samuelbücher, 70 n. 2 (ET 90 note b); Weiser, Samuel, 26. 70. 75. On our view, see below p. 48.

[51] Cf. C. U. Wolf, Traces of Primitive Democracy in Ancient Israel, JNES 6 (1947), 98–108; de Vaux, Les institutions, I 108. 212f. (ET 69. 138); J. L. McKenzie, The Elders in the Old Testament, Bib 40 (1959), 522–540; Malamat, Organs of Statecraft in the Israelite Monarchy (1965), in: BAR 3, 1970, 167f.; Buccellati, Cities and Nations of Ancient Syria, 1967, 130ff.

ry (*g^eḇûl*) of Israel" (v. 3. 7), which indicates that there was a territory where the people of Israel settled. But this does not mean that Israel was already a state, since the totally independent situation of the people of Jabesh confronting Nahash (v. 1–3) shows that Israel was organized too loosely to be called a political unit[52]. The fact that the people of Jabesh had authority to make a treaty with a foreign king clearly indicates its political independence of all external control. However, we must also note that Nahash's cruel condition imposed upon the people of Jabesh was regarded as a "disgrace upon all Israel" (v. 2), the people of Israel wept over the fate of Jabesh (v. 4), and finally they voluntarily joined Saul's campaign for the relief of Jabesh (v. 7–11). We may infer that, on the eve of the formation of the monarchy, the name "Israel" signified a great tribal community which had a common religio-national consciousness in the "dread of Yahweh" (v. 7) and shared a common feeling of close consanguineous bonds, but had no firm political organization to express its solidarity[53].

We have demonstrated elsewhere that the name "Israel" was used in a double sense in the pre-monarchical period[54]. On the one hand, it was the name of a great community comprising all the tribes of Israel. On the other, it was the designation of a local tribal confederation which was organized occasionally by a charismatic war-leader at a critical moment. Therefore, the "men of Israel", whom Saul mustered at Bezek (v. 8)[55], designate a tribal confederation organized *ad hoc* by Saul. But a new development took place at that juncture which no charismatic war-leader could ever achieve. Saul managed to call up the militia "as one man" from "all the territory of Israel" (v. 7–8). To be sure, it appears that Saul's force consisted mainly of the tribes of central Palestine and

---

[52] According to Dus, pre-monarchical Israel was a republic ruled by a "suffete" (ArOr 31, 444ff.). On the other hand, Buccellati regards the "Israelite amphictyony" as a state, because of its supra-tribal institutions and the acknowledgment of a common law (Cities and Nations 111ff.). It seems, however, that their arguments are based on unsound interpretation of the source materials.

[53] Cf. Y. Kaufmann, The Book of Judges, 1962, 36f. (Hebrew).

[54] Ishida, RB 80, 523ff.

[55] Owing to the unrealistic numbers, I Sam 11 8b is sometimes regarded as a later addition, see Noth, Jabes-Gilead, ZDPV 69 (1953), 35 n. 9; Wildberger, ThZ 13, 488; K.-D. Schunck, Benjamin. Untersuchungen zur Entstehung und Geschichte eines israelitischen Stammes, 1963, 90. However, there is no reason to eliminate the whole verse as secondary, although the mention of the "men of Judah" alongside the "men of Israel" seems to reflect a view derived from the monarchical period, see K. Möhlenbrink, Sauls Ammoniterfeldzug und Samuels Beitrag zum Königtum des Saul, ZAW 58 (1940/41), 60; von Rad, Der Heilige Krieg im alten Israel, 1952^2, 20; Weiser, Samuel, 71; cf. also W. Richter, Zu den „Richtern Israels", ZAW 77 (1965), 52.

of the tribes from east of the Jordan[56]. But there is no reason to doubt that the other tribes from "all the territory of Israel" also sent contingents to the campaign. This was not a general mobilization of the "amphictyony", as M. Noth[57] maintains, but the establishment of the first great coalition including all the tribes of Israel. This kind of mobilization from "all the territory of Israel" prior to Saul is mentioned only once, in the account of the assembly of all the tribes of Israel called up against Gibeah (Judg 19 29). It is widely accepted, however, that this story took its present pan-Israelite character from a late embellishment, presumably based on the narrative of Saul's campaign for the relief of Jabesh[58]. Needless to say, Saul's great coalition came into being only after long preparation in the preceding periods, in which consciousness of national unity had been gradually strengthened among the tribes of Israel. But "Israel" as a tribal confederation had never included all "Israel", the great tribal community. When both concepts of "Israel" were superimposed exactly one upon the other under Saul's call-up, the time was about to be ripe for the establishment of the monarchy.

If the *šopeṭ*-regime adopted by Samuel was a heritage of the tribal confederation at Shiloh, the origin of his political ideology can also be traced back to the Shilonite tradition. Although we have little information on the tradition of Shiloh, it is possible to find its characteristic features in the two epithets by which Yahweh was called at Shiloh – Yahweh *ṣ*^{e}*ḇa'ôṯ* (I Sam 1 3. 11 4 4) and Yahweh who sits above the Cherubim (4 4). It appears that both titles first came to be attached to Yahweh at Shiloh, where his presence was symbolized by the Ark standing in the shrine (4 4; cf. II Sam 6 2)[59]. The exact meaning of the first epithet is arguable, but it doubtless shows Yahweh's power and his dominion[60]. Evidently, the second designation indicates invisible

---

[56] Möhlenbrink argues that the tribal league which fought under Saul's command was formed with Benjamin and the tribes from east of the Jordan only (ZAW 58, 57ff.), while Schunck maintains that all the tribes of Israel as well as Judah participated in the campaign (Benjamin 126ff.).

[57] Geschichte 157 (ET 169).

[58] Cf. Eissfeldt, Der geschichtliche Hintergrund der Erzählung von Gibeas Schandtat (1935), in: Kleine Schriften, II 1963, 64–80; Schunck, Benjamin, 57ff.

[59] Cf. Eissfeldt, Jahwe Zebaoth (1950), in: Kleine Schriften, III 1966, 113ff.; de Vaux, Les institutions, II 74f. 129f. 135f. (ET 259. 299. 304); R. E. Clements, God and Temple, 1965, 33ff., especially 34 n. 6. Against this view, J. Maier argues that the title *ṣ*^{e}*ḇa'ôṯ* implied the national levy of Israel and Judah under David's double monarchy (Das altisraelitische Ladeheiligtum, 1965, 51ff.). But his argument is unconvincing.

[60] Cf. Eissfeldt, Jahwe Zebaoth, in: Kleine Schriften, III 107ff.; de Vaux, Les

Yahweh sitting on the Cherubim-throne, a throne supported by sphinxes on each side[61]. Thus, it becomes patent that both titles are perfectly fit for Yahweh as king, whom we frequently meet later in the Jerusalemite cult tradition[62]. Opinions have been divided on the origin of the conception of Yahweh's kingship:

M. Buber[63] has argued for its Mosaic origin. But his argument, based on the character of Yahweh as the leading God and on the interpretation of the Sinaitic covenant as the royal covenant, was criticized by G. von Rad[64]. O. Eissfeldt[65] has once demonstrated that the earliest application of the term king to Yahweh appears in Is 6 5 and all other evidence is later. It is not plausible, however, that Isaiah suddenly began to call Yahweh king[66]. Because of the special relation of the idea of Yahweh's kingship to Jerusalem, A. F. von Gall[67] has maintained that this idea originated in the kingship of the chief god of the pantheon of pre-Davidic Jerusalem. Yet many scholars aver that it came into being in Jerusalem after the kingdom of David was established there[68].

---

institutions, II 136 (ET 304); J. P. Ross, Yahweh *Ṣ^ebā'ôt* in Samuel and Psalms, VT 17 (1967), 76–92; F. M. Cross, Canaanite Myth and Hebrew Epic, 1973, 69ff.

61 See de Vaux, Les chérubins et l'arche d'alliance. Les sphinx gardiens et les trônes divins dans l'ancien Orient (1960), in: Bible et Orient, 1967, 250.

62 The theology of Yahweh's kingship is found mainly in the so-called "enthronement psalms". S. Mowinckel has advanced the theory that "Yahweh's enthronement" was celebrated in the temple of Jerusalem at the New Year festival (Psalmenstudien, II 1921). About the development of this theory and critical remarks on it, see K.-H. Bernhardt, Das Problem der altorientalischen Königsideologie im Alten Testament, 1961, 78f. 192ff. 258ff. 294ff.; J. Schreiner, Sion-Jerusalem. Jahwes Königssitz, 1963, 191ff.; Clements, God and Temple, 69ff.

63 Königtum Gottes, 1932, 1956³, (ET Kingship of God, 1967); cf. J. de Fraine, L'aspect religieux de la royauté israélite, 1954, 117ff.; idem, La royauté de Yahvé dans les textes concernant l'arche, SVT 15 (1966), 134–149.

64 In: Theologisches Wörterbuch zum Neuen Testament, I 1933, 563ff. (ET in: Theological Dictionary of the New Testament, I 1964, 565ff.); cf. V. Maag, Malkût JHWH, SVT 7 (1960), 129–153; but see also Tsevat, Tarbiz 36, 100f. (Hebrew).

65 Jahwe als König (1928), in: Kleine Schriften, I 1962, 172–193; but he changed his opinion afterwards and accepted Alt's suggestion that the ideology of Yahweh's kingship originated from the pre-monarchical period, see below p. 39 n. 69.

66 Cf. A. R. Johnson, The Psalms, in: The Old Testament and Modern Study, 192.

67 Über die Herkunft der Bezeichnung Jahwes als König, in: Wellhausen Festschrift, BZAW 27 (1914), 155f.; cf. H. Schmid, Jahwe und die Kulttraditionen von Jerusalem, ZAW 67 (1955), 168–197; Mowinckel, The Psalms in Israel's Worship, I 1962, 114.

68 E. G. Kraeling, The Real Religion of Ancient Israel, JBL 47 (1928), 153; J. Morgenstern, Psalm 48, HUCA 16 (1941), 40; H.-J. Kraus, Die Königsherrschaft Gottes im Alten Testament, 1951, 90ff.; J. Gray, The Hebrew Conception of the Kingship of God: its Origin and Development, VT 6 (1956), 268–285; L. Rost, Königsherrschaft Jahwes in vorköniglicher Zeit?, ThLZ 85 (1960), 721–724.

Some recent studies, however, have convincingly demonstrated that the conception of Yahweh's kingship was adopted by Israel from the Canaanites in the pre-monarchical period, most probably at Shiloh[69]. It has been suggested that Yahweh first became the king of the deities whom the tribes of Israel encountered in Canaan, by taking over the kingship of El in the Canaanite pantheon[70]. The Shilonite ideology seems to have linked the conception of Yahweh as king over the foreign deities with Yahweh as deliverer of Israel. This idea came from the ancient tradition of the Holy War which was fought under the command of the charismatic war-leaders in the pre-monarchical period[71]. Thus, the elders of the Shilonite confederation, which had been defeated by the Philistines, hoped that by bringing the Ark of Yahweh from Shiloh to the battlefield "he may save them from the power of their enemies" (I Sam 4 3).

This Shilonite ideology was inherited by Samuel who constantly mentioned Yahweh as king (12 12) and deliverer of Israel (7 3 10 18–19 11 13 12 7.11; cf. 7 8 9 16 10 1 LXX). Evidently, the regime based on this ideology was a theocracy, in which the military command was subordinated to the religious leadership. Its characteristic feature can be found in the narrative of the battle near Mizpah, where the people of Israel achieved victory only with the help of Yahweh's direct intervention, invoked by Samuel the prophet-*šopeṭ* (7 5–11). Against this background we can understand Samuel's reaction to the demand of the elders of Israel to appoint a king. "The thing displeased him" (8 6), since their demand was an attempt to make the military command separate from and independent of the religious authority (cf. 8 5. 20)[72]. He must have understood that an independent military leader would soon get the upper hand over the religious authorities, and, in his view, this was a rejection of Yahweh as king and deliverer of Israel (8 7 10 19 12 12)[73]. But the elders certainly held another view. They could maintain that their demand for a monarchy "like all the nations" (8 5.

[69] See Alt, Gedanken über das Königtum Jahwes (1945), in: Kleine Schriften, I 1953, 345–357, especially 353; Eissfeldt, El und Yahweh (1956), in: Kleine Schriften, III 1966, 397; W. H. Schmidt, Königtum Gottes in Ugarit und Israel, 1966², 80ff.; Clements, God and Temple, 34 n. 6; Weiser, Samuel, 33ff.; Bardtke, BiOr 25, 289ff.

[70] Cf. Eissfeldt, El und Yahweh, in: Kleine Schriften, III 396f.; Schmidt, Königtum Gottes, 86f.

[71] Cf. von Rad, Der Heilige Krieg, 9; de Vaux, Les institutions, II 74ff. (ET 258f.); H. J. Boecker, Die Beurteilung der Anfänge des Königtums in den deuteronomistischen Abschnitten des I. Samuelbuches, 1969, 20ff.

[72] Cf. Robertson, Samuel and Saul, in: The Old Testament Problem, 130ff.

[73] Many scholars regard these verses as Deuteronomistic, see Noth, ÜSt, 56ff.; Gray, The Kingship of God in the Prophets and Psalms, VT 11 (1961), 12; Schmidt, Königtum Gottes, 93f.; Boecker, Die Beurteilung, 19ff.; but see Weiser, Samuel, 33f.

20) would not encroach upon Yahweh's kingship[74], since divine rule and human monarchy were generally regarded as complementary rather than contradictory ideas in the ancient Near East[75].

This was the moment when the impotence of Samuel's regime under Philistine supremacy became conspicuous. But what played a decisive role was "the voice of the people" (8 7. 22 12 1). Understanding the general situation, Samuel not only gave in to the demand of the people but also took the initiative in establishing the monarchy. This change of attitude towards the monarchy is not to be regarded as an ideological change on his part. Although it was a sort of concession, his active participation in founding the monarchy must be interpreted as an effort to put the monarchy under his influence, so that he would still have an opportunity to realize his ideology in the new regime (cf. 15 1ff.). His plan was achieved formally in the proclamation of the "manner of the kingdom" (*mišpāṭ hămmᵉlûḵā*) on the occasion of Saul's enthronement at Mizpah (10 25). We are told nothing about the details of this document, but the whole context indicates that the first monarchy was founded as a constitutional regime by Samuel in collaboration with the people[76].

As for the nature and origin of the "manner of the king" (*mišpāṭ hămmœlœḵ*) (8 9. 11–17) and its relation to the "manner of the kingdom" (10 25) and the "law of the king" (Deut 17 14–20), various suggestions have been made:

M. Noth[77] has regarded the "manner of the king" as a Deuteronomistic composition based on the tradition of the "manner of the kingdom". Similarly, H. J. Boecker[78] has found the same Deuteronomistic judgement of the kingship as a social burden in both the "manner of the king" and the "law of the king". Against the view that the "manner of the king" is an anti-monarchical document based on bad experiences

---

[74] Alt argues that a later theologian stigmatized the establishment of the kingdom as the people's imitation of other nations (Die Staatenbildung, in: Kleine Schriften, II 17 [ET 189]), while Weiser regards the people's desire as a genuine historical motive (Samuel 32. 42f.). Seebass interprets "No!" in the people's answer (v. 19) as "No!" to Samuel's assertion that the people rejected Yahweh's kingship (ZAW 77, 287). But this interpretation is unwarranted, see Boecker, Die Beurteilung, 18f.

[75] As an example of the harmonious relationship between divine and human kingship we can mention the Assyrian coronation ritual in which a priest called out: "Aššur is king!", see Frankfort, Kingship and the Gods, 246.

[76] G. Fohrer regards the "manner of the kingdom" as a document of the covenant between the king and the people (Der Vertrag zwischen König und Volk in Israel [1959], in: Studien zur alttestamentlichen Theologie und Geschichte [1949–1966], 1969, 332f.); cf. Alt, Die Staatenbildung, in: Kleine Schriften, II 23 (ET 195).

[77] ÜSt 58.

[78] Die Beurteilung 16ff.

in the later monarchy, I. Mendelsohn[79] has argued that it bespeaks the condition of the semi-feudal Canaanite society before and during the time of Samuel. According to A. Weiser[80], the "manner of the king" was the king's rights according to the model of the foreign kings, while the "manner of the kingdom" was the law for the Israelite king from the viewpoint of Yahweh's rulership. K. Galling[81] has found the ideology of the charismatic kingship in the "law of the king". But A. Caquot[82] could not find such a view in the "law of the king", which was, as he saw it, a programme for Josiah's reform, although some ancient traditions are included. S. Talmon[83] has advanced a thesis that the "manner of the king" served as the fundamental directions for the negotiations between the elders and Samuel concerning the formation of the monarchy. Since Samuel quoted part of it in his argument against the monarchy, the present text gives a negative impression. Still, we cannot fail to discern the positive character of the original form in the assertion that the king has the right as well as the duty to establish a national standing army, the system of taxation and the royal court. It is to be supposed that the present text is a tendentious excerpt from a full original called the "manner of the kingdom", and that other parts of it are to be found in the "law of the king". Z. Ben-Barak[84] contended that in drawing up the constitution, that is, the "manner of the kingdom", Samuel had recourse to the Canaanite principles of kingship, that is, the "manner of the king". Recently, R. E. Clements[85] has argued that the "manner of the king" was a document stemming from a bad experience under the despotic regime of Solomon but later associated with Saul by the Deuteronomists who regarded all other monarchies than the Davidic kingship as those rejected by Yahweh.

It is not our purpose to enter into this much debated problem. We are interested only in the fact that, whatever mutual relations and attitudes towards the monarchy the three documents may have, it is not easy to find in them any rejection of the dynastic principle. On the contrary, in the "law of the king" dynastic stability is guaranteed by Yahweh on condition of the king's obedience to him (Deut 17 20). We may assume that the "manner of the kingdom" included a similar article about the dynastic succession of the royal house. This assumption will be discussed in the next section.

---

79 Samuel's Denunciation of Kingship in the Light of Akkadian Documents from Ugarit, BASOR 143 (1956), 17–22. 80 Samuel 67.

81 Das Königsgesetz im Deuteronomium, ThLZ 76 (1951), 133–138.

82 Remarques sur la "loi royale" du Deutéronome 17/14–20, Semitica 9 (1959), 21–33. On the other hand, S. Yeivin is of the opinion that the "law of the king" stemmed from the period of Solomon (The Time of the Book of Deuteronomy [1950/51], in: Studies in the History of Israel and His Country, 1959/60, 227ff. [Hebrew]).

83 "*Mišpaṭ hămmælæḵ*" (I Sam 8), in: Biram Festschrift, 1956, 45–56 (Hebrew).

84 "The Manner of the King" and "The Manner of the Kingdom", Diss. Jerusalem, 1972, 213ff. (Hebrew).

85 The Deuteronomistic Interpretation of the Founding of the Monarchy in I Sam. VIII, VT 24 (1974), 398–410.

C. THE IDEOLOGICAL DEVELOPMENT UNDER THE MONARCHY OF SAUL

Despite the effort of the final redactor to make a continuous history of Saul's elevation to be king, we can still distinguish three narratives concerning his election, namely, I Sam 9 1–10 16, 10 17–27 and 11 1–15. Attempts have been made to reconstruct from them the sequence of events in the rise of the monarchy (cf. above p. 29).But not a few scholars have concluded that no theory can explain satisfactorily all the details of the historical process, owing to the condition of the source material[86]. We agree with this conclusion. But we do not think that the difficulty is caused by a theological distortion of history in later times or by the characteristics of the saga in the narratives[87]. It seems that the differences between the narratives arose from the different viewpoints of the narrators, who were more or less contemporaneous with each other. In other words, each narrative was composed for its own purpose and followed its own tendency. Since the differences are inherent, it is futile from the outset to attempt reconstruction of a harmonious history from all the narratives. Rather, we must learn the nature of the various positions from the obvious discrepancies between them.

The first monarchy was prepared by Samuel and the people. But, when it was established, Saul, the first king, appeared as its third factor. Undoubtedly, it was these three factors that constituted main elements determining the course of the rise of the monarchy and influencing its development. Therefore, we may expect to find expressions of all three in the narratives. In the following inquiries we shall ask what place the three occupy in each narrative. In the process, we will be able to find a particular theme in each narrative which must have been composed to express the viewpoint of one or other factor.

The first narrative of Saul's election (9 1–10 16) is analyzed variously by some scholars into two traditions from different times:

According to H. W. Hertzberg[88], there were originally two independent sources behind the present text. One tells of Saul's searching for the lost asses and his future

[86] Robertson argues that Saul, whom Yahweh had appointed as *nagîḏ* years before, was naturally chosen by sacred lot, and "the first (10 17–27) was merely a stage in the process which reached its culmination in the second (11 1–15)" (Samuel and Saul, in: The Old Testament Problem, 115f.). According to Wildberger, 10 21b–27 and 11 15 are two traditions about one and the same thing (ThZ 13, 468). However, this sort of harmonious explanation is unconvincing, see Alt, Die Staatenbildung, in: Kleine Schriften, II 15 (ET 187); Noth, Geschichte, 156 (ET 168); Soggin, Das Königtum in Israel, 30f.; Bright, A History of Israel, 1972², 183.

[87] Against Gressmann, Die älteste Geschichtsschreibung, 26f. 34f.; Alt, Die Staatenbildung, in: Kleine Schriften, II 13ff. (ET 185ff.).

[88] Die Samuelbücher 60ff. (ET 78ff.).

kingship revealed by an unknown seer, the other describes a visit of Saul to Samuel and his anointing. H. Wildberger[89] has maintained that the narrative can be divided into the ancient nucleus (9 22–10 1. 3–4) and its legendary expansion. B. C. Birch[90] has argued that an editor from the prophetic circle made up Saul's call narrative by combining an old folk-tale (9 1–14. 18–19. 22–24 10 2–4. 9. 14–16a) with the old aetiology of a popular proverb (10 10–13). L. Schmidt[91] has maintained that an old story about Saul as a warrior was changed by an editor in c. 850–800 B. C. into a narrative about his anointing by Samuel.

It is true that the narrative reveals literary discrepancies from the modern critical point of view. But the theory that it can be divided into two sources is by no means convincing. Hertzberg[92], who assumes two original sources, has admitted that we can no longer separate them clearly. According to H. J. Stoebe[93], these literary discrepancies occured in the process of expanding the original narrative to give it a new climax, that is, the secret anointing. On the other hand, A. Weiser[94] and W. Richter[95] have argued for the unity of the narrative, with the exception of some secondary expansion or additions. It would seem that the fundamental unity of the narrative and its ultimate origin from the time of Saul cannot be contested.

Now, let us inquire into the respective places of Samuel, the people and Saul in the narrative. It is very clear that Samuel plays the leading part. He is introduced into the story as a "man of God who is held in honour; all that he says comes true" (9 6). Before anyone knew how Israel would be liberated from the Philistines, and even before Saul himself had any idea about his future, Samuel received Yahweh's command to designate Saul as *nagîḏ* over the people of Israel to be their deliverer (9 15–17). He carried out his mission by anointing Saul (10 1 LXX). On the other hand, according to the story, the people contributed scarcely anything to Saul's election. Some scholars assume that the ritual meal of thirty guests (9 22–24; cf. 9 12–13) was actually a secret meeting of the representatives of the people called by Samuel to confer on Saul's designation[96]. But this is a highly hypothetical suggestion[97].

---

[89] ThZ 13, 450ff.

[90] The Development of the Tradition on the Anointing of Saul in 1 Sam 9:1–10:16, JBL 90 (1971), 55–68.

[91] Menschlicher Erfolg und Jahwes Initiative, 1970, 58ff.

[92] Die Samuelbücher 61 (ET 79).

[93] Noch einmal die Eselinnen des Ḳîš, VT 7 (1957), 364; idem, Das erste Buch Samuelis, 200; cf. Schunck, Benjamin, 85f.

[94] Samuel 48ff.

[95] Die sogenannten vorprophetischen Berufungsberichte, 1970, 13ff.

[96] Wildberger, ThZ 13, 453f.; Seebass, ZAW 79, 158. L. Schmidt regards it as an anticipated coronation meal (Menschlicher Erfolg 85).

[97] So Weiser, Samuel, 51 n. 8.

The narrative pointedly records that Saul's anointing was carried out secretly without the knowledge of anyone but Samuel and Saul (9 27; cf. 10 16). It is to be pointed out, however, that the people's cry to Yahweh was the initial cause of Saul's designation (9 16). This role of the people is not different in its nature from that in the narrative in the previous chapter concerning their desire for a king. In both, Yahweh's decision, represented by Samuel, was preceded by the people's initiative in finding a way out of difficulties. An important difference in emphasis can be shown: the people's initiative is in the foreground in ch. 8, in our story it is minimized.

The narrative begins with the genealogy of Saul[98] as a sign of his membership of a noble family, and with a description of his imposing and handsome figure (9 1–2). The respectful attitude towards Saul does not change throughout the narrative. His questioning of Samuel's allusion about his family's glorious future (9 21) should not be interpreted literally. It is one of the typical elements of the call narrative (cf. Judg 6 15)[99]. Opinions are divided on the interpretation of the story of Saul's prophetic ecstasy and the proverb: "Is Saul also among the prophets?" (10 10–13; cf. 19 24)[100]. But whatever be the original meaning of the proverb, this event is doubtless regarded as positive in the present context (cf. 10 6–7. 9)[101]. Another remarkable feature of the narrative is the literary setting, which suggests that Saul was not yet an independent adult, but was sent by his father, accompanied by one of his father's servants, to look for his father's lost asses (9 3)[102]. The

[98] About Saul's genealogy, see Malamat, King Lists of the Old Babylonian Period and Biblical Genealogies, JAOS 88 (1968), 171ff.; A. Demsky, The Genealogy of Gibeon (I Chronicles 9:35–44): Biblical and Epigraphic Considerations, BASOR 202 (1971), 16–23.

[99] Wildberger finds a contradiction between 9 1 and 9 21 (ThZ 13, 453). Richter regards 9 20f. as additional (Die sogenannten vorprophetischen Berufungsberichte 21). But Birch finds all the elements of the call narrative in 9 15ff. including v. 21. About the form of the call narrative, see N. Habel, The Form and Significance of the Call Narratives, ZAW 77 (1965), 297–323. According to L. Schmidt, Saul's questioning was composed by a compiler of the old story on the model of the formula of the call narrative in Ex 3 and Judg 6 (Menschlicher Erfolg 88f.).

[100] While V. Eppstein maintains that this proverb was fashioned when the prophecy declined into a superstitious folk institution in the ninth century (Was Saul also among the Prophets?, ZAW 81 [1969], 287–304), J. Sturdy argues that it was derived from Davidic propaganda against Saul (The Original Meaning of "Is Saul also among the Prophets?", VT 20 [1970], 206–213). On the other hand, L. Schmidt assumes that its origin can be found in Saul's illness (Menschlicher Erfolg 103ff.).

[101] Cf. Hertzberg, Die Samuelbücher, 67 (ET 86); J. Lindblom, Prophecy in Ancient Israel, 1963, 74.

[102] Saul's search for the lost asses is sometimes interpreted as symbolic, see M. Bič, Saul sucht die Eselinnen (1 Sam IX), VT 7 (1957), 92–97; Stoebe, VT 7, 362–370; idem,

event took place in Saul's youth before anyone expected him to become king.

In the second narrative (10 17–27), O. Eissfeldt[103] has discovered a trace of the amalgamation of different traditions between v. 21bα and v. 21bβ. The story of Saul's absence (v. 21bβ) cannot be consistent with the tradition of his being taken by lot out of the family of the Matrites (v. 21bα LXX), since a person must be present when the lot falls to him[104]. On the basis of this observation, Eissfeldt has divided the narrative into two sources. In one, Saul was chosen by lot, in the other his imposing stature was taken to be a sign of choice by divine oracle[105]. In a modification of the two-source theory, M. Noth[106] argued that the old tradition of choice by oracle was transformed into the present narrative by the Deuteronomist, who thought it primitive to regard Saul's imposing stature as the mark of the future king. In fact, both the source theory and the modification theory are untenable. On the one hand, if we try to divide the narrative into sources, they become too fragmentary to be considered independent sources[107]. On the other, if the Deuteronomistic invention of the story of Saul's election by lot stemmed from the Deuteronomist's theological point of view, he could have completely deleted the old tradition of choice by oracle instead of making a clumsy halfway modification. It seems that the narrative was composed from the beginning as a literary unit. Presumably, a number of traditions were employed, but they served only to produce the thematic unity of the narrative that Saul was chosen by Yahweh directly in a miraculous way.

In this story Samuel appears as a man who holds official authority. He called the assembly of the people at Mizpah (v. 17) and expressed his opinion, opposing the people's desire for a king (v. 18–19a). Nonetheless, he took the initiative in choosing the king (v. 19b–22), introduced the newly elected monarch to the people (v. 24), established the "manner of the kingdom" as the constitution of the monarchy (v. 25a), and dis-

---

Das erste Buch Samuelis, 202; this interpretation is criticized by Hertzberg, Die Samuelbücher, 62 n. 1 (ET 80f. note a).

103 Die Komposition der Samuelisbücher 7f. 10; cf. Fohrer, Der Vertrag, in: Studien, 332; against this theory Weiser, Samuel, 66 n. 41. According to Seebass, there were originally two different versions of the lottery (ZAW 77, 288 n. 9).

104 About the lottery, see R. Press, Das Ordal im Alten Testament, das Losordal, ZAW 51 (1933), 227–231; Lindblom, Lot Casting in the Old Testament, VT 12 (1962), 164–178.

105 About the oracle of royal designation, see Lods, Le rôle des oracles dans la nomination des rois, des prêtres et des magistrats chez les Israélites, les Égyptiens et les Grecs, in: Mélanges Maspéro, I/1 1934, 91–100.

106 ÜSt 58; cf. Boecker, Die Beurteilung, 44ff.

107 Cf. Noth, ÜSt, 58.

missed the assembly (v. 25b). In short, he presided over the popular assembly. From chapters 7, 8 and 12, we can learn that his authority was derived from the office of *šop̄eṭ,* the leader of the tribal confederation. As we have shown, the extent of this confederation covered only part of central Palestine, but the concept "Israel" in our narrative is manifestly expanded to the great tribal community, comprising all the tribes of Israel, out of which the tribe of Benjamin was taken by lot (10 20). It is obvious that this expansion could be made only after the establishment of the kingdom, which brought all the tribes under a crown.

In contrast to the first narrative, here the people actively participated in the election of the king. Despite Samuel's opposition, their demand for a king was accepted (v. 19). All the people took part in the election (v. 19b–21bα). When they did not find a proper person, they looked for him eagerly until he was discovered, and brought him out to the public (v. 21bβ–23a). But in their reaction to the newly elected king they were divided among themselves. Although Saul was hailed by acclamation (v. 24b), he was followed by part of them only (v. 26b), and some openly expressed their disagreement with the result of the election (v. 27a)[108]. The most passive role in this narrative is played by Saul. The episode of his hiding among the baggage, while the people were looking for him (v. 22), shows that the narrative tries to create the impression that Saul did not covet the kingship but that the people compelled him to be king. Although he was publicly chosen by Yahweh, and the assembly recognized his election, he acted very leniently towards the dissenters (v. 27)[109]. There is no question that the tone of the narrative is, as a whole, very favourable to Saul[110].

As for the literary unity of the third narrative (11 1–15), many scholars have regarded v. 12–14 as a redactional addition, based on the episode of Saul's opponents in 10 27[111]. But a close examination shows that 10 27 and 11 12–14 differ in nature as well as in the situation described. In the former, Saul's military capability is doubted after his

---

[108] Weiser maintains that 10 27 and 11 12f. form the framework of the story of Saul's campaign against the Ammonites (Samuel 72ff.). Against this view, see Seebass, ZAW 78, 159 n. 30; Boecker, Die Beurteilung, 57f.

[109] It has been generally accepted to emend *k^emăḥ^arîš* (MT) into *k^emeḥodæš* according to LXX, see S. R. Driver, Notes on the Hebrew Text and the Topography of the Books of Samuel, 1913², 85. But the emendation is not necessary, see Buber, in: Werke, II 780f.

[110] Weiser assumes that a Benjaminite circle was responsible for this tradition (Samuel 68).

[111] Wellhausen, Die Composition, 241f.; Wildberger, ThZ 13, 449. 468; Hertzberg, Die Samuelbücher, 73f. (ET 94); Stoebe, Das erste Buch Samuelis, 228f.

election, in the latter his kingship is opposed before his accession[112]. It seems that even after his decisive victory there were opponents to Saul's elevation to the throne, apparently opponents of a different kind from those whom he met after his election at Mizpah. Nor can we accept the suggestion that the campaign against the Ammonites actually took place long before the enthronement at Gilgal and that there was no direct relationship between the two events[113]. There is no reason to doubt that Saul's overwhelming victory inspired the people to make him king (cf. 12 12).

In this narrative Saul is the leading figure. Being enraged at the disgrace brought upon all Israel by Nahash the Ammonite, he became a charismatic war-leader on receiving Yahweh's spirit (11 5–6). Immediately he called up Israel, mustered them at Bezek, and took command in the campaign against the Ammonites besieging Jabesh (v. 7–11). In his resounding triumph the people found the divine designation of Saul as king. An enthusiastic party wanted to execute the dissenters (v. 12), but Saul settled the matter without bloodshed (v. 14). He was made king with tremendous popular rejoicing (v. 15). He is described here as a hero of the people.

As has been pointed out, this narrative testifies to social conditions in the pre-monarchical period, where a people's self-government ruled each local community. The men of Jabesh (v. 1. 5. 9. 10) or the elders of Jabesh (v. 3) were the representatives of Jabesh-gilead in political matters. They made a treaty with a foreign king on behalf of their community, sent messengers to the tribes of Israel, and received answers from them. Clearly, the people of Gibeah of Saul (v. 4) and those of the other communities in all the territory of Israel (v. 3. 7) had the same authority. They came voluntarily to join the campaign launched by Saul. But they never lost their fundamental right to determine their own political matters. Therefore, it was the people who gave answer to the messengers from Jabesh (v. 9)[114], tried to punish the opponents to Saul's kingship (v. 12), and made him king at Gilgal (v. 15). In contrast, Samuel's contribution both to the campaign and to the establishment of the monarchy looks very small. Indeed, many scholars think that the name of Samuel was inserted secondarily into this narrative (v. 7. 12. 14)[115]. But we cannot accept this suggestion. It appears that the narrative is faithful to the historical situation in which Samuel still held the office of *šop̱eṭ* but the people began to look for a

---

[112] Cf. Seebass, ZAW 79, 165 n. 42.

[113] Against Lods, Israël, 409ff. (ET 352ff.); Wildberger, ThZ 13, 466; Schunck, Benjamin, 109ff.; Seebass, ZAW 79, 155ff.

[114] But εἶπεν in LXX, see S. R. Driver, Notes on the Hebrew Text, 86.

[115] See above p. 35 n. 50.

king as their new leader. Accordingly, Saul exploited Samuel's authority for his mobilization (v. 7)[116]. It was Samuel whom the people asked to hand over the dissenters (v. 12), since he had official jurisdiction in internal political matters. Moreover, he took the initiative to go to Gilgal to "renew" (*neḥăddeš*) the kingdom there (v. 14). Although the word "renew" seemingly came from the redactor, it is not necessary to attribute the whole verse to him. As a man of official competence, Samuel could appeal to the people for unification under the new regime at a time of crisis[117]. He was certainly present at Saul's accession at Gilgal (v. 15), although his name is not specifically mentioned there[118], an omission that brings out the nature of the tendency of this narrative.

Now we can clarify the theme and viewpoint of each narrative. First of all, we agree with the accepted view that the last narrative (11 1–15) presents in large measure the historical situation in which the event took place. But this does not imply that it is the sole "authentic history"[119], for it has also its own tendency. Its assertion is that the foundation of Saul's monarchy rested on the will of the people. It is evident that the people had a strong voice in the monarchy of Saul, at least at the beginning. The fact that he did not take any action against the dissenters (10 27 11 13) attests his inability rather than his generosity[120]. Against the will of the people, he could neither execute Jonathan (14 45) nor carry out the command of Samuel (15 24). But it must be regarded as a tendentious exaggeration that Samuel's part in the whole affair is minimized to such an extent in this narrative. This attitude towards Samuel articulates the viewpoint of the people who disagreed with him about the establishment of the monarchy. There must have been, in the rejection of Samuel's regime of *šōpeṭ*, a declaration that the monarchy was established by the people. This view could be formed in the early days of Saul's monarchy, when his first appearance was still remembered as that of the hero whom the people sought against Samuel's will. Moreover, Saul's elevation to the kingship was regarded

---

116 Cf. H. M. Wiener, The Composition of Judges II 11 to I Kings II 46, 1929, 12.

117 Möhlenbrink assumes that, when Saul was made king by the Gilgal amphictyony, whose members were Benjamin, Gad and Reuben, Samuel as the representative of the Ephraim-Shiloh amphictyony contributed to the unification of the two amphictyonies under Saul's monarchy (ZAW 58, 57ff.).

118 The name of Samuel is found in LXX (v. 15).

119 So Irwin, AJSL 58, 113; cf. Alt, Die Staatenbildung, in: Kleine Schriften, II 17f. (ET 189); Noth, Geschichte, 156 (ET 168).

120 Knierim argues that the people asked here for sacral justice against the slanderers of Yahweh's messiah but not for petty vengeance. Accordingly, Saul's acquittal shows not his magnanimity but a new law established by the certified messiah (The Messianic Concept, in: Colwell Festschrift, 33f.). It is difficult to assume, however, that Saul was recognized as Yahweh's messiah before his elevation to king at Gilgal.

as an election by the popular assembly, which still had a powerful voice in the administration of the monarchy.

The characteristic feature of the second narrative (10 17–27) is the miraculous divine intervention in the choice of the king. Although the people took part in the election of the king, they had no longer any authority to decide on the candidate. It was God who chose the future king. In this narrative, the monarchy was founded on the ideology of the divine election. The comparison between this and the previous narrative, where the people's voice was the decisive factor, reminds us of the early development of political ideology in Mesopotamia analyzed by T. Jacobsen (see above p. 11). According to his thesis, the ruler, who was originally elected by the popular assembly, introduced the ideology of the divine election in order to give a solid ideological foundation to his regime, which became more and more independent of the authority of the popular assembly. We may assume that a similar development took place in the early monarchy in Israel. It is likely that, as the monarchy of Saul developed rapidly into a sophisticated royal regime, Saul felt the necessity of a stronger control over the people. For this purpose, he must have wanted ideological support. So he exploited Samuel's authority as an instrument against the people. Presumably, Samuel was interested in Saul's proposal, since he was looking for an opportunity to carry out his original plan of bringing the monarchy under his influence. From the previous narrative (11 1–15), we can learn that the plan was thwarted under strong popular pressure after the establishment of the monarchy. We may assume, therefore, that co-operation between the king and the religious authority came into being as an outcome of common interest, during the developing stage of Saul's monarchy. This cooperation produced the second narrative, which gave the king divine sanction completely independent of the authority of the popular assembly, and confirmed the validity of religious authority over the monarchy[121].

If this assumption is sound, it is self-evident that the first narrative (9 1–10 16) was produced by the same co-operation at a later stage[122]. In it, the people's part in the establishment of the monarchy is

---

[121] Cf. Lods, Le rôle des oracles, in: Mélanges Maspéro, I/1 99f. According to Weiser, the theme of this narrative is to show that there were equal conditions for all the tribes at the election of the king. Therefore, it was a reply to the jealous rivalry of the other tribes against Benjamin (Samuel 65).

[122] Lods points out that both narratives are two variations on the same theme (in: Mélanges Maspéro, I/1 99). Weiser regards this narrative as an apology to the group which did not accept Saul's authority (Samuel 53); but Richter is of the opinion that the purpose of the narrative is to show how a *baḥûr* became the *nagîḏ* in an unexpected way (Die sogenannten vorprophetischen Berufungsberichte 43ff.).

minimized to an extreme degree. By contrast, the figure of Samuel is dominant, and Saul's anointing by him presupposes his kingship[123]. But, because of the pre-monarchical setting of the narrative, the title "king" is carefully avoided except for a suggestive mention of the "matter of the kingdom" at the end (10 16)[124]. Instead, Saul is anointed to be *nagîḏ* (9 16 10 1). We must discard the theory that *nagîḏ* was originally the title of the charismatic war-leader in the pre-monarchical period[125]. There is no evidence of its attribution to anybody prior to Saul[126]. Since the term *nagîḏ* is mentioned here for the first time in biblical traditions, it seems that it was adopted for the "king designate"[127] in the process of producing the narrative of young Saul[128], and

[123] Richter differentiates the anointing for king from that for *nagîḏ*, which Samuel gave Saul (Die *nāgîd*-Formel. Ein Beitrag zur Erhellung des *nāgîd*-Problem, BZ NF 9 [1965], 71–81). But this view is untenable, since Saul's anointing was a royal anointing to show his predesignation to king, see E. Kutsch, Salbung als Rechtsakt im Alten Testament und im Alten Orient, 1963, 52ff.; cf. also de Vaux, Les institutions, I 160 (ET 103); Noth, Geschichte, 156f. (ET 168f.); Weiser, Samuel, 51ff.; L. Schmidt, Menschlicher Erfolg, 79ff. 86ff.

[124] Some scholars regard the "matter of the kingdom" as a secondary addition, see Richter, Die sogenannten vorprophetischen Berufungsberichte, 22. It is likely, however, that the term "kingdom" here is mentioned with a special intention, see Buber, in: Werke, II 774f.; Hertzberg, Die Samuelbücher, 67 (ET 86); Birch, JBL 90, 67; L. Schmidt, Menschlicher Erfolg, 81ff.

[125] Against Alt, Die Staatenbildung, in: Kleine Schriften, II 23f. (ET 195f.); Richter, BZ NF 9, 71ff.; cf. also Soggin, Charisma und Institution im Königtum Sauls, ZAW 75 (1963), 60; L. Schmidt, Menschlicher Erfolg, 152ff.

[126] Cf. J. Liver, in: EncBib, V 1968, 753–755 (Hebrew).

[127] Cf. Noth, Geschichte, 156f. 156 n. 2 (ET 169. 169 n. 1). T. C. G. Thornton maintains that the title *nagîḏ* had nothing to do with charismatic leadership but implied merely "heir apparent to the throne" (Charismatic Kingship in Israel and Judah, JThS NS 14 [1963], 8). R. A. Carlson is of the opinion that "the term *nāgīd* is a pure synonym for the term *mælæk*" and regards the former as "a form of Deuteronomic definition of the national leader" (David, the Chosen King, 1964, 52ff.). On the basis of the reading נגדי in Sefîre III 10 (Fitzmyer, The Aramaic Suzerainty Treaty from Sefîre in the Museum of Beirut, CBQ 20 [1958], 448), Albright assumes that both Saul and David were anointed not as kings but as military leaders over the tribal confederation called *nagîḏ* (Samuel and the Beginning of the Prophetic Movement 16). It is by no means clear, however, that the third letter of the term should be read ד instead of ר, as נגרי, see A. Dupont-Sommer, Les inscriptions araméennes de Sfiré, 1958, 128; J. J. Koopmans, Aramäische Chrestomathie, I 1962, 65; KAI I § 224 10; KAI II 208; R. Degen, Altaramäische Grammatik der Inschriften des 10.–8. Jh. v. Chr., 1969, 21. Recently, E. Lipiński suggested that the original meaning of the term *nagîḏ* was "crown prince", and as such it is employed at the designation of Solomon (I Kings 1 35) and of Abijah (II Chron 11 22) (*Nāgīd*, der Kronprinz, VT 24 [1974], 497–499). But his argument seems to be based on arbitrary evaluation of the historicity of source materials.

[128] The term *nagîḏ* as a title of kings of Israel and Judah is mentioned twelve times for

the connotation of a future king designated by Yahweh for the people was also attached to it under the influence of the narrative[129].

The foregoing review has shown that the power relationships between the people, Samuel and Saul contributed to the development of the political ideology under Saul's monarchy. This observation requires us to reconsider the controversy over the thesis of the "Israelite charismatic monarchy" advanced by A. Alt (see above p. 2), that the idea of dynastic succession had from the beginning no place in Saul's monarchy, whose fundamental structure rested on his personal designation as a charismatic war-leader by Yahweh and his personal acclamation as a king by the people[130]. Against this view, G. Buccellati[131] submits that Saul's monarchy is to be regarded as dynastic both *de jure* and *de facto*. W. Beyerlin[132] also underlined that Saul was neither a mere charismatic war-leader nor a king made by the people's acclamation. It seems, however, that we must examine each part of the evidence more closely by distinguishing one viewpoint from the other.

To begin with, it should be asked what sort of monarchy the people intended to build when they made Saul king at Gilgal after his military success (11 15). In this tradition, Saul appeared as a charismatic war-leader called deliverer-*šop̱eṭ* but the people made him "king" (*mœlœk̠*). This fact clearly shows that they differentiated the monarchy from the regime of *šop̱eṭ*[133]. It should be also supposed that the people's political action at Gilgal was taken after long preparation for the new regime in the stead of the government of *šop̱eṭ*. Then it becomes very difficult to

---

the following seven kings: Saul (I Sam 9 16 10 1), David (I Sam 25 30 II Sam 5 2 6 21 7 8; cf. I Sam 13 14), Solomon (I Kings 1 35), Abijah (II Chron 11 22), Jeroboam I (I Kings 14 7), Baasha (I Kings 16 2), and Hezekiah (II Kings 20 5). Except Hezekiah's case, the term is used in connection with the designation of a future king.

129 Except the cases of Solomon and Abijah, the designator of *nagîd̠* is always Yahweh or a prophet of Yahweh; about the formula of the designation of *nagîd̠*, see Richter, BZ NF 9, 73ff. As for the etymology of the term, J. J. Glück suggested that it relates with *noqed̠* (Nagid-Shepherd, VT 13 [1963], 144–150). Although the suggestion has been criticized from the philological point of view (Richter, BZ NF 9, 72f. n. 7), the semantic relation between both terms is conspicuous (cf. II Sam 5 2 7 8).

130 Alt, Die Staatenbildung, in: Kleine Schriften, II 32f. (ET 204); idem, Das Königtum in den Reichen Israel und Juda, in: Kleine Schriften, II 119 (ET 244).

131 Cities and Nations 195ff.

132 Das Königscharisma bei Saul, ZAW 73 (1961), 186–201.

133 Some scholars are of the opinion that the difference between the regime of *šop̱eṭ* and the monarchy was one not of character but of degree, see D. A. McKenzie, VT 17, 121; G. W. Ahlström, Solomon, the Chosen One, History of Religion 8 (1968/69), 99. Although *šop̱eṭ* was actually a "ruler", he never exercised "kingship", as Gideon's refusal of the offering of hereditary rulership (Judg 8 22–23) shows.

accept Alt's formula: "a designation of Yahweh and an acclamation of the people", as the unique process of the founding of the monarchy in Israel. Truely, the people hailed Saul as king by acclamation when they recognized his victory as a sign of his designation by Yahweh. But the monarchy as a new regime was prepared long before. In other words, the people of Israel had designed the structure of monarchy as a political institution on the model of the neighbouring countries before Saul appeared. They were simply looking for a man who would be able to function as a leader of the new institution. If our assumption is correct, the people's acclamation of Saul at Gilgal should be regarded as their expression of recognition of him as a leader of the new regime which they had prepared in expectance. We must conclude, therefore, that both divine designation and popular acclamation played essentially no part in determining the characteristic feature of the Israelite monarchy.

In comparison to the regime of *šōpēṭ*, the characteristic features of the monarchy must have been expected to be a strong military power and a stable leadership, both of which the regime of *šōpēṭ* failed to offer, to defend the people from the increasingly severe attacks of the neighbouring countries. Apparently, the people felt the necessity for a standing army since their militia had been utterly routed by the professional Philistine army (I Sam 4 1b–18). In this respect, too, we cannot concede Alt's thesis that Saul established his standing army by adopting the Philistine military institutions as "a considerable departure from the original conception of the army in the kingdom of Israel as a national levy"[134]. There is reason to assume that Saul's standing army had its origin at the moment of his elevation to be king (10 26b)[135]. Indeed, its establishment must have been one of the most important articles in the people's programme for the monarchy from the very start (cf. 8 11–12). Needless to say, a powerful standing army cannot be sustained without a stable leadership. Thus, we can only assume that the people planned to build a hereditary monarchy, having realized long since that a stable leadership could be founded only on the hereditary principle. We have suggested that the Shilonite confederation had already attempted to make the leadership hereditary (see above p. 33). In addition, it is extremely difficult to assume that the people of Israel could invent the idea of a non-dynastic kingship at the preparatory stage of the monarchy, inasmuch as the monarchies of "all the nations", on which the Israelite monarchy was modelled, were

---

[134] Alt, Die Staatenbildung, in: Kleine Schriften, II 27 (ET 199).

[135] Cf. A. van Selms, The Armed Forces of Israel under Saul and David, in: Studies on the Books of Samuel, ed. A. H. van Zyl, 1960, 55ff.; L. Schmidt, Menschlicher Erfolg, 194ff.

without exception hereditary, as we have shown in the previous chapter.

Secondly, let us examine Samuel's conception of monarchy. From his theocratic point of view, the monarchy was given by Yahweh to the people (8 4–9. 19–22 9 16 10 17–24 12 12–13). Accordingly, it was Yahweh who designated Saul to be king (9 16–17 10 1 LXX 10 19b–24 12 13 15 1. 11. 17. 35), and the enthronement was carried out by Samuel as Yahweh's representative (9 16 10 1. 16b. 19b–24 12 1 15 1). But this conception does not exclude the dynastic principle from the monarchy. On the contrary, we have some evidence that Samuel accepted that principle as an integral part of the monarchy: a) he pointedly told Saul that "all that is desirable in Israel" belongs not only to him but also to his "father's house" (9 20) – without doubt, in these words he alluded to the dynastic establishment of Saul's house[136]; b) when the co-operative relationship between Samuel and Saul deteriorated, he declared that Saul's kingdom would neither be established nor would it continue (13 13–14) – words that allow us to conjecture that Samuel once gave a favourable oracle in which Yahweh promised to establish the dynasty of Saul[137]; c) in the light of this evidence, the "manner of the kingdom", which Samuel proclaimed on the occasion of Saul's enthronement (10 25), seems to have included an article on the dynastic succession identical to in the "law of the king" (Deut 17 20).

Thirdly, Saul's idea on the nature of the monarchy. As soon as he became king, the standing army was established (I Sam 10 26b; cf. 14 52). Abner was appointed its commander (14 50)[138], and the royal court was formed (cf. 16 14ff.) around the family of Saul (14 49–50). The most remarkable figure among the king's entourage was Jonathan, his eldest son. The fact that Jonathan was heir-apparent is plainly indicated by Saul's words (20 31) as well as by the special mention of his name alongside that of Saul (II Sam 1 22–27). Moreover, Jonathan's words: "My father does nothing either great or small without disclosing it to me" (I Sam 20 2), would show, in our opinion, that he was, in effect, co-

[136] Cf. L. Schmidt, Menschlicher Erfolg, 81ff.

[137] Cf. Buccellati, Cities and Nations, 198. Seebass assumes that the original form of I Sam 13 13b was a prophecy of victory given before a campaign (ZAW 78, 155). On the other hand, Birch finds here a "reminiscence of the promises given to David establishing his dynasty in II Sam 7 12. 16" (The Rise of the Israelite Monarchy: The Growth and Development of I Sam. 7–15, Diss. Yale University, 1970, 136f.); cf. also R. Hallevy, Charismatic Kingship in Israel, Tarbiz 30 (1960/61), 240 (Hebrew).

[138] *Śăr hăṣṣaḇa'* "commander of the army" was the most important official in the monarchies of the neighbouring countries (Gen 21 22. 32 Judg 4 2. 7 II Sam 10 18 II Kings 5 1), see B. Maisler (Mazar), The Scribe of King David and the Problem of the High Officials in the Ancient Kingdom of Israel (1946/47), in: Canaan and Israel, 1974, 208 (Hebrew).

regent. Undoubtedly, Saul took it for granted that Jonathan would succeed him.

Thus it becomes patent that the idea of the "charismatic monarchy" was held neither by the people nor by Samuel, let alone by Saul. It is, however, in some biblical narratives, Saul's monarchy was seemingly based on the charismatic principle. These are the narratives about Saul's rejection (I Sam 13 7b–15a 15 1–35) and the episodes in the "history of the rise of David" (I Sam 16–II Sam 8). In the first, Samuel exercises authority over Saul, king of Israel, as though he could freely depose him (I Sam 15 23. 26) as well as proclaim a change of the royal house (13 13–14) on the basis of the divine will. In the same way, the second begins with Yahweh's spirit forsaking Saul and being received by David (16 13–14). Owing to the shift of charisma from Saul to David, the latter was already proclaimed king during the former's reign (23 17 24 21). According to A. Alt[139], this evidence, together with the short-lived reign of Ishbaal, implies that the idea of the "charismatic monarchy" prevailed in Israel during the early monarchy. But it is very evident that the narratives were composed in the Davidic court to show how David had been chosen by Yahweh instead of Saul. Indeed, no one can fail to identify a "man after his own heart" (13 14) and a "neighbour of yours, who is better than you" (15 28; cf. 28 17), who will receive Saul's kingship. We must conclude that the assertion that Saul's kingship was transferred directly to David on the basis of the charismatic principle is a tendentious interpretation of the actual course of history from the viewpoint of the defence of David.

---

[139] Die Staatenbildung, in: Kleine Schriften, II 32f. (ET 204); idem, Das Königtum, in: Kleine Schriften, II 119 (ET 244).

Chapter 4: The Legitimation of the Kingship of David

A. THE "DEFENCE OF DAVID"

In 1926, L. Rost[1] demonstrated that, instead of parallel narrative strands, two independent complexes, called the "history of the rise of David" and the "history of the succession to David", are placed consecutively in the latter half of I Samuel, II Samuel and the first two chapters of I Kings. Since then, while the demarcation of the second complex has been generally recognized by scholars, the existence of the first complex as a literary unit is still controversial. For instance, both the literary-critical method of O. Eissfeldt[2] and the traditio-historical approach of R. A. Carlson[3] have rejected Rost's thesis. According to H. W. Hertzberg[4], the continuity of the story of David's rise can be recognized "with nothing like the same degree of certainty" as the "succession history", and both theories of fixed sources and of an author for this complex are hypothetical[5]. Under these circumstances, it is not strange that scholars who accept Rost's suggestion do not reach a consensus on the exact points at which the "history of the rise of David" begins and ends:

A. Alt[6] thought that it begins at I Sam 16 14 and ends in II Sam 8. M. Noth[7] found the same starting-point but regarded II Sam 5 25 as the end of the story; this view

---

[1] Die Überlieferung von der Thronnachfolge Davids (1926), in: Das kleine Credo und andere Studien zum Alten Testament, 1965, 119–253. He contends that a continuous story of David's rise is to be found in I Sam 23 1–13 27 1–28 2 29 1–30 26 II Sam 1 1 2 4a 3 20–29. 31–37 4 1a. 5–12 5 3. 17–25 (ch. 8?), (ibid. 238).

[2] Einleitung in das Alte Testament, 1964³, 182ff. 362ff. (ET The Old Testament. An Introduction, 1965, 137ff. 271ff.).

[3] David, the Chosen King, 1964, 43.

[4] Die Samuelbücher, 1960², 10 (ET I & II Samuel, 1964, 19).

[5] Ibid. 199f. (ET 244).

[6] Die Staatenbildung der Israeliten in Palästina (1930), in: Kleine Schriften, II 1953, 15 n. 3 (ET The Formation of the Israelite State in Palestine, in: Essays on Old Testament History and Religion, 1966, 187 n. 35); idem, Zu II Samuel 8 1, ZAW 54 (1936), 149–152.

[7] ÜSt 62ff., especially 62 n. 2. 63 n. 5; idem, Geschichte Israels, 1954², 165 n. 1 (ET The History of Israel, 1960², 179 n. 1).

has been followed by R. L. Ward[8]. H.-U. Nübel[9] maintained that the *Grundschrift* of David's rise can be found in I Sam 16–II Sam 9, and II Sam 10–12 are also attributed to this work as a later expansion. F. Mildenberger[10] has shown that an old Saul-David tradition in I Sam 13–II Sam 7 makes a literary unit. A. Weiser[11] argued that the work begins with David's anointing (I Sam 16 1–13) and concludes with Nathan's prophecy (II Sam 7). J. H. Grønbaek[12] demonstrated that the beginning of the work is to be found in I Sam 15 and the end in II Sam 5. According to H. M. Wolf[13], the complex of I Sam 15-II Sam 8 is the "defence of David". J. W. Flanagan[14] held that I Sam 1–II Sam 8 form a literary unit compiled as a two-part history: David's rise to power and the court history (II Sam 9–20).

We will not re-examine here all these literary-critical and traditio-historical problems of the complex which lies between the "Samuel-Saul complex" (I Sam 7–15) and the "history of the succession to David" (II Sam 9–20 I Kings 1–2). Yet it seems possible to find in that complex a literary unit such as the "history of David's rise", as a working hypothesis. For we cannot dismiss the impression that one theme – David's rise to power supplanting Saul – runs through the whole of it.

The dominant view in the complex describes the relationship between Saul and David as follows. After Saul was rejected by Yahweh (I Sam 15), David was chosen and anointed as the future king (16 1–13); when David received Yahweh's spirit, it departed from Saul (16 13–14 18 12); Yahweh was always with David, answered him and protected him (16 18 17 37 18 12. 14. 28 22 5. 10. 13. 15 23 2. 4. 10–12. 14 30 6. 8 II Sam 2 1 3 9–10. 18 4 9 5 2. 10. 12. 19–20. 23–25 7 1. 8–9. 18; cf. I Sam 20 13 I Kings 1 37), but Saul was denied the divine oracle (I Sam 28 6. 15; cf. 14 18–19. 37); although David was innocent (19 4 20 1. 32 24 10–16 26 18–20), Saul repeatedly attempted to kill him (18 11. 17. 21 19 1–2. 5. 10–11 20 1. 3. 31–32 22 23 23 7–12. 14–15. 25–26 24 3 26 3; cf. 27 1); nevertheless, David "repaid him good" (24 18; cf. 24 5–8. 18 26 9–11. 21. 23); "David

---

[8] The Story of David's Rise: A Traditio-Historical Study of I Samuel XVI 14–II Samuel V, Diss. Vanderbilt University, 1967.

[9] Davids Aufstieg in der Frühe israelitischer Geschichtsschreibung, Diss. Bonn, 1959, 76ff. 122ff.

[10] Die vordeuteronomistische Saul-David-Überlieferung, Diss. Tübingen, 1962; cf. idem, ThLZ 87 (1962), 778f. (Since this dissertation was not available to me, I have referred for this information to J. H. Grønbaek, Die Geschichte vom Aufstieg Davids, 1971, 27ff.).

[11] Die Legitimation des Königs David, VT 16 (1966), 325–354.

[12] Die Geschichte vom Aufstieg Davids 16ff.

[13] The Apology of Hattusilis Compared with Other Political Self-Justifications of the Ancient Near East, Diss. Brandeis, 1967, 118ff.

[14] A Study of the Biblical Traditions Pertaining to the Foundation of the Monarchy in Israel, Diss. Notre Dame University, 1971, 55ff.; idem, Court History or Succession Document? A Study of 2 Samuel 9–20 and 1 Kings 1–2, JBL 91 (1972), 172–181.

had success in all his undertaking" (18 14; cf. 18 5. 30), and was loved by Jonathan (18 1. 3 19 1 20 3. 17), by Michal (18 20; cf. 19 11–17), and by all the people (18 16. 22. 28 LXX), but Saul was disobedient to Yahweh's behest (13 7b–15a 15 1–35), was stupid enough to trouble the people by an unnecessary vow which jeopardized Jonathan's life (14 24–46), was afraid of Goliath (17 11) and of the army of the Philistines (28 5), was crazy owing to an evil spirit sent by Yahweh (16 14–23 18 10 19 9; cf. 19 23–24), quarrelled with Jonathan (20 30–34), massacred the priests of Nob (22 11–19), consulted a medium of Endor (28 3–25; cf. I Chron 10 13–14), and, finally, since Yahweh became his enemy (I Sam 28 16), fell in battle (31 1–7 I Chron 10 1–7); in contradistinction, Yahweh designated David as *nagîḏ* and king over Israel instead of Saul (I Sam 25 30 II Sam 3 9–10 5 2. 12 6 21 7 8).

In this summary, the verdict on Saul as a villain makes a striking contrast to that on David as guiltless. But it should be noted that the complex includes informations which reveal another aspect of the relationship between them. From the main stories we get the impression that David did not resist Saul but simply flee from his pursuit. According to certain traditions, even when Saul fell into David's hands, David spared his life and did not do him harm (I Sam 24 4–8 26 6–12). But according to others, as soon as David was purged from Saul's court, he gathered round himself in the wilderness of Judah a band of people, in addition to his family and clansmen, who were discontented with the regime of Saul (22 1–2; cf. I Chron 12 1–22), which fact, as well as Saul's complaint about David's ambush (I Sam 22 8. 13), teaches us that, in fact, he resisted Saul vigorously by guerrilla warfare. Otherwise, how can we understand why Saul pursued David deep into the wilderness of Judah again and again (23 15. 25–26 24 3 26 2)? The story that David was prepared to take part in the Philistine campaign against Saul at Gilboa (28 1–2 29 2.8) also shows that he wanted to overthrow Saul's regime at all costs. Indeed, if he had been loyal to Saul and his House, he would not have contended with Ishbaal for hegemony over Israel after Saul's death (II Sam 2 12–3 1).

The cause of discord between Saul and David is attributed in the main traditions to Saul's jealousy of David (I Sam 18 6–9; cf. 18 12. 15. 28–29). But we are sceptical about the historicity of this information, since there is much evidence testifying to Saul's popularity. In spite of his breach with Samuel, he always had the people's support. In contrast, David was the target of several uprisings (II Sam 15–18 20 1–2. 4–22). It is true that Saul once said to his servants: "You have all conspired against me" (I Sam 22 8). But these words must be interpreted as an overstatement made by the mistrustful king[15]. And, beyond peradven-

[15] Cf. Hertzberg, Die Samuelbücher, 151 (ET 187).

ture, he is described positively and with sympathy in his traditions (I Sam 9–14 28 31)[16], which tell that he was the handsomest and tallest man among the folk (9 2; cf. 10 23–24), and the deliverer of Israel (11 3 14 48; cf. 9 16 10 1 LXX). From another tradition we know that he was so zealous for the people of Israel that he persecuted the Gibeonites by breaking the ancient covenant between the two peoples (II Sam 21 2; cf. Josh 9 3–27). A vivid reflection of his popularity in Israel is the gallantry of the people of Jabesh-gilead in saving the bodies of his sons and his own from Bethshan (I Sam 31 11–13) as well as the David's praise of Saul and Jonathan in his elegy over their death (II Sam 1 19–27). David, on the other hand, was a mere upstart without any important background in Israel (cf. I Sam 18 18. 23). After having been expelled from the court, he tried to defy Saul in the wilderness of Judah. But since Saul's prestige in the southern tribes was overwhelming (23 12. 19–20 26 1), David had finally no choice but to take refuge in the land of the Philistines (27 1–4; cf. 21 11–16 26 19). Under these circumstances, the tradition which sees Saul's jealousy as the main incentive of events must answer the question why Saul, king of Israel, who was stronger and more popular should have become madly jealous of David. As this attitude was unreasonable, the answer can be found only in Saul's mental sickness (16 14–16. 23 18 10 19 9; cf. 19 23–24)[17]. Saul seems to have been excitable by temperament (10 10 20 33 24 17). But had he been really insane as described, he could hardly have played successfully the most difficult role of the first king of Israel (14 47–48)[18] for a considerable length of time[19].

---

[16] Cf. H. Schulte, Die Entstehung der Geschichtsschreibung im alten Israel, 1972, 105ff.

[17] Ward maintains that the information on Saul's sickness reflects the psychology and theology of that time and has nothing to do with Saul's vilification (The Story of David's Rise 18). It is clear, however, that Saul's sickness is mentioned in connection with his rejection by Yahweh, cf. Grønbaek, Die Geschichte vom Aufstieg Davids, 79. On the other hand, Nübel ascribes the description to a later editor (Davids Aufstieg 32).

[18] Evidently, the word *yăršîʿă* "he acted wickedly" in MT (14 47) is derived from later anti-Saulide distortion. The original reading is to be supposed as either *wăyyiwwašeʿă* "he was saved" (LXX) (S. R. Driver, Notes on the Hebrew Text and the Topography of the Books of Samuel, 1913², 120) or *yôšîʿă* "he did saving acts" (Hertzberg, Die Samuelbücher, 94f. [ET 119f.]).

[19] The text of MT for the regnal year of Saul (I Sam 13 1) is corrupted. Noth holds that Saul reigned for two years according to the text in which the term *šᵉnaṭăyim* "two years" is written in an unusual way (*šᵉṭê šᵃnîm*) (ÜSt 24; idem, Geschichte, 163 [ET 176f.]). However, H. Tadmor suggests that either 12, 22 or 32 stood in the original text (in: EncBib, IV 1962, 299 [Hebrew]). K.-D. Schunck argues that we may emend the text into either "nine years" or "twelve years" (Benjamin, 1963, 120ff.), while Hertzberg assumes that the number forty may have originally stood

In the light of the foregoing, we cannot doubt that the complex is strongly coloured by a pro-Davidic and anti-Saulide bias[20]. In other words, the main theme of the complex is the "defence of David" against Saul[21]. In view of the condition of the source material at our disposal, to reconstruct the true course of history we must first find out the aim of the defence in each narrative. Palpably, the central question with which the narratives are concerned is the kingship in Israel, or, more precisely, the transfer of the kingship from Saul to David. In the very beginning, when Saul became suspicious of David, he said to himself: "What more can he have but the kingship?" (18 8). When

---

here, as in Josephus, Antiquitates Judaicae, 6.14.9 and in Acts 13 21 (Die Samuelbücher 81 [ET 103]); but the number twenty stands in Josephus, Antiquitates Judaicae, 10.8.4; cf. also H. Seebass, I Sam 15 als Schlüssel für das Verständnis der sogenannten königsfreundlichen Reihe . . ., ZAW 78 (1966), 156f. n. 22.

[20] It is possible to assume that in some narratives either pro-Saulide or anti-Davidic traditions originally stood behind the present texts. Grønbaek finds sympathy for Saul in I Sam 15 and 31 and animosity towards David in I Sam 25 (Die Geschichte vom Aufstieg Davids 62f. 109. 172). Ward argues that in the Nob traditions (I Sam 21 2–10 22 1–23) David is described as a desperado but Saul is not depicted as a villain (The Story of David's Rise 189f. 211). Nonetheless, it is clear that in the final compilation of the complex "the friendly disposition towards the first king" is overlaid by the view which "regarded the development from Samuel to Saul as a mistaken one", Hertzberg, Die Samuelbücher, 11 (ET 20).

[21] Alt maintains that "the precise purpose of this work was to provide a historical justification for the handing over of the Israelite kingship to David" (Die Staatenbildung, in: Kleine Schriften, II 38f. n. 4; cf. 40 n. 1 [ET 210 n. 94; cf. 211 n. 99]). A. Bentzen holds that "the description of David's history before his accession to the throne is probably a defence of David against Saul" (Introduction to the Old Testament, I 1952², 244). Weiser defines the purpose of "David's rise" as "den David als den rechtmäßigen Nachfolger Sauls im Königtum über Israel zu legitimieren" (VT 16, 340). According to Grønbaek, however, that the purpose of this work was a polemic of Rehoboam against Jeroboam by claiming the legitimate kingship of David over all Israel (Die Geschichte vom Aufstieg Davids 260ff.). J. Conrad assumes that the complex was composed by a Jerusalemite group which denounced the bloodshed of Jehu in his revolt against the House of Ahab (Zum geschichtlichen Hintergrund der Darstellung von Davids Aufstieg, ThLZ 97 [1972], 321–332). The late date of the composition, that is, after the division of the united kingdom, is supported also by F. Schicklberger, Die Davididen und das Nordreich. Beobachtungen zur sog. Geschichte vom Aufstieg Davids, BZ NF 18 (1974), 255–263. Against these views, Nübel argues that "aus dem Bemühen, von David jeden Verdacht voreiliger und gewaltsamer Machtergreifung fernzuhalten, läßt sich allerdings diese Schrift nicht zureichend erklären" (Davids Aufstieg 141). On the other hand, R. Rendtorff has tried to show that the author of "David's rise" not only collected traditions but also supplemented them with short informations to complete the description of the course of history (Beobachtungen zur altisraelitischen Geschichtsschreibung anhand der Geschichte vom Aufstieg Davids, in: von Rad Festschrift, 1971, 428–439).

he discovered that Jonathan had let David go, he angrily told his son: "As long as the son of Jesse lives on the earth, neither you nor your kingship shall be established" (20 31). From these words we may surmise that David hatched a plot to take over Saul's kingship. Naturally, his innocence of this charge is emphatically defended both by David himself (20 1 24 10–16 26 18–20) and by Jonathan (19 4–5 20 32)[22]. But, in any case, David took over the kingship from the House of Saul after his death (cf. II Sam 16 8). It is exactly because of the vehement advocacy of David's innocence that we are inclined to believe Saul's suspicion to be true, though we have no positive evidence of the plot[23], which appears to have been schemed so cunningly (cf. I Sam 23 22) that neither Jonathan (19 1–5 20 1–21 1 22 8; cf. 23 15–18) nor Michal (19 11–17) sensed it but only Saul, and certainly not Ahimelech, the priest of Nob (21 2–10 22 14–15)[24].

During David's flight to the wilderness of Judah, the relationship between him and the king can be described as a state of war. But no tradition gives us any information of David's campaigning against Saul, beyond some suggestive hints, which we have pointed out above. On the contrary, although Saul pursued David ruthlessly, David spared Saul's life twice (24 4–8 26 6–12)[25]. However, it is unlikely that, as the tradition has it, the inviolability of the anointed of Yahweh restrained

---

[22] J. Liver has pointed out that Jonathan is described not as a real person but as an ideal one in contrast to Saul (in: EncBib, III 1958, 534 [Hebrew]). Therefore, it is not easy to extract any historical fact from the friendship between David and Jonathan, because it is obscured by the legitimation of David's future kingship, cf. Grønbaek, Die Geschichte vom Aufstieg Davids, 102. On the other hand, J. A. Thompson finds a political implication in the term *'ahăḇ* "love" in the narratives of David and Jonathan (Significance of the Verb *love* in the David-Jonathan Narratives in 1 Samuel, VT 24 [1974], 334–338).

[23] Samuel's anointing of David (I Sam 16 1–13) and Jonathan's help for David's flight (I Sam 20) were clearly rebellious acts against the rule of Saul. Is it possible, however, to find any historical recollection in these tendentious sources that both Samuel and Jonathan were involved in David's conspiracy to overthrow the regime of Saul?

[24] M. A. Cohen argues that the priests of Nob instigated David to engineer a palace conspiracy against Saul (The Role of the Shilonite Priesthood in the United Monarchy of Ancient Israel, HUCA 36 [1965], 59–88). But this view cannot be accepted, since Ahimelech, the priest of Nob, was evidently innocent of David's flight (I Sam 21 2 22 14f.).

[25] K. Koch assumes that both traditions go back to the same source (Was ist Formgeschichte? Neue Wege der Bibelexegese, 1967², 174f. [ET The Growth of the Biblical Tradition, 1969, 142f.]), while Grønbaek contends that there were two independent traditions which were influenced by each other in the course of oral transmission (Die Geschichte vom Aufstieg Davids 168f.). In any case, it appears that both stories are set side by side in order to attain a dramatic culmination, cf. Weiser, VT 16, 336f.

David from raising his hand against Saul (24 7. 11 26 9. 11)[26]. The only historical fact which we can sift out from the traditions is, it seems, that David could not defeat Saul by any means. On the other hand, the Davidic defence is very clear in both narratives. David is defended most effectively, not least by putting his defence in the mouth of Saul: the king not only admits David's innocence (24 18–20 26 21) but also confirms his future kingship over Israel (24 21), which has been predicted by Jonathan (23 17). When Saul and David part for good, they are not enemies any more, but have become friends. Saul blesses David and speaks of his great success to come (26 25), In this way, suspicion of David's disloyalty towards Saul is completely dispelled. Moreover, his succession is authorized by Saul, the reigning king, and consented to by Jonathan, the crown prince. This perfect exculpation of David cannot be historical. Nor can we learn from the narratives that Saul's monarchy was not hereditary[27]. On the contrary, exactly because it was hereditary, David badly needed Saul's authorization to become his legitimate heir. Jonathan's consent simply enhanced it. Remerkably, Saul is here called "my father" by David (24 12) and David "my son" by Saul (24 17 26 17. 21. 25). Although K. Koch[28] finds a loyal relationship between Saul and David in this form of address, we are of the opinion that the common formula of adoption in the ancient Near East (cf. II Sam 7 14 Ps 2 7 89 27) must be detected here[29]. By making David Saul's adopted son, his succession to Saul was legitimatized

---

[26] T. C. G. Thornton is of the opinion that the doctrine of the inviolability of the anointed of Yahweh was invented in the Davidic court to defend the Judaean kings from attempts at assassination (Studies in Samuel, CQR 168 [1967], 416). According to Nübel, this was a royal ideology formed by the *Bearbeiter* under the influence of Elijah (Davids Aufstieg 147). On our view, see below pp. 75–76.

[27] J. Morgenstern argues that both Saul's authorization and Jonathan's consent show that David had the legitimate successorship to Saul by his marriage with Michal (Beena Marriage [Matriarchate] in Ancient Israel and its Historical Implications, ZAW 47 [1929], 93ff.; idem, David and Jonathan, JBL 78 [1959], 322–325). But see below pp. 72–73.

[28] Was ist Formgeschichte? 171 (ET 139).

[29] In both Babylonian laws and adoption contracts from Mesopotamia and Syria, we find a formula of dissolution of adoption such as *ul māruni attā* "you are not my son", *ul abī attā* "you are not my father" or *ul ummī attī* "you are not my mother", for instance, CH § 192 XL 6–7; ANET 175. On the other examples, see H. Donner, Adoption oder Legitimation? Erwägungen zur Adoption im Alten Testament auf dem Hintergrund der altorientalischen Rechte, OrAnt 8 (1969), 115ff. From this formula it is assumed that the formula "you are my son", "you are my father", "you are my mother", etc., was declared as *sollemnia verba* when the contract of adoption was established, see M. David, Die Adoption im altbabylonischen Recht, 1927, 78f.; G. R. Driver & J. C. Miles, The Babylonian Laws, I 1952, 402.

impeccably[30]. Of the adoption of a crown prince, we have a good example in the Hittite Old Kingdom. After having disinherited his own sons as well as an adopted son because of their disloyalty, Hattusili I adopted a boy called Mursili and designated him to be his successor[31]. According to A. Alt[32], Abbael, king of Aleppo, also adopted Yarimlim, son of Hammurapi, to install him as his successor[32], but this suggestion has been disputed[33]. It is interesting to note that Eupolemos (c. 160 B. C.) mentions David as Saul's son:

> "After that, Samuel became prophet; then, by the will of God Saul was chosen as king by Samuel; he died after a reign of twenty-one years; then his son David took the power."[34]

But we do not know whether he regarded David mistakenly as Saul's real son or as an adopted one.

It goes without saying that this adoptive relationship between Saul and David was a fiction invented by David's defender. The same defender knew that the House of David finally prevailed over the House of Saul after a long and bloody struggle. It seems that this historical situation is implicit in Saul's plea for David's mercy on his descendants in the same narrative (I Sam 24 22). The plea was also made by Jonathan (20 15–16; cf. 20 42). No one can fail to find in it an echo of David's later position (cf. II Sam 9 1–13 21 1–14). It becomes plain that the effect of the narrative concering the fictitious adoption was twofold. On the one hand, it tried to testify to David's legitimate status as Saul's heir on the basis of the dynastic principle. On the other, it showed the

---

[30] It seems that the Israelites had no custom of adoption in the full sense of the term, see de Vaux, Les institutions de l'Ancien Testament, I 1958, 85ff. (ET Ancient Israel, 1961, 51f.); Donner, OrAnt 8, 87–119, especially 113ff. But it is widely accepted that there was a concept of divine adoption in the Judaean royal ideology, see Alt, Die Staatenbildung, in: Kleine Schriften, II 63 (ET 235); G. von Rad, Das judäische Königsritual (1947), in: Gesammelte Studien, I 1971⁴, 209 (ET The Royal Ritual in Judah, in: The Problem of the Hexateuch and Other Essays, 1966, 226f.); de Vaux, Les institutions, I 171ff. (ET 111ff.). Although Donner argues against it (OrAnt 8, 113f.), it seems difficult to exclude a notion of divine adoption from the Judaean royal ideology, see H. J. Boecker, Anmerkung zur Adoption im Alten Testament, ZAW 86 (1974), 86–89. It is possible to assume, therefore, that the author of the "defence of David" applied the formula of divine adoption to the fictitious royal adoption.

[31] HAB I–II 37–38; O. R. Gurney, The Hittites, 1961[3], 171.

[32] Bemerkungen zu den Verwaltungs- und Rechtsurkunden von Ugarit und Alalach, WO 3/1–2 (1964), 14f.

[33] See M. B. Rowton, Chronology – Ancient Western Asia, CAH I ch. VI, 1962, 43f.; J. R. Kupper, Northern Mesopotamia and Syria, CAH II ch. I, 1963, 34.

[34] Eusebius Werke, VIII. Die Praeparatio Evangelica, I, ed. K. Mars, 1954, 538 30 2–3; cf. J. Giblet, Eupolème et l'historiographie du Judaïsme hellénistique, EThL 39 (1963), 541. 548.

historical reality – that David was not a king of the Saulide dynasty but the founder of his own.

The founder of a dynasty always derived his authority from divine election. Therefore, Yahweh's choice of David is one of the most important themes throughout the "defence of David". It recounts that Yahweh chose David as the future king of Israel (I Sam 16 1. 12), the spirit of Yahweh came on him (16 13), Yahweh was with him (16 18 18 12. 14. 28 II Sam 5 10 7 9; cf. I Sam 17 37 20 13), answered him (I Sam 22 15 23 2. 4. 10–12 30 8 II Sam 2 1 5 19. 23–24 7 5–16), protected him (I Sam 17 37 23 14 25 29 II Sam 7 9; cf. I Sam 25 26 30 6), guided him (22 5 II Sam 7 18), designated him *nagîḏ* (I Sam 25 30 II Sam 5 2 6 21 7 8; cf. 3 18) and king of Israel (II Sam 3 9–10 5 12), and established his House (I Sam 25 28 II Sam 7 11–12. 16; cf. 7 18–29). The effect of David's divine election is further intensified by explaining it as the inevitable consequence of Saul's rejection by Yahweh (I Sam 13 14 15 28 16 1 28 17 II Sam 6 21 7 15).

This double nature of the "defence of David" reflects the development of the relationship between the House of David and the House of Saul. In the beginning, the House of David had to pretend that it had dynastic continuity with the House of Saul. But after its authority was consolidated all over Israel, it no longer cared about this fictitious nexus. Instead, it claimed its divinely legitimatized right to the kingship over Israel in place of the House of Saul[35].

B. DAVID KING OF JUDAH: THE FOUNDER OF THE DYNASTY OF DAVID

The only information that we have about the beginning of the Davidic monarchy and the establishment of the kingdom of Judah is very brief and inadequate (II Sam 2 1–4a), since the "defence of David" is not interested in reporting about it in detail[36]. But even from this scant material it becomes clear that the very person of David was a decisive factor in the establishment of the monarchy in Judah[37]. When David came up to Hebron from Ziklag with his family and mercenaries after Saul's defeat at Gilboa (2 3), he doubtless planned to found the

[35] H. M. Wolf assumes that the "defence of David" (I Sam 15–II Sam 8) was composed under the literary influence of the "apology of Hattusilis III", the king of the Hittite empire (1275–1250) (The Apology of Hattusilis 161). But his comparison is unconvincing, see M. Tsevat, JBL 87 (1968), 458–461.

[36] Cf. Alt, Die Staatenbildung, in: Kleine Schriften, II 40 n. 1 (ET 211 n. 99); Weiser, VT 16, 333.

[37] Cf. Alt, Die Staatenbildung, in: Kleine Schriften, II 40 (ET 212); Noth, Geschichte, 168 (ET 182).

kingdom of Judah. The account that he consulted Yahweh by oracle as to whether he should go up and to which place (2 1) shows that it was a truly critical moment. A propitious oracle of Yahweh encouraged him to go up to Hebron[38]. But we know that there was a long preparation for it on his part.

As we have pointed out, it appears that David already had aspiration to the throne when still a successful commander in Saul's army. After he was expelled from court, his political stance was revealed in a struggle for power with Saul. He organized a powerful band of six hundred men, originally four hundred (I Sam 22 1–2 23 13 25 13 27 2 30 10), with whom he traversed the land of Judah[39]. With them, he waged a campaign against the Philistines who went attacking Keilah (23 1–5), protected the herdsmen of Nabal (25 7), and laid an ambush against Saul (22 8. 13). In addition, he succeeded in forming ties with the king of Moab (22 3–4), and perhaps with Nahash the Ammonite (cf. II Sam 10 2). In this period, he married Ahinoam of Jezreel and Abigail of Carmel to establish a connection with the Calebite families in the south of Judah (I Sam 25 42–43 27 3 30 5 II Sam 2 2; cf. II Sam 3 2–3 I Chron 3 1)[40]. But when he understood that his power was not yet strong enough to challenge Saul's supremacy in Judah, he sought asylum in the land of the Philistines and received Ziklag as his estate from Achish, king of Gath (I Sam 27 1–7; cf. 21 11–16). Even so, he did not refrain from developing his influence on the southern tribes, his fellow countrymen (27 8–12 30 26–31). It is likely that, as a result of these activities, there were already some supporters of his cause among them before he went up to Hebron. On the other hand, we can assume that his departure for Hebron was made with the consent of the Philistines, who desired to weaken what was left on the power of Saul's kingdom by separation of south from north[41]. Thus, both external and in-

[38] J. A. Soggin assumes that the oracle which David received was later referred to by Abner (II Sam 3 9–10. 18) and by the elders of Israel (5 2) (Das Königtum in Israel, 1967, 64ff.).

[39] On the regular army of David, see A. Malamat, Military Rationing in Papyrus Anastasi I and the Bible, in: Mélanges Robert, [1957], 117ff.; B. Mazar, The Military Élite of King David, VT 13 (1963), 310–320; Y. Yadin, The Art of Warfare in Biblical Land, II 1963, 275ff.

[40] Both Jezreel and Carmel later belonged to the seventh district of the kingdom of Judah (Josh 15 55–57), see Y. Aharoni, The Land of the Bible, 1966, 300; Z. Kallai, The Tribes of Israel, 1967, 328f. (Hebrew). It appears that they were originally Calebite settlements, see Kallai, in: EncBib, IV 1962, 323 (Hebrew). They are definitely not Jezreel and Carmel in northern Palestine, against Schicklberger, BZ NF 18, 261 n. 22.

[41] Alt assumes that the kingdom of Judah was established as a sort of vassal state of the Philistines (Die Staatenbildung, in: Kleine Schriften, II 40 [ET 212]); cf. Noth, Geschichte, 169 (ET 183); J. Bright, A History of Israel, 1972², 191.

ternal conditions were ripe for David to establish the kingdom of Judah[42].

It is remarkable, that, unlike Jephthah (Judg 11 4–11), David did not receive an invitation from the inhabitants of Judah. This shows that the "house of Judah" over which he was made king (II Sam 2 4a) had not yet crystallized as a political entity before his accession. Evidently, the "house of Judah" here signifies "greater Judah", which included, apart from the tribe of Judah, all the southern tribes, such as the Calebites, the Kenazites (or Otheniel), the Jerachmeelites, the Kenites and Simeon. A. Alt and M. Noth have argued that the Davidic kingdom of Judah was based on a sacral league of these six tribes with its centre at the tree sanctuary of Mamre in the vicinity of Hebron[43]. But it is difficult to accept the thesis of the "Mamre amphictyony"[44], for we cannot find any evidence of greater Judah as a political entity before David's enthronement at Hebron. The Calebites, the Kenazites, the Jerachmeelites and the Kenites originally belonged to different ethnic groups (cf. Gen 15 19 36 11. 15. 42 I Chron 1 36. 53; cf. also Num 24 21–22). They were never counted as members of the twelve-tribe system of Israel, like Judah and Simeon. It would seem that these foreign tribes came from the south, while Judah and Simeon came from the north[45]. The foreign tribes and the latter group retained their ethnic

---

[42] It is worth noting that Rezon, son of Eliada, established the kingdom of Damascus in a similar situation, as Malamat has pointed out (Aspects of the Foreign Policies of David and Solomon, JNES 22 [1963], 5).

[43] Alt, Der Gott der Väter (1929), in: Kleine Schriften, I 1953, 54f. (ET The God of the Fathers, in: Essays, 53f.); idem, Die Staatenbildung, in: Kleine Schriften, II 41 (ET 213); Noth, Das System der zwölf Stämme Israels, 1930, 107f.; idem, Geschichte, 167 (ET 181f.); cf. Aharoni, The Land of the Bible, 234f. Apart from the thesis of the Mamre amphictyony, H.-J. Zobel assumes that a political consolidation among the southern tribes was under way already prior to the days of David (Israel und die Völker 8ff. 214ff. – Since this *Habilitationsschrift* was not available to me, I have referred for this information to G. Wallis, Die Tradition von den drei Ahnvätern, ZAW 81 [1969], 30); see now Zobel, Beiträge zur Geschichte Gross-Judas in früh- und vordavidischer Zeit, SVT 28 (1975), 253–277. It is true that the "elders of Judah" mentioned as the representatives of the towns in southern Palestine (I Sam 30 26) would show as if there already existed "greater Judah" when David was in Ziklag, see Grønbaek, Die Geschichte vom Aufstieg Davids, 209. It seems, however, that the name Judah here stemmed from the author of the "rise of David".

[44] Cf. de Vaux, The Settlement of the Israelites in Southern Palestine and the Origin of the Tribe of Judah, in: H. G. May Festschrift, 1970, 133 (= Histoire ancienne d'Israël. Des origines à l'installation en Canaan, 1971, 509f.). Mazar argues that the Kohathites in Hebron took an active part in the crowning of David (The Cities of the Priests and the Levites, SVT 7 [1960], 197).

[45] Cf. Aharoni, The Land of the Bible, 198. But there is a possibility that both Judah and Simeon, too, came from the south, see M. Weippert, Die Landnahme der

independence side by side until the days of David (I Sam 15 6 25 3 27 10 30 14. 29; cf. Judg 4 11. 17 5 24). Their integration into greater Judah can be documented only from the accounts of the conquest (Num 13–14 32 12 34 19 Deut 1 36 Josh 14 6ff. 15 13ff. Judg 1 2ff.; cf. 3 9ff.) and from the genealogical tables (I Chron 2–4), both dating from the days of David[46]. As to the integration of Simeon into Judah, we may surmise that it took place at about the same time or a little earlier, since the term "Negeb of Judah" in the days of David (I Sam 27 10 30 14 II Sam 24 7) was actually identical with the tribal area of Simeon[47]. But we must draw attention to the note about the cities of Simeon: "There were their cities unto the reign of David" (I Chron 4 31; cf. Josh 15 21–32 19 1–9)[48]. This history of the settlement of the southern tribes shows that the unification of greater Judah, comprising all those tribes, was first achieved under the rule of David as the king of Judah.

Y. Aharoni[49] has argued that Judah and Simeon formed one of the six administrative districts of Saul's kingdom. The following evidence, however, implies that the land of Judah was outside Saul's direct rule: a) David managed to form the band of six hundred men with whom he resisted Saul in the territory of the southern tribes; b) Saul had to make frequent campaigns against David in the land of Judah; c) David married women from the Calebite families; d) the elders of Judah received presents from David in Ziklag. If Saul had ruled over them directly, they would have been punished by him like the priests of Nob. On the other hand, Saul's influence over the southern tribes can be discovered in the following facts: a) the men of Judah participated in Saul's campaign against the Amalekites (I Sam 15 4; cf. 14 48) – the aim of the campaign was doubtless the protection of the southern tribes from nomad incursions (cf. 27 8); b) the sons of Jesse the Bethlehemite served at Saul's court and followed him to the battlefield (16 14–23 17 12–15); c) both the men of Keilah (23 11–12) and the Ziphites (23 19–20 26 1) tried to hand David over to Saul; d) David was finally compelled to escape from Saul's pursuit to Achish, king of Gath (27 1–4; cf. 21

israelitischen Stämme, 1967, 49f. (ET The Settlement of the Israelite Tribes in Palestine, 1971, 44f.); de Vaux, in: May Festschrift, 130f. (= Histoire 506f.).

[46] See Aharoni, The Land of the Bible, 197f. 224ff.; J. Liver, The Israelite Tribes, in: WHJP, III 1971, 211.

[47] Cf. Aharoni, The Negeb of Judah, IEJ 8 (1958), 26–33.

[48] Cf. Y. Kaufmann, The Biblical Account of the Conquest of Palestine, 1953, 23. 83; Aharoni, The Land of the Bible, 265; Kallai, The Tribes of Israel, 295 (Hebrew).

[49] The Districts of Israel and Judah, in: The Kingdoms of Israel and Judah, ed. Malamat, 1961, 114f. (Hebrew); idem, The Land of the Bible, 255ff. For other arguments for the inclusion of Judah in the kingdom of Saul, see Schunck, Benjamin, 124ff.; C. E. Hauer, The Shape of the Saulide Strategy, CBQ 31 (1969), 158ff.; A. D. H. Mayes, Israel in the Pre-Monarchy Period, VT 23 (1973), 169f.

11–16). The inference is that the southern tribes were in Saul's firm grip, but that his rule was not as direct as over the northern tribes[50]. Moreover, each tribe in the south had a different relationship to Saul's rule. For instance, the Ziphites were loyal to him, the Calebites linked up with David. This also shows that the southern tribes had no political unity before the establishment of the kingdom of Judah by David.

The foundation of that kingdom rested on the national consolidation of the southern tribes. David brought about this political development by taking advantage of two conditions among the Israelite tribes, prevailing since the day of their settlement in Canaan: a) the deep rift between the northern and southern tribes; b) a special, though loose, tie binding the southern tribes. The unification of greater Judah was a result of the positive exploitation of the second condition. But it was only achieved by widening the rift through the setting up of the kingdom of Judah alongside the kingdom of Israel[51]. Under the strong impact of David's political success, the southern tribes appear to have been then assimilated into the tribe of Judah[52]. Therefore, the kingship of David must have been recognized by the people of greater Judah at the beginning of his reign as a symbol of their consolidation. This, unquestionably, is the origin of the dynastic stability of the House of David in Judah.

Although David played the leading role in the establishment of the kingdom of Judah, we cannot overlook the initiative taken by the people: "And the men of Judah came, and there they anointed David king over the house of Judah" (II Sam 2 4a). This is a clear indication of the "democratic" tradition of ancient Israel[53]. In fact, the people of Israel never ceased to express their sovereignty against the centralized

---

[50] Cf. Alt, Die Staatenbildung, in: Kleine Schriften, II 19f. n. 3 (ET 191 n. 47); Flanagan, A Study of the Biblical Traditions, 154ff. According to Grønbaek, it was the intention of the author of "David's rise" to show that Judah had been included in Saul's kingdom in order to legitimatize David's rule over both Israel and Judah as Saul's successor (Die Geschichte vom Aufstieg Davids 23). But we are of the opinion that there was no need for David to legitimatize his kingship over Judah.

[51] Cf. Alt, Die Staatenbildung, in: Kleine Schriften, II 40 (ET 211); Noth, Geschichte, 168 (ET 182).

[52] Cf. S. Mowinckel, „Rahelstämme" und „Leastämme", in: Eissfeldt Festschrift, BZAW 77 (1958), 137f.; idem, Tetrateuch-Pentateuch-Hexateuch, 1964, 66; M. A. Cohen, HUCA 36, 94ff.; de Vaux, in: May Festschrift, 131ff. (= Histoire 507ff.).

[53] According to Soggin, the Israelite kingship was established upon the tension between three ways of thinking, that is, democratic, charismatic and institutional, and the first two principles had an opposing relation to the last (Zur Entwicklung des alttestamentlichen Königtums, ThZ 15 [1959], 401–418; idem, Charisma und Institution im Königtum Sauls, ZAW 75 [1963], 54ff.; idem, Das Königtum in Israel, 45f.).

authority of the king throughout the monarchical period[54]. Obviously, David could not establish the kingdom without the people's consent. In this respect, A. Alt seems right in the assumption that a covenant must have been made between David and the men of Judah at his enthronement, though it is not mentioned explicitly. He has explained this relationship as follows: "the initiative of the one matches the initiative of the other, and together the two provide the mutual bond on which the body politic was based."[55]

Nonetheless, David created the monarchy by the exclusive instrumentality of his personal troops, and the people could have had only a passive part in the structure of his regime. The relationship between David and the people appears to have been already tense at the start of the monarchy, and it became the fundamental cause of the later crisis.

As the kingdom grew rapidly into an empire, that basic schism between the king and the people widened increasingly. The power on which David relied was his mercenaries, who pledged allegiance to his person and had followed him since his wandering in the wilderness of Judah. David's system of administration was a highly developed officialdom organized on the Egyptian-Canaanite model[56]. Moreover, he chose as his residence Jerusalem, that had been a foreign city until its capture by David. Surrounded by his family, officials and mercenaries, all of whom were the "servants" of the king, David governed the people from Jerusalem, which lay outside the tribal territory. Since all these drastic political and administrative changes took place within a few decades, it was certainly not easy for the people, who still lived in a traditional tribal-patriarchal society, to cope with the resulting radical social transformation. In the beginning, David completed the formation of the empire so quickly and successfully that the people simply had no time to raise a critical voice against the regime. But when he

---

[54] Cf. Malamat, Organs of Statecraft in the Israelite Monarchy (1965), in: BAR 3, 1970, 163–198; Buccellati, Cities and Nations of Ancient Syria, 1967, 133ff.; H. Tadmor, "The People" and the Kingship in Ancient Israel: The Role of Political Institutions in the Biblical Period, JWH 11 (1968), 34–50.

[55] Die Staatenbildung, in: Kleine Schriften, II 41 (ET 213); cf. G. Fohrer, Der Vertrag zwischen König und Volk in Israel (1959), in: Studien zur alttestamentlichen Theologie und Geschichte (1949–1966), 1969, 332f.

[56] On the officials of the kingdom of David and Solomon, see de Vaux, Titres et fonctionnaires égyptiens à la cour de David et de Salomon (1939), in Bible et Orient, 1967, 189–201; idem, Les institutions, I 195ff. (ET 127ff.); J. Begrich, Sōfēr und Mazkīr (1940), in Gesammelte Studien, 1964, 67–98; B. Maisler (Mazar), The Scribe of King David and the Problem of the High Officials in the Ancient Kingdom of Israel (1946/47), in: Canaan and Israel, 1974, 208–221 (Hebrew); T. N. D. Mettinger, Solomonic State Officials. A Study of the Civil Government Officials of the Israelite Monarchy, 1971.

went too far along this path without proper consideration for the authority of the people on whom his kingdom was based, or for their demands, their dissatisfaction exploded in Absalom's rebellion[57].

Still, the ring-leaders of the rebellion belonged to, or were connected with, the House of David. Absalom was the third son of David, born at Hebron of Maacah, daughter of Talmai, king of Geshur (II Sam 3 3 I Chron 3 2; cf. II Sam 13 37). The commander of the army appointed by Absalom was Amasa, whose mother was Abigail, daughter of Nahash, sister of Zeruiah, Joab's mother (II Sam 17 25; cf. I Chron 2 16–17). According to another tradition, Zeruiah and Abigail were sisters of David (I Chron 2 16). The details of Amasa's ancestry are obscure, however[58]. Absalom's adviser was Ahithopel (II Sam 15 31. 34 16 15. 20ff.), apparently the grandfather of Bathsheba, wife of Uriah the Hittite (II Sam 11 3 23 34), and also a counsellor of David (II Sam 15 12 I Chron 27 33)[59]. In the circumstances the rebellion was not a people's rising but the insurrection of a disgruntled party in the royal court in Jerusalem. But it is plain that Absalom exploited popular disillusionment with David's monarchy, and the people wanted to establish an ideal monarchy under him (cf. II Sam 15 2–6)[60]. In any case, Absalom's revolt was no indication of a revolution against the House of David. In spite of the deep displeasure of the people with David's regime, the prestige and authority of the House of David were already firmly rooted in Israel, and especially in Judah[61].

---

[57] Alt contends that the rebellion of Absalom and Sheba's revolt were caused by Israel's disapproval of David's campaign against the countries east of the Jordan (Die Staatenbildung, in: Kleine Schriften, II 56ff. [ET 228f.]). On the other hand, J. Weingreen regards David's policy of ruthlessness towards the people as the cause of the rebellion (The Rebellion of Absalom, VT 19 [1969], 263–266). According to H. Bardtke, the cause of the rebellion is to be found in disappointment of the Judaean amphictyony that David was not fit for the figure of its ideal king (Erwägungen zur Rolle Judas im Aufstand des Absalom, in: K. Elliger Festschrift, 1973, 1–8). It seems, however, that the people were concerned not with any ideological problem but with David's failure in the domestic administration (Cf. II Sam 15 2–6), cf. Tadmor, JWH 11, 53f.

[58] Cf. Hertzberg, Die Samuelbücher, 294 (ET 357); S. Aḥituv, in: EncBib, VI 1971, 306 (Hebrew).

[59] Cf. S. Yeivin, The Beginning of the Davidids (1944/45), in: Studies in the History of Israel and His Country, 1959/60, 200ff. (Hebrew); B. Maisler (Mazar), in: EncBib, I 1950, 226f. (Hebrew).

[60] Tadmor points out that Absalom established his consultative body with the men of Israel and the elders of Israel whom David neglected (JWH 11, 53ff.).

[61] Alt maintains that Judah was not involved in the rebellion and remained neutral (Die Staatenbildung, in: Kleine Schriften, II 57f. [ET 228f.]). This thesis is followed by some scholars, see Hetzberg, Die Samuelbücher, 277 (ET 337); Soggin, Das Königtum

It is important for the present study to analyse the political settlement by means of which David overcame the very difficult situation that he had to face after quelling the rebellion. Notwithstanding his decisive victory in battle, David's position was still precarious in the kingdom. He was, at that moment, a dethroned king (II Sam 19 10–11; cf. 15 10). Now, he skilfully manoeuvred himself into the restoration of his kingship (19 23). First of all, he abstained from all retaliatory punishment and endevoured to prevent further disturbances (II Sam 19 17–31). Secondly, he repeated the tactics by which he had become king of Judah and Israel. He took the initiative in appealing to the elders of Judah on the reasoning of "bone and flesh", the basis of the tribal-patriarchal society (19 13–14; cf. Gen 2 23 29 14 Judg 9 2 II Sam 5 1)[62], and proved his conciliatory policy by the appointment of Amasa as commander of the army in the place of Joab (19 14). By this explicit manifestation of his preference for Judah, he made use again of the old feud between north and south, which had in the past served to consolidate the southern tribes as greater Judah and now "swayed the heart of all the men of Judah as one man" (19 15). He must have been well aware that this policy would arouse the resentment of the northern tribes. But he had no alternative – first he had to regain the support of the people of Judah, for he could handle the problem of the northern tribes only after his regime was solidly based on the kingdom of Judah. In the same order he built his monarchy first in Judah, then in Israel, which demonstrates that the dualism between Israel and Judah in the kingdom of David was derived from the very nature of his monarchy. The grievances of the northern tribes flared up in Sheba's revolt (20 1–2. 4–22). David at once realized that Sheba would "do more harm than Absalom" (20 6), since Sheba, unlike Absalom, rejected the rule of the House of David over Israel (20 1).

It appears that Sheba's revolt deflected the interest of the people of Judah from the shortcomings of David's monarchy to self-defence. Although Amasa was assassinated by Joab, the people followed Joab to pursue Sheba (20 8–13). But it can also be assumed that David realized the vital importance of popular support in Judah for his regime and for the future primacy of his House. Although explicit mention is lacking, we may assume that he made considerable modifications in his relations with the people of Judah after the rebellion. One of the greatest

in Israel, 75. But it is hardly acceptable, see Noth, Geschichte, 184f. (ET 201); Tadmor, JWH 11, 51; Bright, A History, 204f.; Bardtke, in: Elliger Festschrift, 1ff.

[62] Cf. J. Pedersen, Israel, I–II 1926, 267f.; de Vaux, Les institutions, I 18 (ET 5); Buccellati, Cities and Nations, 99ff. W. Reiser calls the expression "bone and flesh" the "kinship formula" (Die Verwandtschaftsformel in Gen 2, 23, ThZ 16 [1960], 1–4).

privileges granted to them seems to have been exemption from tax. We may surmise this from the absence of Judah in the list of the administrative districts organized by Solomon for taxation (I Kings 4 7–19)[63]. Otherwise, it is hard to explain the source of the steadfast support which the people of Judah gave to the House of David at the time of the schism after the death of Solomon (12 20). Thus did David succeed in founding his dynasty in Judah. But he could not solve the problem of the dualism between Judah and Israel.

C. DAVID KING OF ISRAEL: THE SUCCESSOR TO SAUL

As soon as David became king of Judah, he went into action to realize his long cherished ambition to rule over Israel. Apparently, kingship over Judah was nothing for him but a step towards this ultimate end. He sent a message to the men of Jabesh-gilead in a bid to make a treaty with them (II Sam 2 4b–7)[64]. By the treaty, David meant to undermine Ishbaal's regime in Mahanaim, which had been established under the guardianship of Abner, commander of Saul's army, after the catastrophe at Gilboa (2 8–9). Although the result of David's proposal to Jabesh is not reported, we need not think that he failed[65]. There is reason to assume that he achieved a fair amount of success in making anti-Ishbaal treaties during his reign at Hebron. His marriage to Maacah, daughter of Talmai, king of Geshur (II Sam 3 3 I Chron 3 2; cf.II Sam 13 37) can be regarded as one of his successes. We may also assume that he made a treaty with Nahash, king of Ammon, against the House of Saul in this period (cf. II Sam 10 2), unless that event should be placed in the period of his wanderings in the wilderness of Judah (see above p. 64)[66]. The abortive treaty with Abner (3 6–39) was, in effect, the climax of a series of diplomatic offensives against Ishbaal's regime.

---

[63] See Aharoni, The Land of the Bible, 279; but the view is disputed, see de Vaux, Les institutions, I 208 (ET 135).

[64] On the expression עשה הטובה in reference to the act of treaty-making, see W. L. Moran, A Note on the Treaty Terminology of the Sefîre Stelas, JNES 22 (1963), 173–176; D. R. Hillers, A Note on Some Treaty Terminology in the Old Testament, BASOR 176 (1964), 46–47; Malamat, in: BAR 3, 196f.; Soggin, Das Königtum in Israel, 65 n. 2; M. Weinfeld, King-People Relationship in the Light of 1 Kings 12:7, Lešonenu 36 (1970/71), 10ff. (Hebrew); M. Fox, *ṬÔB̲* as Covenant Terminology, BASOR 209 (1973), 41f.

[65] Cf. Hertzberg, Die Samuelbücher, 203 (ET 249).

[66] Cf. N. Glueck, Das Wort *ḥesed*, 1927, 16 (ET *Ḥesed* in the Bible, 1967, 50). On the activity of David in Hebron, see Mazar, David's Reign in Hebron and the Conquest of Jerusalem, in: Silver Festschrift, 1963, 235–244.

It appears that the House of Saul laid claim to rulership over Judah, though Saul's goverance there was not as stable as over the norhern tribes (see above pp. 66–67). It follows, therefore, that Ishbaal regarded David's accession to the throne of Judah as a rebellion, and it became the *casus belli* of a long war between the two Houses (2 12–3 1. 6)[67]. But when Abner decided to make a treaty with David, Ishbaal had no power to prevent him from negotiating. Nor could he reject David's demand for Michal, Saul's daughter and David's former wife (3 13–16). Some scholars are of the opinion that the story of David's marriage to Michal during Saul's lifetime is unhistorical[68]. But this view is untenable[69]. According to the present form of the account of it, David's marriage to Michal grew out of Saul's evil design against David (I Sam 18 17–27). It can be assumed, however, that, in the original story, David married Michal with her father's full approval and at a time when Saul esteemed David, before he began to mistrust him[70]. When David, a promising young warrior, heard of Saul's intention to give him his daughter, he was embarrassed, because he came neither from the northern tribes (18 18) nor from a family good enough to match with the royal family (18 23). Nonetheless, Saul encouraged him to take Michal to wife: it was David who was "the most faithful among Saul's servants, the king's son-in-law, the captain over king's bodyguard, and honoured in the royal house" (22 14). J. Morgenstern[71] has argued that this was a *beena*-marriage, in which the lineage was transmitted on the distaff side, and so, through it, David acquired his "real and substantial claim to the successorship to Saul". It is not an acceptable theory, as we have no decisive evidence of matriarchate in ancient Israel[72]. Still, it is a plain fact that David became a member of the House of Saul through the marriage, and that this status enabled him, even without a legal claim based on a *beena*-marriage, to be a natural pretender to the throne. Of course, Saul deprived him of the status immediately after the breach (25 44; cf. II Sam 3 15). That David demanded Michal's return from Abner as the first condition of making a treaty (II Sam 3

---

[67] Cf. Eissfeldt, Ein gescheiterter Versuch der Wiedervereinigung Israels (2 Sam 2, 12–3, 1) (1951), in: Kleine Schriften, III 1966, 132–146.

[68] Recently Noth, Geschichte, 170 n. 1 (ET 184 n. 1); for the other bibliography, see H. J. Stoebe, David und Mikal. Überlegungen zur Jugendgeschichte Davids, in: Eissfeldt Festschrift, BZAW 77 (1958), 228 n. 41.

[69] Cf. R. Kittel, Geschichte des Volkes Israel, II 1925[7], 109 n. 5.

[70] Hertzberg tries to reconstruct the original story by means of putting v. 17b. 21a. 25b in parenthesis (Die Samuelbücher 128 [ET 159f.]); cf. also Grønbaek, Die Geschichte vom Aufstieg Davids, 103f.

[71] See above p. 61 n. 27.

[72] See Pedersen, Israel, I–II 75f. 94; de Vaux, Les institutions, I 37f. (ET 19f.); W. Plautz, Zur Frage des Mutterrechts im Alten Testament, ZAW 74 (1962), 18ff.

13) shows that he attached importance to his marital tie with Saul's daughter in establishing his legitimate claim to be his successor[73].

The marriage can be compared to that of the general Haremhab with Mutnodjme[74]. In the transition between the 18th and the 19th dynasties of Egypt, this pharaoh married a princess of royal blood with the intention of bringing legitimacy to the royal throne into his House, which sprang from a commoner[75]. We, however, take it that David had no intention, from the start, of having a prince of the royal blood of the House of Saul as an heir to his own throne born of his resumed espousal of Michal. It seems, as we will show, that the real cause of Michal's sterility was not the punishment of Yahweh (II Sam 6 20–23) but David's avoidance of her.

When David received the news of Saul's death in battle, as well as of Ishbaal's assassination, he executed the informers then and there, against their expectations (II Sam 1 1–16 4 5–12). David maintained that the Amalekite who allegedly killed Saul should be put to death since he laid hands on the anointed of Yahweh, and Ishbaal's assassins likewise, to avenge the blood of the guiltless. Apart from these reasons, we cannot fail to find here a definite political gesture. Like the informers, everybody knew that David wished to remove both Saul and Ishbaal. Just because of this situation, David must have hastened to prove his own innocence, especially in the matters of Ishbaal's death. When Abner was assassinated by Joab, David similarly proclaimed his innocence in public (3 28–39); although he could well be suspected (cf. 3 37), it is unlikely that he wanted Abner's death at that stage; Abner, like Amasa, was killed by a Joab jealous of David's attention to others (cf. I Kings 2 5–6. 31–33). It appears that David was innocent also of any part in Ishbaal's murder. But he had to demonstrate it by the most convincing of acts – the execution of the assassins, for he was liable to be suspected more seriously in this than in the case of Abner's assassination. It seems that David's political gesture at the death of Saul and Ishbaal carried a deeper implication, going beyond a simple demonstration of personal innocence. He expressed his profound sorrow at Saul's death in battle together with Jonathan by fasting (II Sam 1 11–12), as well as by composing a funeral dirge (1 17–27). He wanted to manifest his close relationship with the House of Saul: when he played the role of

[73] About the implication of the expressions "Michal, Saul's daughter" and "Michal, David's wife", see D. J. A. Clines, X, X *ben* Y, *ben* Y: Personal Names in Hebrew Narrative Style, VT 22 (1972), 269ff.

[74] See J. H. Breasted, Ancient Records of Egypt, III 1906, § 28.

[75] See C. J. Bleeker, The Position of the Queen in Ancient Egypt, in: The Sacral Kingship. Studies in the History of Religions, Suppl. to Numen 4 (1959), 266; A. Gardiner, Egypt of the Pharaohs, 1962, 242.

gô'el of that House by executing both the Amalekite and the murderers of Ishbaal, the relationship was attested as familial[76]. In fact, on Ishbaal's death he had recovered his membership of the House of Saul through his remarriage to Michal.

His taking over of Saul's harem (II Sam 12 8) should be regarded as a further important testimony of the legal transfer of the kingship from Saul to David. We have some evidence of monarchical legitimacy acquired by taking the previous king's harem, both in Israel and in the ancient Near East[77]. Before Sargon of Akkad usurped the throne of Lugalzagesi, he took one of his wives[78]. In his testament, Arihalbu, king of Ugarit, forbade anyone to take his wife from his brother[79]. M. Tsevat[80] has argued that this testament shows that Niqmepa, the brother of Arihalbu, succeeded to the throne of Ugarit through a levirate marriage in order to keep the kingship in the same royal family, since marriage with the wife of a former king legitimized the succession. Against this background, we can correctly understand the implication of Ahithopel's advice to Absalom to take possession of David's harem (16 21–22), as well as the troubles concerning women from the royal harem between Ishbaal and Abner (3 6–11) and between Solomon and Adonijah (I Kings 2 13–25). We do not know when David took possession of Saul's harem. But we may suppose that it was soon after Ishbaal's death, as being another decisive step towards acquire legitimacy as Saul's successor.

After these preparations, whereby David convinced to the people of Israel that he possessed the claim to the throne of Israel as legitimate successor to Saul, he received the visit of the elders of Israel at Hebron and got their offer of the kingship over Israel. Their offer was based on three grounds: a) the people of Israel were David's bone and flesh (II Sam 5 1); b) David was the leader of the army of Israel under Saul (5 2a); c) Yahweh designated him *nagîḏ* over Israel (5 2b). Remarkably, these three grounds ensured the legitimate continuity of the Israelite monarchy from Saul to David, that is, a) since David was a member of Saul's House, he belonged to the northern (*sic*) tribes[81]; b) like Saul, he

---

[76] Cf. Morgenstern, JBL 78, 325. About blood vengeance as the duty of a *gô'el*, see Pedersen, Israel, I–II 396; de Vaux, Les institutions, I 40f. (ET 21f.).

[77] Cf. U. Oldenburg, The Conflict between El and Baʿal in Canaanite Religion, 1969, 114f. According to his analysis of the Canaanite myth, Baal usurped Ashera, El's consort, when he took over the throne of El (ibid. 115ff.). But this assumption has only indirect and vague support in the text.

[78] See V. Scheil, Nouveaux renseignements sur Šarrukin d'après un texte sumérien, RA 13 (1916), 117. 178 rev. II 1–2.

[79] PRU, III 1955, 76 (RS. 16.144).

[80] Marriage and Monarchical Legitimacy in Ugarit and Israel, JSS 3 (1958), 237–243.

[81] So Hertzberg, Die Samuelbücher, 218 (ET 266). But Malamat argues that the

was a leader of the army of Israel; c) he was the legitimate successor to Saul as *nagîḏ* (see above p. 50).

According to A. Alt[82], this direct application of the ideal scheme of the Israelite monarchy to David bespeaks the absence of the idea of dynastic continuity in Israel at that time. On the contrary, in our opinion, the grounds adduced show that both the elders of Israel and David took much pains to establish the constitutional as well as the dynastic continuity of the Israelite monarchy from Saul to David.

As to the constitutional continuity, it is important to mention the motif of David's reverence for Saul as "Yahweh's anointed", to which the "defence of David" repeatedly refers with special emphasis (I Sam 24 7. 11 26 9. 11. 16. 23 II Sam 1 14. 16). Royal anointing in Israel appears to have its origin in a Hittite enthronement rite or in an Egyptian installation ceremony of vassals (cf. EA § 51 6. 8), and was adopted through the Canaanites (cf. Judg 9 8. 15). While M. Noth[83] has argued for a Hittite origin, R. de Vaux[84] has emphasized Egyptian influence. According to E. Kutsch[85], the pattern of royal anointing in Israel can be divided into the anointing by the people and that by Yahweh. While the former reflects Hittite influence, the latter shows an Egyptian character. Kutsch[86] has further maintained that the title "Yahweh's anointed" is a theological expression for the special relationship between the king and Yahweh as a royal legitimation. But David's intention in his homage to this title went further than a mere royal legitimation: he was expressing his full recognition of the validity of the royal anointing performed at Saul's enthronement (I Sam 11 15 LXX). Since he was made king over Israel by the same rite of anointing (II Sam 5 3), his succession to the title of Saul (12 7 19 22 22 51 = Ps 18 51 II Sam 23 1) was legitimate from the constitutional point of view. On the other hand, the "defence of David" never calls Ishbaal "Yahweh's anointed", although it is very likely that he, too, was anointed at his

---

expression "your bone and flesh" here implies "a positive conclusion to the royal covenant, which is the antithetical to the formula: we have no portion in David, and we have no inheritance in the son of Jesse" (in: BAR 3, 170).

82 Die Staatenbildung, in: Kleine Schriften, II 32f. 42 (ET 204. 214).

83 Amt und Berufung im Alten Testament (1958), in: Gesammelte Studien, I 1960², 321 (ET Office and Vocation in the Old Testament, in: The Laws in the Pentateuch and Other Essays, 1966, 239).

84 Le roi d'Israël, vassal de Yahvé (1964), in: Bible et Orient, 1967, 299f. (ET The King of Israel, Vassal of Yahweh, in: The Bible and the Ancient Near East, 1972, 165).

85 Salbung als Rechtsakt im Alten Testament und im Alten Orient, 1963, 52ff.

86 Ibid. 61ff. This view has been criticized, see de Vaux, Le roi d'Israël, in: Bible et Orient, 300f. n. 5 (ET 166 n. 68); J. A. Emerton, JSS 12 (1967), 126ff.

accession[87]. This does not imply, as Alt[88] thinks, that Ishbaal's kingship was based on Abner's arbitrary experiment and was supported neither by Yahweh nor by the people. Why did Abner choose to make Ishbaal king? Simply because he was a son of Saul. Had the hereditary principle not been accepted in Israel, Abner could have proclaimed himself king, it being visible from the beginning that Ishbaal was Abner's puppet. But, by reason of the legitimacy of dynastic succession, the people of Israel recognized Ishbaal as their king. It was David who rejected Ishbaal's legitimacy as the successor to Saul, on the ground that the legitimate successor was not Ishbaal but David, according to his assertion.

A pertinent parallel is furnished by the "defence of Nabonidus". Nabonidus, the last king of the Neo-Babylonian empire (555–539), did not belong to the royal family by descent. Nonetheless, he declared without hesitation:

> "I am the real executor of the wills of Nebuchadnezzar and Neriglissar, my predecessors."[89]

On the other hand, although Labaši-Marduk, son of Neriglissar, was the legitimate successor from the genealogical point of view, Nabonidus rejected his legitimacy as king:

> "His son Labaši-Marduk, a minor (who) had not (yet) learned how to behave, sat down on the royal throne against the intentions of the gods."[90]

What Nabonidus argued is that he did not usurp the throne but legitimately succeeded the former kings of the Chaldean dynasty, although Labaši-Marduk was the former king's real son and Nabonidus not of royal lineage. This is not a dismissal of the dynastic principle. Since dynastic continuity was important to him, Nabonidus did not found a new dynasty. Instead, he became the legitimate successor to the former kings by divine election. It seems that David made just the

---

[87] It appears that all the kings of Israel and Judah were anointed at their accession, although it is not explicitly mentioned for all of them except Saul (I Sam 11 15 LXX), David (II Sam 2 4 5 3), Solomon (I Kings 1 34. 39. 45 5 15 I Chron 29 22), Jehu (II Kings 9 3. 6), Joash (II Kings 11 12 II Chron 23 11) and Jehoahaz (II Kings 23 30), and perhaps Zedekiah (Lam 4 20). Absalom was also anointed (II Sam 19 11), see de Vaux, Les institutions, I 160ff. (ET 103ff.); Liver, in: EncBib, IV 1962, 1100ff. (Hebrew); Kutsch, Salbung, 59f. Malamat observes that the royal anointing is mentioned in the Bible only in instances of founders of dynasties or of contested successions (The Last Kings of Judah and the Fall of Jerusalem, IEJ 18 [1968], 140).

[88] Die Staatenbildung, in: Kleine Schriften, II 30ff. (ET 202ff.); cf. Bright, A History, 191 n. 31.

[89] ANET 309; NBKI 276 V 14–18.

[90] ANET 309; NEKI 276 IV 37–42.

same sort of excuse in declaring that he was the legitimate successor to Saul by Yahweh's will, and that Ishbaal was not, even though he was the real son of Saul.

A later development is reflected in the account of David's anointing by Samuel in his youth (I Sam 16 1–13).The narrative not only attributes the origin of David's kingship to Yahweh's pre-election, but also associates David with Samuel, who, as the great religious-political leader, was the chief actor in the establishment of Saul's monarchy. It is likely that this narrative was composed on the model of the story of young Saul's anointing by Samuel (I Sam 9 1–10 16)[91]. Fictitious as it is, it no longer seeks to show David as the legitimate successor to Saul. It underlines his divine election in lieu of Saul. Accordingly, David must have been anointed directly by Samuel, who thus gave divine sanction to his kingship over Israel[92].

David always felt that a threat existed from the House of Saul, which was still in possession of the potential claim to the kingship of Israel. Beyond any doubt, he wanted to get rid of Saul's descendants. This is unmistakable in the narrative of the execution of seven members of Saul's family by the Gibeonites (II Sam 21 1–14). Although the executioners were the Gibeonites and the reason for the act was the appeasement of Yahweh's anger caused by Saul's violation of the covenant between the Israelites and the Gibeonites, it is impossible not to detect David's initiative in this event[93]. The primary motive was, to be sure, David's anxiety about the dynastic claim of Saul's House to the kingship of Israel[94]. It seems that other members of Saul's House were also extinguished in similar ways (cf. 16 7–8 19 29). After the liquidation was completed, David finally asked: "Is there still any one left of the House of Saul?" (9 1). When Meribbaal, the lame son of Jonathan, was found, David took him into his own direct custody on the pretext of keeping the covenant between him and Jonathan (9 2–13; cf. 4 4 19 25–31 21 7).

In this connection, the relationship between David and Michal should be reconsidered. According to a biblical tradition, Michal's love

---

[91] Cf. Wellhausen, Die Composition des Hexateuchs und der historischen Bücher des Alten Testaments, 1899³, 248ff.; Grønbaek, Die Geschichte vom Aufstieg Davids, 71ff.

[92] Weiser finds in this story the characteristic tendency of the "history of David's rise" (VT 16, 325ff.); cf. Nübel, Davids Aufstieg, 20. 124ff.

[93] Cf. A. S. Kapelrud, King and the Sons of Saul, in: The Sacral Kingship, Suppl. to Numen 4 (1959), 299 (= König David und die Söhne des Saul, ZAW 67 [1955], 202).

[94] J. Blenkinsopp argues that the event took place towards the beginning of the reign of David (Gibeon and Israel, 1972, 89f.). Although his thesis may be accepted, it is to be underlined that the Saulide challenge still survived in the time of Absalom's rebellion (II Sam 16 3. 5–8).

for David was the beginning of it (I Sam 18 20). It seems, as we have suggested, that Saul approved of her love and gave her to David (18 27). But after David's flight from the court, Saul gave her to Palti, the son of Laish, a man of Gallim (25 44). Eventually, by negotiation with Abner, David recovered her forcibly from her second husband (II Sam 3 13–16). Thereafter, her name is mentioned twice in the biblical source: a) since she reproached David for his dancing before Yahweh, she remained childless until her death (6 20–23); b) the five sons, whom she bore to "Adriel the son of Barzillai the Meholathite", were delivered to the Gibeonites by David (21 8). But the name of Michal in the second story is generally emended into Merab, because of the name of the father of the five sons and the contradiction with the account of Michal's sterility[95]. But if her sterility was merely a symptom of David's intentional avoidance of her, she could have five sons by her second marriage. Yet a difficulty still remains, since Adriel, son of Barzillai the Meholathite, was Merab's husband (I Sam 18 19). Therefore, we must either emend "Michal" into "Merab" or "Adriel" into "Paltiel". The first emendation – the traditional one – appears to betray the influence of moral considerations for David. It looks gruesome, indeed, that David should deliver to their doom the sons of his own wife by her previous marriage. But if Michal really had sons from her second marriage, it must have been very urgent for David to get rid of them, since they had a double claim to the kingship of Israel, as Saul's grandsons and as the stepsons of David. Even Meribbaal, who had no qualification for kingship owing to his bodily defects (II Sam 4 4), dreamt of the restoration of his House (16 3). We may assume that Michal's sons had more than one prospects of becoming the nucleus of a movement to restore Saul's monarchy. We can conclude, therefore, that, from the dynastic-political point of view, there were stronger reasons for Michal's sons to be removed by David than Merab's. Hence, we prefer the emendation of "Adriel" into "Paltiel"[96].

Why was David so cautious about his elimination of Saul's descendants that he never officially admitted his responsibility? By contrast, later usurpers of the kingdom of Israel always finished off every member of the former king's family at one stroke (I Kings 14 10–11 15 29 16 3–4. 11–12 II Kings 9 8–9 10 11). David, however, executed the

---

[95] S. R. Driver regards the name Michal here as "a *lapsus calami*" for Merab (Notes on the Hebrew Text 352). For the other emended texts, see J. J. Glück, Merab or Michal, ZAW 77 (1965), 75 n. 21.

[96] Cf. Glück, ZAW 77, 72–81. According to Stoebe, Michal's second husband was Adriel and a late elaboration changed his name into Paltiel (in: Eissfeldt Festschrift, BZAW 77 [1958], 234). But this thesis seems unconvincing, see Hertzberg, Die Samuelbücher, 316 n. 3 (ET 383 note e).

Saulides only on good pretexts and by another's hand, as in the narrative of the Gibeonite revenge. There must have been special grounds for it. First of all, the House of Saul probably had great influence on the people of Israel even in the later years of David's reign. We can observe this from David's lenient treatment of Meribbaal and Shimei after Absalom's rebellion. Although both these men of the family of Saul were disloyal to David during the uprising, he forgave them (II Sam 19 17–31). This indulgence shows not his magnanimity but his political respect for the Saulide influence on the people of Israel. In fact, Shimei's execution was only postponed until Solomon has firmly consolidated the rule of the House of David over Israel (I Kings 2 36–46; cf. 2 8–9). Secondly, David must have taken into account that he was not as popular as Saul among the northern tribes, whose bitter feelings towards him are in the slogan of Sheba's revolt: "We have no portion in David, and we have no inheritance in the son of Jesse" (II Sam 20 1; cf. I Kings 12 16). Although David managed to quell the revolt, this animosity towards the rule of the House of David flared up again in the schismatic movement of Jeroboam, which in the end made the northern tribes independent of the rule of the Judaean dynasty (I Kings 11 26–40 12 1–20). Their hatred of David exploded at his obvious favouritism of the southern tribes. As we have observed, this fatal dualism was deeply rooted in the very nature of David's monarchy. Enquiry into the origin of the dualism would involve us in the complicated problems of the formation of Israel in the pre-monarchical period. Although we have no intention of discussing it here, it appears that the dualism in David's monarchy originated in the historical gulf between the northern and the southern tribes from the days of their settlement in Canaan. That is why we baulk at accepting the hypothesis that the twelve tribes of Israel already had a formal unity, such as an amphictyony, prior to the monarchical period[97].

---

[97] M. Noth demonstrated the classical hypothesis of the "amphictyony of Israel" organized by the Israelite twelve tribes in the pre-monarchical period (Das System der zwölf Stämme Israels, 1930; idem, Geschichte, 83ff. [ET 85ff.]). This thesis is still accepted as a working hypothesis by many scholars, see Buccellati, Cities and Nations, 111ff.; Soggin, Das Königtum in Israel, 12 n. 1; Bright, A History, 156ff. 158 n. 45. But it has been also critically re-examined recently, see Mowinckel, in: Eissfeldt Festschrift, BZAW 77 (1958), 129–150; H. M. Orlinsky, The Tribal System of Israel and Related Groups in the Period of the Judges, OrAnt 1 (1962), 11–20; S. Herrmann, Das Werden Israels, ThLZ 87 (1962), 562–574; idem, Autonome Entwicklung in den Königreichen Israel und Juda, SVT 17 (1968), 139–158; G. Fohrer, Altes Testament – „Amphiktyonie" und „Bund"? (1966), in: Studien, 84–119; de Vaux, La thèse de l'"amphictyonie israélite", HThR 64 (1971), 415–436 (= Histoire ancienne d'Israël, II. La période des juges, 1973, 19–36); A. D. H. Mayes, VT 23, 151–170.

In Judah, David succeeded in establishing the dynasty by his own initiative. But in Israel, where the people's alien feelings towards Judaean rule were hardly dispelled, he made a great effort, to begin with, to legitimatize his kingship by pretending to be a member of the House of Saul. Once its authority over the northern tribes was stabilized, however, the House of David launched out into a new argument for the legitimacy of the Davidic monarchy in Israel. In this polemic, the emphasis swayed from David's legitimate successorship to Saul to his election by Yahweh in place of Saul. This argument came to a climax in the "prophecy of Nathan" (II Sam 7 1–16 I Chron 17 1–14), in which Yahweh promised David an eternal dynasty in Israel.

Chapter 5: The Royal-Dynastic Ideology of the House of David

A. THE CHARACTER AND PURPOSE OF NATHAN'S PROPHECY

The divine election of the dynastiy of David was promulgated by Nathan's prophecy, which is preserved in two parallel texts (II Sam 7 1–17 I Chron 17 1–15) and in its numerous quotations and allusions in the Bible[1]. As for the priority among these texts and their mutual relations, opinions are divided: Some scholars hold that Ps 89 contains a poetic recension of the original prophecy on which both II Sam 7 and I Chron 17 are dependent[2]. This view is rejected by others[3]. J. L. McKenzie[4] has

---

1 "David's prayer" (II Sam 7 18–29 I Chron 17 16–27) is a direct continuation of Nathan's prophecy, and they make a literary unit. Main references to Nathan's prophecy are found in the following passages: I Sam 25 28. 30 II Sam 22 51 23 5 I Kings 2 4. 24. 45 3 6 5 19 8 15–20. 23–26. 66 9 5 11 13. 32. 36. 38 15 4 II Kings 8 19 19 34 20 6 21 7 Is 37 35 55 3 Jer 33 17. 20–26 Ps 18 51 89 4–5. 20–38 132 11–12. 17 I Chron 22 7–10 28 2–7 II Chron 1 8–9 6 4–10. 14–17. 42 7 17–18 13 5 21 7 23 3 33 7–8; cf. C. J. Labuschagne, Some Remarks on the Prayer of David in II Sam 7, in: Studies on the Books of Samuel, ed. A. H. van Zyl, 1960, 29; S. Amsler, David, roi et messie, 1963, 38ff.; A. Caquot, La prophétie de Nathan et ses échos lyriques, SVT 9 (1963), 213–224; M. Tsevat, Studies in the Book of Samuel, III. The Steadfast House: What was David promised in II Sam 7:11b–16?, HUCA 34 (1963), 74ff.; J. Coppens, Le messianisme royal dynastique. La prophétie de Nathan, II Sam VII 1–16, NRTh 90 (1968), 233ff.

2 R. H. Pfeiffer, An Introduction to the Old Testament, 1948², 368ff.; S. Mowinckel, He that cometh, 1954, 100f. n. 3; G. W. Ahlström, Psalm 89. Eine Liturgie aus dem Ritual des leidenden Königs, 1959, 182ff.; E. Lipiński, Le poème royal du Psaume LXXXIX, 1–5, 20–38, 1967, 91.

3 H. van den Bussche, Le texte de la prophétie de Nathan sur la dynastie davidique (II Sam., VII–I Chron., XVII), EThL 24 (1948), 354f. n. 2; E. S. Mulder, The Prophecy of Nathan in II Sam 7, in: Studies on the Books of Samuel, 36; J. Ward, The Literary Form and Liturgical Background of Psalm LXXXIX, VT 11 (1961), 321–339; N. M. Sarna, Psalm 89. A Study in Inner Biblical Exegesis, in: Biblical and Other Studies, ed. A. Altmann, 1963, 29–46; Coppens, NRTh 90, 229.

4 The Dynastic Oracle: II Sam 7, ThS 8 (1947), 187–218; cf. also J. W. Rothstein & J. Hänel, Kommentar zum ersten Buch der Chronik, 1927, 332ff.; G. von Rad, Das judäische Königsritual (1947), in: Gesammelte Studien, I 1971⁴, 210 (ET The Royal Ritual in Judah, in: The Problem of the Hexateuch and Other Essays, 1966, 227); Labuschagne, in: Studies on the Books of Samuel, 29; Caquot, SVT 9, 221; G. Cooke, The Israelite King as Son of God, ZAW 73 (1961), 203.

argued that all three recensions of the prophecy in II Sam 7, I Chron 17 and Ps 89 are derived from a common original source. But N. M. Sarna[5] has made it clear that "Psalm 89 vss 20–38 actually constitute, not a recension of the original oracle, but an interpretation of it." H. van den Bussche[6] has suggested the priority of the text of Chronicles, but this suggestion has been criticized[7]. After weighing these arguments, it seems difficult to resist the priority of the text of II Sam 7.

As for the literary-critical problems, the analysis of L. Rost[8] of the prophecy was once widely accepted. He suggested that the oldest nucleus of the prophecy is II Sam 7 11b. (+16), and that the chapter consists of three strata from four periods, that is, the oldest stratum from the time of David (v. 1–4a. 4b–7. 11b. 16. 18–21. 25. 26*. 27–29), the second from the time of Isaiah (v. 8–11a. 12. 14. 15. 17), and the third Deuteronomistic (v. 13 from the time of Josiah and v. 22–24 from the exilic period). But recently many scholars have defended the fundamental unity of the chapter[9]. Recent studies also agree on the origin of the prophecy in the Davidic-Solomonic period[10].

Despite the consensus on these issues, a problem remains unsolved which is of great importance to the understanding of the character and purpose of the prophecy, namely, the interpretation of the "temple

---

[5] In: Biblical and Other Studies 29.

[6] EThL 24, 354–394.

[7] R. de Vaux, Jérusalem et les prophètes, RB 73 (1966), 482f. 483 n. 6. n. 7; Coppens, NRTh 90, 229f.; cf. S. Japhet, Interchanges of Verbal Roots in Parallel Texts in Chronicles, Lešonenu 31 (1967/68), 165–179. 261–279 (Hebrew); idem, The Ideology of the Book of Chronicles and its Place in Biblical Thought, Diss. Jerusalem, 1973, 443ff. (Hebrew).

[8] Die Überlieferung von der Thronnachfolge Davids (1926), in: Das kleine Credo und andere Studien zum Alten Testament, 1965, 168ff.; cf. Noth, ÜSt, 64f.

[9] S. Mowinckel, Natanforjettelsen, 2 Sam. kap. 7, SEÅ 12 (1947), 220–229; S. Herrmann, Die Königsnovelle in Ägypten und Israel, WZ Leipzig 3 (1953/54), 51–62; Noth, David und Israel in 2 Sam 7 (1957), in: Gesammelte Studien, I 1960², 334–345 (ET David and Israel in II Samuel VII, in: The Laws in the Pentateuch and Other Essays, 1966, 250–259); E. Kutsch, Die Dynastie von Gottes Gnaden. Probleme der Nathanweissagung in 2 Sam 7, ZThK 58 (1961), 137–153; A. Weiser, Tempelbaukrise unter David, ZAW 77 (1965), 153–168.

[10] Noth, David und Israel, in: Gesammelte Studien, I 334ff. (ET 250ff.); Kutsch, ZThK 58, 137ff.; Caquot, SVT 9, 213 ff.; Weiser, ZAW 77, 153ff.; de Vaux, RB 73, 482; N. Poulssen, König und Tempel im Glaubenszeugnis des Alten Testamentes, 1967, 51f. However, some scholars regard II Sam 7 as a Deuteronomistic composition, see R. A. Carlson, David, the Chosen King, 1964, 97ff.; H. Gese, Der Davidsbund und die Zionserwählung, ZThK 61 (1964), 26f.; D. J. McCarthy, II Sam 7 and the Structure of the Deuteronomic History, JBL 84 (1965), 131–138; F. M. Cross, Canaanite Myth and Hebrew Epic, 1973, 241ff.

episode'' (II Sam 7 1–7), with which the prophecy introduces the subject. The difficulty lies in the ambiguity of the text, where it is by no means clear why Yahweh rejected David's plan to build a temple for his dwelling. Generally, scholars try to find either religious or political conflicts behind the divine refusal[11]. The suggested solutions fall into the following four categories: a) a conflict between the traditions of the Tabernacle and the Ark, related to the northern and the southern traditions, respectively[12]; b) a conflict between Canaanite religion and genuine Yahwism which categorically declined a temple[13]; c) a theological conflict about the definition of a temple[14]; d) a political conflict between the Jebusite party headed by Nathan and the Judahite party[15].

But none of the explanations is satisfactory. Apart from these suggestions, S. Herrmann[16] has proposed that II Sam 7 was composed after a literary type called the "Egyptian royal novel" whose main themes are the building of the temple and the royal theology. In his opinion, the chapter contains all the literary elements of the "royal novel", in both style and content. Thus, Yahweh's rejection of David's plan is, according to Herrmann, nothing but an application of the literary technique of the "royal novel" where the greatness of the king's decision is underlined by the successful accomplishment of his plan in spite of the opposition of the courtiers. But Herrmann admits that, on this very point, a "Copernican renovation of the royal novel" took place on Israelite soil, where the king's place was taken by Yahweh and the king became a servant (who is a courtier in the "royal

---

[11] For a survey of the main discussion on this problem, see J. Schreiner, Sion-Jerusalem. Jahwes Königssitz, 1963, 80ff.; R. E. Clements, God and Temple, 1965, 56ff.; cf. also T. E. Fretheim, The Priestly Document: Anti-Temple?, VT 18 (1968), 328 n. 2.

[12] See von Rad, Zelt und Lade (1931), in: Gesammelte Studien, I 124 (ET The Tent and the Ark, in: Essays, 119); A. Kuschke, Die Lagevorstellung der priesterschriftlichen Erzählung, ZAW 63 (1951), 89. 96; cf. M. Newman, The People of the Covenant. A Study of Israel from Moses to the Monarchy, 1962, 55ff.

[13] See M. Simon, La prophétie de Nathan et le temple, RHPhR 32 (1952), 57; de Vaux, Les institutions de l'Ancien Testament, II 1960, 171ff. (ET Ancient Israel, 1961, 329f.); idem, RB 73, 485; Poulssen, König und Tempel, 45; V. W. Rabe, Israelite Opposition to the Temple, CBQ 29 (1967), 228–233; Fretheim, VT 18, 322ff.; Cross, Canaanite Myth, 241ff.

[14] See H. W. Hertzberg, Die Samuelbücher, 1960^2, 233 (ET I & II Samuel, 1964, 285); Schreiner, Sion-Jerusalem, 89ff.; Weiser, ZAW 77, 158ff.; cf. Gese, ZThK 61, 21.

[15] See Ahlström, Der Prophet Nathan und der Tempelbau, VT 11 (1961), 113–127. Clements proposes a combination of these conflicts (God and Temple 59f.).

[16] WZ Leipzig 3, 51–62.

novel") before God[17]. This thesis has found wide approval among scholars[18].

But, as E. Kutsch[19] has rightly pointed out, it is difficult to find in the "Egyptian royal novel" the main theme of Nathan's prophecy, formed by the contrast between the king's plan to build a temple, or, strictly speaking, Yahweh's rejection of the plan, and the divine promise of dynastic prosperity. Since Herrmann ignored this fundamental difference between Nathan's prophecy and the "Egyptian royal novel", he was compelled to give David a twofold role in the "royal novel", so that David plays not only the king's role but also that of the courtiers. We cannot but regard this as a forced analogy[20]. Egyptian influences on the court of David and Solomon have been traced by many scholars, especially in court ceremonial[21], the organization of the officials and the training of the scribes[22]. It is, however, impossible to find, in any Egyptian literature, where the king is always an incarnate god, a parallel to the tension existing between king and God as implied in Nathan's prophecy. We should rather look for comparative material in Mesopotamia, where the king was a mere servant of the gods and always anxious to have divine blessing bestowed on his reign and dynasty[23].

---

[17] Ibid. 59.

[18] Noth, David und Israel, in: Gesammelte Studien, I 342ff. (ET 256f.); von Rad, Theologie des Alten Testaments, I 1957, 48ff. (ET Old Testament Theology, I 1962, 48f.); Amsler, David, roi et messie, 34f.; Caquot, SVT 9, 215f.; Carlson, David, the Chosen King, 98. 113f.; Weiser, ZAW 77, 154ff.; R. N. Whybray, The Succession Narrative. A Study of II Sam. 9–20 and I Kings 1 and 2, 1968, 100ff.; K. Seybold, Das davidische Königtum im Zeugnis der Propheten, 1972, 27ff.

[19] ZThK 58, 151ff.

[20] Accepting Herrmann's thesis, de Vaux points out that "c'est au prix d'un renversement total de la formule" and "l'influence dumeure extérieure" (RB 73, 484f.). On the other hand, some scholars discredit the validity of Herrmann's comparison, see Schreiner, Sion-Jerusalem, 75f.; Cross, Canaanite Myth, 247ff.; cf. also M. Weinfeld, Deuteronomy and the Deuteronomic School, 1972, 250ff.

[21] Cf. von Rad, Das judäische Königsritual (1947), in: Gesammelte Studien, I 205–213 (ET 222–231); S. Morenz, Ägyptische und davidische Königstitulatur, ZÄS 79 (1954), 73–74; H. Cazelles, La titulature du roi David, in: Mélanges Robert, [1957], 131–136; de Vaux, Le roi d'Israël, vassal de Yahvé (1964), in: Bible et Orient, 1967, 287–301 (ET King of Israel, Vassal of Yahweh, in: The Bible and the Ancient Near East, 1972, 152–180).

[22] See above p. 68 n. 56; cf. also Whybray, The Succession Narrative, 1ff.

[23] Cf. H. Frankfort, Kingship and the Gods, 1948, 231ff.; T. Jacobsen, Mesopotamia, in: Before Philosophy, by Frankfort et al., 1949, 200ff. E. A. Speiser has stressed a sharp contrast concerning the concept of kingship between Egypt and Mesopotamia, and has shown Israel's affiliation to the latter's cultural sphere (The Biblical Idea of

In Mesopotamia[24], the decay of the sanctuaries was regarded as a sign of the wrath of the gods, the existence of a temple showed the gods' dwelling among the people[25]. Therefore, one of the most important tasks of the king as the representative of society *vis-à-vis* the divine world was the building or repairing of a temple[26]. But he could not undertake the construction on his own initiative, since it depended on divine will whether the gods would stay or not. He must first ask the gods for permission to build a temple for them. In view of his grave responsibility, he often expressed anxiety whether he had understood the divine will correctly and whether he would be able to accomplish the task[27]. When Esarhaddon, king of Assyria (680–669), found the temple of Aššur in decay, he was first embarrassed, and then asked divine licence to repair it:

> "I was afraid, I was alarmed, feared and hesitated to rebuild that temple. However, Šamaš and Adad answered me an affirmative yes by the offering bowl of the observer of the offering and as to the building of that temple and the renovation of the chamber they made a liver oracle."[28]

It is against this background that we should understand the implication of David's words to Nathan the prophet (II Sam 7 2). As the title "prophet" shows, Nathan was not a mere representative of the courtiers[29], but the king's adviser who mediated between king and God. He was a court prophet[30]. Without asking Yahweh's approval, David could not undertake the building of a temple. It is true that Nathan's ready consent to the king's plan (7 3) looks enigmatic, and we shall deal

---

History in its Common Near Eastern Setting, IEJ 7 [1957], 201–216; idem, Mesopotamia – Evolution of an Integrated Civilization, in: WHJP, I 1964, 255ff.).

[24] Cf. M. Ota, A Note on 2 Sam 7, in: J. M. Myers Festschrift, 1974, 403–407.

[25] See Frankfort, Kingship and the Gods, 269.

[26] Cf. ibid. 267ff.; A. S. Kapelrud, Temple Building. A Task for Gods and Kings, Or NS 32 (1963), 56–62.

[27] Divine sanction for the building of a temple was asked especially by kings in southern Mesopotamia, from Gudea of Lagaš down to Nabonidus of Babylon, but in Assyria only by Esarhaddon, see R. S. Ellis, Foundation Deposits in Ancient Mesopotamia, 1968, 6f.

[28] Borger, Asarh., § 2 III 43–IV 6.

[29] Against Herrmann, WZ Leipzig 3, 58.

[30] About court prophets, see J. Lindblom, Prophecy in Ancient Israel, 1963, 74ff. Outside Israel we can find court prophets in Byblos in the 11th century (ANET 26) and in Hamath in the eighth century B. C. (KAI § 202 A 12). We can also compare them with prophets in Mari in the 18th century B. C., see A. Malamat, Prophetic Revelations in New Documents from Mari and the Bible, SVT 15 (1966), 212; H. B. Huffmon, Prophecy in the Mari Letters (1968), in: BAR 3, 1970, 199–224; J. F. Ross, Prophecy in Hamath, Israel, and Mari, HThR 63 (1970), 1–28. About the court prophets in Neo-Assyria, see below pp. 90–92.

with this point below. But it does not change the whole situation. After all, David received Yahweh's answer through Nathan on the same night: "But it was in that same night, the word of Yahweh came to Nathan saying: 'Go and tell my servant David. Thus says Yahweh. . .'" (7 4–5). L. Rost[31] has suggested that v. 4a was the introduction to the original oracle transmitted directly to David, which is now missing. This assumption is unwarranted[32]. If we ignore Nathan's role of mediator between king and God, we shall miss the point. An inscription of Aššurbanipal, king of Assyria (668–627), is pertinent:

> "(And indeed) in the midst of the (very same) night in which I addressed myself to her (i. e. Ištar), a *šabru*-priest went to bed and had a dream. He woke up with a start and Ištar made him see a nocturnal vision. He reported (it) to me as follows: The goddess Ištar . . . called you to give you the following order: Wait with the attack . . ."[33]

Both Ištar and Yahweh gave the kings negative answers through mediators on the very night when the kings enquired of their oracles.

In Mesopotamia, the possibility was always present that the gods would reject the king's proposal. Therefore, he was anxious to receive a favourable answer from them when he wanted to undertake the building of a temple. Since only those who succeeded in building a temple with divine consent left their inscriptions, it is not easy to find unsuccessful cases. Still, we know of several kings who failed to receive divine sanction for their building plans. First of all, the king who succeeded in building a temple sometimes refers to previous kings as having failed to win divine approval. An inscription of Nebuchadnezzar II, king of Babylon (605–562), reads:

> "At that time Ebabbarra, the temple of Šamaš which is in Sippar, which fell into decay long time before me, was like a heap of ruine. Šamaš, the great lord, did not favour any previous kings and did not order to build (it). (But) me, his servant, the wise, the pious, the reverent of his divinity, he desired for the building of the sanctuary."[34]

Secondly, a Sumerian text: "The curse of Akkad" (c. 2000 B.C.) tells of Naram-Sin, king of Akkad (2254–2218), who failed to receive Enlil's favourable answer when he wanted to rebuild Ekur, Enlil's temple at Nippur, to appease the god's wrath:

> "For the house (that is, Ekur) he sought an oracle (for the permission) to build the

---

[31] Die Überlieferung von der Thronnachfolge, in: Das kleine Credo und andere Studien, 179; cf. Herrmann, WZ Leipzig 3, 60.

[32] Cf. Hertzberg, Die Samuelbücher, 233 n. 1 (ET 284 note a).

[33] A. L. Oppenheim, The Interpretation of Dreams in the Ancient Near East, 1956, 249; ANET 606; Streck, Asb., 116 49–52. 58–59.

[34] NBKI 100 I 25–II 10.

house, (but) there was no oracle for him. He sought an oracle a second time for the house (for the permission) to build the house, (but) there was no oracle for him."[35]

Getting no answer from Enlil, Naram-Sin became angry and destroyed Ekur. This blasphemous act, according to the Sumerian historiographer, was the cause of the permanent desolation of Akkad.

As a third example, we can mention a letter to Zimrilim, king of Mari (c. 1750), about a divine revelation:

"He said the following (dream): 'You shall not build this deserted house. If this house is built, I will make it collapse into the river.' The day he saw this dream, he said nothing to anyone. The next day he again saw the following dream: 'It was a god. You shall not build this house. If you build it, I will make it collapse into the river.' "[36]

Although we do not know whether the house was a temple or not, as A. Malamat[37] has pointed out, this prophecy reminds us of Yahweh's rejection of David's plan revealed by Nathan.

In Mesopotamia, there was a long history of the "building or foundation inscriptions", to which the great majority of royal records belong. The simplest form of inscription consists only of the name of the king as builder of the temple and the name of the god to whom it was dedicated. Because of a greatly diversified stylistic development, it is not easy to find a common pattern. Yet in essential character there was no change from the Sumerian period down to the time of the Greek rulers in Syria[38]. Clearly, Nathan's prophecy does not fall into this literary *genre*: while it speaks the words of God to the king, the inscriptions speak the words of kings addressed to gods. Nevertheless, it seems that the real nature of Nathan's prophecy can be elucidated by comparison with the inscriptions: both treat of the same subjects, that is, the building of a temple by the king and the prosperity of the royal dynasty, and both reflect a similar spiritual *milieu*, where the king was constantly seeking divine grace.

From among the inscriptions of Mesopotamia we shall choose those

---

[35] A. Falkenstein, Fluch über Akkad, ZA 23 (1965), 55. 68 96–99. Our translation is dependent on his German rendering. S. N. Kramer translates these lines differently: "(But then) seeking on oracle at the house, in the 'built' house there was no oracle . . ." (ANET 648).

[36] ANET 624; ARM XIII § 112 rev. 1'–11'.

[37] SVT 15, 224.

[38] About the building inscriptions, see S. Mowinckel, Die vorderasiatischen Königs- und Fürsteninschriften. Eine stilistische Studie, in: Gunkel Festschrift, I 1923, 278–322; W. Baumgartner, Zur Form der assyrischen Königsinschriften, OLZ 27 (1924), 313–317; H. W. F. Saggs, The Greatness that was Babylon, 1962, 369f.; Oppenheim, Ancient Mesopotamia, 1964, 146ff. 234f.; E. Sollberger & J.-R. Kupper, Inscriptions royales sumériennes et akkadiennes, 1971, 24ff.

of Neo-Babylonia as material of our comparative study, because they appear to be most suitable for it in both theme and style. Their typical formula has three parts: a) the name of the king with a long series of titles; b) the narrative, which is generally composed of the *inūma* (when)-clause, whose main theme is divine election and help of the king, and the *inūmīšu* (at that time), *inūšu* (then), or *ina umīšu* (on that day)-clause, which recounts the building of a temple; and c) the king's prayer for the prosperity of his reign and dynasty[39]. For instance, an inscription of Nabopolassar (625–605) reads:

> "Nabopolassar, the viceroy of Babylon, the king of Sumer and Akkad .. when (*inūma*) on the command of Nebo and Marduk ... I subjugated the Assyrians, ... at that time (*inūmīšu*) Marduk, the lord, ordered me firmly to found the base of Etemenanki ... as deep as the nether world and to make its top compete with heaven ... I asked the oracle of Šamaš, Adad and Marduk, and the great gods showed me through the decision of an oracle (the place) where I should put my heart and take the measurements into consideration ... I built a temple after the copy of Ebabbarra with joy and jubilation, and I elevated its top as high as a mountain ... O Marduk, my lord, look joyously at my pious work! By your noble command, that will be never changed, may the work, the work of my hand, last for ever! As the bricks of Etemenanki are firm for ever, establish the foundation of my throne for all time to come!"[40]

Because of Yahweh's rejection of David's plan to build a temple, we cannot compare Nathan's prophecy directly with the inscription of Nabopolassar, who succeeded in building Etemenanki. Still, if we examine the unique structure of the prophecy, in which God as builder of a dynasty (*băyiṯ*) takes the place of the king as builder of a temple (*băyiṯ*) in mid-course, it becomes clear that II Sam 7 includes substantially the same themes as the Babylonian inscription, except for the king's name and titles.

II Sam 7 begins with the theme of the *inūma*-clause of the inscription, that is, the subjugation of the enemies as the basic condition preceding the building of a temple (v. 1; cf. Deut 12 10–11 I Kings 5 17–19). Then follows the theme of the *inūmīšu*-clause: the building of a temple; in the inscription it is ordered by Marduk but in the prophecy David proposes it (v. 2); in both, the kings seek divine will. But this theme does not lead to the building of a temple in the prophecy as it does in the inscription. Instead of permitting David to build a temple

---

[39] See S. Langdon, Die neubabylonischen Königsinschriften, **1912**, 5f.; Mowinckel, in: Gunkel Festschrift, I **282**; P.-R. Berger, Die neubabylonischen Königsinschriften, **1973**, **84**ff.

[40] NBKI **60**ff. I **9–12**. **23–24**. **29**. **32**. **36–41** II **31–39** III **19–25**. **31–49**; cf. F. H. Weissbach, apud F. Wetzel, Das Hauptheiligtum des Marduk in Babylon, in: Esagila und Etemenanki, **1938**, **42**f.

(v. 4–7), Yahweh enumerates the works of mercy which he has wrought for David (v. 8–11a): 1) he has chosen David to be *nagîḏ* over Israel (v. 8aβb); 2) he has abided with David (v. 9aα); 3) he has destroyed David's enemies (v. 9aβ); 4) he has made David's name great (v. 9b)[41]; 5) he has given Israel peace (v. 10–11aα); 6) he has given David peace (v. 11aβ). These are precisely the themes of the *inūma*-clause of another inscription of Nabopolassar:

> "1) When I was a son of nobody in my youth . . . he (i. e. Marduk) appointed me to be the head in the land where I was born, (and) I was designated to be the ruler of the land and the people, 2) he made a good tutelary deity go by my side . . . he made Nergal, the mighty one among the gods, go as a messenger by my side, 3) he killed my enemies and overthrew my opponents, 5) as to the Assyrians, who ruled over all the peoples since ancient time and had tortured the people of the land by their heavy yoke, I, the weak and powerless, trusted in the lord of the lords and with the mighty power of Nebo and Marduk, my lords, cut their foot from the land of Akkad and cast away their yoke."[42]

Although theme 4) is missing in the inscription, the expression *zikir šumīja ušarbû* "they (i. e. the gods) made my name great" is not uncommon in the building inscriptions[43]. And theme 6) belongs to the king's prayer (see below).

Because of the shift of builder from David to Yahweh, and of the implication of the term *băyiṯ* from temple to dynasty, the theme of the building of a temple gives way to that of the king's prayer for the prosperity of his reign and dynasty in the last part of the prophecy (v.

---

[41] It is not clear whether the tense of the verbs in v. 9b–11a denotes perfect or imperfect. Rost holds that the statements refer to the past (Die Überlieferung von der Thronnachfolge, in: Das kleine Credo und andere Studien, 170f.); cf. Kutsch, ZThK 58, 141 n. 2. On the other hand, O. Loretz maintains that the statements express not past history but future promises (The Perfectum Copulativum in 2 Sam 7, 9–11, CBQ 23 [1961], 294–296); cf. Gese, ZThK 61, 23f. n. 34. Hertzberg renders them in the present tense, "because it is expected that what the Lord has done hitherto will remain effective afterwards" (Die Samuelbücher 234 [ET 285f.]). A. Gelston argues that the tense of these verbs should be understood as future, since the term *maqôm* in v. 10 implies not the promised land but the temple of Jerusalem (A Note on II Samuel 7 10, ZAW 84 [1972], 92–94). In our view, Yahweh's guidance in the past is described here, since we regard them as themes of the *inūma*-clause.

[42] NBKI 66ff. no. 4 4. 11–21.

[43] For instance, J. Seidmann, Die Inschriften Adadniràris II, 1953, 10 line 9; Borger, Asarh., § 65 rev. 32; Streck, Asb., 134 B VIII 36. 202 K. 2802 V 20; T. Bauer, Aššurbanipal, 1933, 80 XVIII 27 (Šamaš-šum-ukin); see AHw 940a; H. Tawil, Some Literary Elements in the Opening Section of the Hadad, Zākir, and the Nērab II Inscriptions, Or NS 43 (1974), 58ff. S. Morenz argues that "to make a great name" in II Sam 7 9a was a direct translation of one of the Egyptian royal titles (ZÄS 79, 73f.). This view is followed by Herrmann, WZ Leipzig 3, 59. But Cross points out that this notion is a common Hamito-Semitic concept (Canaanite Myth 248f.).

11b–17). It includes the following themes: 7) Yahweh promises a dynasty, the succession of a son to David and the establishment of his kingdom and throne (v. 11b. 12. 13b. 16); 8) this son of David will build a temple for Yahweh (v. 13a); 9) Yahweh will be a father to him (v. 14); 10) he will not remove his steadfast love from him (v. 15). We can find these themes, together with theme 6), in a prayer of Nebuchadnezzar II in one of his building inscriptions:

> "O Marduk . . . 9) you have begotten me (and) entrusted me with the kingship over the entire people . . . I am really the king, the provider, 10) the beloved of your heart . . . 8) By your command, merciful Murduk, may the temple, which I built, be strong for ever! . . . 6) From the west to the east, where the sun rises, may my enemy not be, nor have I adversary! 7) May my descendants rule for ever in it over the black-headed people."[44]

In the end, II Sam 7 has a long prayer of David for the establishment of his dynasty (v. 18–29). It is patent that it is comparable with the king's prayer in the building inscriptions of Babylonia in substance and style alike.

Our comparison between Nathan's prophecy and the building inscriptions has demonstrated that many themes are shared by both. But the comparison has its limitation, since the prophecy does not belong to the literary type of the inscriptions. However, we have other interesting material with which Nathan's prophecy can be compared. That is the "Neo-Assyrian prophecy"[45]. This collection of the prophecies to Esarhaddon and Aššurbanipal includes all the themes cited from 1) to 10), except 8) which deals with the building of a temple. (The following Akkadian transliteration is quoted from K. Deller & S. Parpola, Neuassyrische Prophetensprüche, [unpublished manuscript], but the English renderings are mine).

> 1) Divine election of the king:
> *a-na-ku* ^{d}15 *ša* ^{uru}*Arba-il Aš+šur is-si-ka ú-sa-lim ṣi-ḫi-ra-ka a-ta-ṣa-ak-ka* "I am Ištar of Arbela. I appeased Aššur with you. When you were young, I singled you out."[46]
> 2) Divine abiding with the king:
> *a-na-ku* ^{d}15 *ša* ^{uru}*Arba-il ina pa-na-tu-u-ka ina ku-tal-li-ka a-la-KA* "I am Ištar of Arbela. I am going before you and behind you."[47]

---

[44] NBKI 120f. 36–38. 42. 47–48. 52–55.

[45] K. Deller & S. Parpola, Neuassyrische Prophetensprüche, (unpublished manuscript). I would like to express here my sincere thanks to Prof. K. Deller, who kindly showed me his unpublished manuscript and gave me many valuable explanations and suggestions during my stay in Heidelberg in the summer of 1970. The same texts are partly translated into English in ARAB II § 618–638. 860–861; ANET 449–451. 605–606; cf. M. Weippert, Heiliger Krieg in Israel und Assyrien, ZAW 84 (1972), 473f.

[46] IVR 61 II 30–32.

[47] Ibid. 61 I 21–25.

3) Divine help to destroy the king's enemies:
a-na-ku d15 *ša* uru*Arba-il ša na-KA-ru-te-ka ina* IGI GÌR2.meš-*ka ak-kara-ru-u-ni* "I am Ištar of Arbela, who put your enemies before your feet."[48] *na-ka-ru ša* MAN KUR *Aš+šur* [*a*]-*na ṭa-ba-aḫ-ḫi a-da-na* "I will deliver up the enemy of the king of Assyria to slaughter."[49]
4) Making the king's name great:
[LUGAL-*ku-nu* lú K]ÚR-*šú ik-ta-šad* [LUGAL-*ku-n*]*u* lú KÚR-*šú* [KI.TA G]ÌR-*šú is-sa-kan* [TA *ra-b*]*a* dUTU-*ši* [*a-di na-pa*]-*aḫ* dUTU-*ši* [TA *na-pa*]-*aḫ* dUTU-*ši* [*a-di ra*]-*ba* dUTU-*ši* . . . *a-ḫap-pi* "[Your king] destroyed his [en]emy, y[our king] put his enemy [under his f]oot. [From] sun[set to] sun[rise, from] sun[rise to] sunset . . . I will destroy."[50] This prophecy is not a direct parallel, but its implication is similar (cf. Ps 89 26).
5) Peace for the land:
KUR *Aš+šur ú-ta-qa-a*[*n ina* KI.TA] AN-*e ú-ta-qa-a*[*n na-p*]*a-aḫ* dUTU-*ši* [*ra-ba* dUTU-*ši*] "The land of Assyria will be safe [under] the heaven, (and) will be safe (from) sunrise [(to) sunset.]"[51]
6) Peace for the king:
[*ni*]-*ir-ri-ṭu* [TA] ŠÀ É.GAL-*ja* [*ú*]-*še-ṣa ak-lu taq-nu ta-kal* Ameš *taq-nu-ti ta-šá-at-ti ina lìb-bi* É.GAL-*ka ta-taq-qu-un* "I will expel the trembling [from] the midst of my palace. You will eat well-prepared food and you will drink well-prepared water. You will be safe in the midst of your palace."[52]
7) Divine promise of a dynasty and the succession of the king's son:
DUMU-*ka* DUMU.DUMU-*ka* LUGAL-*u-tu ina bur-ki šá* dMAŠ *ú-pa-áš* "Your son and your son's son will exercise kingship on the lap of Ninurta."[53] IBILA-*ka* IBILA.IBILA-*ka* LUGAL-*u-tu* IGI dMAŠ *up-pa-áš* "Your son and your son's son will exercise kingship before Ninurta."[54]
9) Divine paternity of the king:
a-na-ku AD-*ka* AMA-*ka bir-ti a-gap-pi-ja ur-ta-bi-ka* "I am your father and your mother. I have brought you up between my wings."[55] *sa-ab-su-ub-ta-k*[*a*] *ra-bi-tu a-na-ku mu-še-niq*(!)-*ta-ka de-eq-tu a-na-ku* "I am your great midwife and your good nurse."[56] I*Aš+šur*-PAP-AŠ *ap-lu ke-e-nu* DUMU dNIN-LÍL "Esarhaddon, legitimate heir, son of Ninlil!"[57] (cf. Ps 89 27–28).
10) Divine love for the king:
ḫi-is-sa-at-[*ka*] *ḫa-sa-*[*ku*] *ar-ta-am-k*[*a*] *a-dan-*[*niš*] "I am always thinking about you and I love you very much."[58]

---

[48] Ibid. 61 I 13–15.
[49] Ibid. 61 I 32–33.
[50] J. A. Craig, Assyrian and Babylonian Religious Texts, I 1895, 23 I 28–35.
[51] S. Langdon, Tammuz and Ishtar, 1914, Pl. II–III II 28–30.
[52] IVR 61 VI 19–26.
[53] Ibid. 61 VI 27–30.
[54] Langdon, Tammuz and Ishtar, Pl. II III 14–15.
[55] Ibid. Pl. II–III II 21.
[56] IVR 61 III 23–26.
[57] Ibid. 61 IV 5–6. 20–21.
[58] Ibid. 61 IV 22–25.

In addition, the following two themes can be found in both Nathan's prophecy and in the collection of Neo-Assyrian prophecies.

11) The unchangeability of the divine promise to the king (II Sam 7 15; cf. Ps 89 34–36):

a+a-ú-te di-ib-bi-ja ša AQ-QA-ba-kan-ni ina muḫ-ḫi la ta-zi-zu-u-ni "What are my words, which I have spoken to you, upon which you could not rely!"[59] *la ta-pa-làḫ* LUGAL *aq-ṭi-ba-AK la as-li-k[a] ú-ta-ki-i[l-ka] la ú-ba-áš-[ka]* "Fear not, my king! I have spoken to you, I have not told you a lie. I have given you encouragement, I will not let you come to shame."[60]

12) Divine promise of the king's everlasting reign (II Sam 7 16):

a-na-ku ^{d}15 *ša* ^{ur}[^{u}*Arba-il*] ^{I}*Aš+šur*-PAP-AŠ MAN KUR *Aš*[*+šur*] *ina* ^{uru}ŠÀ.URU ^{uru}NIN[A] ^{uru}*Kal-ḫa* ^{uru}*Arba-i*[*l*] UD^{meš} *ar-ku-u-t*[*e*] MU.AN.NA^{meš} *da-ra-t*[*e*] *a-na* ^{I}*Aš+šur*-PAP-AŠ LUGAL-*j*[*a*] *a-da-an-na* "I am Ištar of Arbela. Esarhaddon, king of Assyria! In Aššur, Nineveh, Calah and Arbela I will give long days and everlasting years to Esarhaddon, my king."[61] *ša* u_4*-me ar-ku-te* MU.AN.NA^{meš} *da-ra-te* ^{giš}GU.ZA-*ka ina* KI.TA AN-*e ra-bu-te uk-ti-in* "For long days and everlasting years I have established your throne under the great heavens."[62]

The comparison makes it plain that Nathan's prophecy resembles the Neo-Assyrian prophecies much more closely than the Egyptian royal novel both in themes and in the relation of the king to the god. It is also worth noting that prophecy as a means of communication between god and Man was not usual in ancient Mesopotamia[63]. As far as we know, prophetic activities in Mesopotamia are attested exclusively in Mari and in Neo-Assyria[64]. Because of the characteristic features of both societies, it has been assumed that the prophets in Mesopotamia emerged under West Semitic influence[65]. There is no reason, therefore, to doubt that Nathan's prophecy and the Neo-Assyrian prophecies ultimately stemmed from a common West Semitic tradition. Besides, it should be remembered that prophecy as such is not attested in ancient Egypt[66].

Now to re-examine the implications of the "temple episode" (II

---

[59] Ibid. 61 I 16–18.

[60] Ibid. 61 III 38–IV 2.

[61] Ibid. 61 III 15–22.

[62] Ibid. 61 III 27–30.

[63] Cf. Oppenheim, Ancient Mesopotamia, 221f.

[64] Cf. ibid. 221; Huffmon, in: BAR 3, 201f.

[65] See Oppenheim, Ancient Mesopotamia, 221; cf. Noth, Geschichte und Gotteswort im Alten Testament (1949), in: Gesammelte Studien, I 234ff. (ET History and Word of God in the Old Testament, in: Essays, 185ff.); Malamat, SVT 15, 207ff.; idem, Mari, BA 34 (1971), 20f.

[66] Cf. G. Fohrer, Geschichte der israelitischen Religion, 1969, 226 (ET History of Israelite Religion, 1972, 226).

Sam 7 1–7). J. Wellhausen[67] has maintained that it implies Yahweh's rejection of a temple as such. Therefore, v. 13 must be omitted as a Deuteronomistic addition, since it alludes to Solomon's building of the temple. This view has been followed by many scholars up to the present day[68]. However, S. Mowinckel[69] argued that the verse is the main point of the whole prophecy, since II Sam 7 is "a *teologisk aition* which gives an answer to the question why a king as devoted David did not build a temple for Yahweh". Our starting-point must be the historical fact that David could not build a temple in Jerusalem, but Solomon could and did. The fact already puzzled people in biblical times, and there are at least two different explanations for it in biblical traditions. According to the first, David was too busy to build a temple "because of the enemies by whom he was encompassed, until Yahweh had put them under the soles of his feet" (I Kings 5 17); the second recounts that Yahweh forbade him to build a temple because "he was a man of wars and had shed blood" (I Chron 22 8 28 3). The second explanation, which develops into a word-play on the name Solomon as signifying a man of peace (22 9), seems a late derivation from the first[70]. Although this is generally regarded as a Deuteronomistic invention[71], it is very likely that the historical truth is reflected in it, as the building inscriptions from

---

[67] Die Composition des Hexateuchs und der historischen Bücher des Alten Testaments, 1899³, 254. 268.

[68] Rost, Die Überlieferung von der Thronnachfolge, in: Das kleine Credo und andere Studien, 167f. 175. 177ff.; Noth, ÜSt, 99; idem, David und Israel, in: Gesammelte Studien, I 335f. 344 n. 27 (ET 251f. 258 n. 27); M. Simon, RHPhR 32, 50ff.; Hertzberg, Die Samuelbücher, 235 (ET 287); Mulder, in: Studies on the Books of Samuel, 40f.; Amsler, David, roi et messie, 35 n. 5; de Vaux, RB 73, 482; Kutsch, ZThK 58, 140. 144.

[69] SEÅ 12, 221 (quoted from Labuschagne, in: Studies on the Books of Samuel, 28); cf. idem, Israelite Historiography, ASTI 2 (1963), 11; idem, He that cometh, 101 n. 3. On other grounds the authenticity of v. 13 is defended by the following scholars: van den Bussche, EThL 24, 382ff.; Labuschagne, in: Studies on the Books of Samuel, 32; Caquot, SVT 9, 213ff.; Gese, ZThK 61, 23; Weiser, ZAW 77, 155ff. Poulssen argues that v. 13 served as a connection between three independent sources, i. e. an old tradition of the rejection of a temple (v. 5–7), a critical view against the monarchy (v. 8–11a) and the original prophecy (v. 11b. 16), and this fusion took place immediately after the erection of Solomon's temple (König und Tempel 44ff.). According to Tsevat, v. 13b–16 are, together with v. 13a, a Solomonic gloss to the original prophecy (HUCA 34, 71ff.; idem, The House of David in Nathan's Prophecy, Bib 46 [1965], 353–356).

[70] Cf. J. Botterweck, Zur Eigenart der chronistischen Davidsgeschichte, in: Christian Festschrift, 1956, 12ff.; J. M. Myers, The Book of I Chronicles, 1965, 154. On the name Solomon, see J. J. Stamm, Der Name des Königs Salomo, ThZ 16 (1960), 285–297.

[71] Noth, ÜSt, 99; idem, Könige, I 1968, 89f.; Weiser, ZAW 77, 158.

Mesopotamia also mention political stability as a fundamental condition for the royal building of a temple.

As we shall show in the next chapter, it appears that David had already conceived the idea of building a temple in Jerusalem at the very beginning of his reign in his new capital. According to the Chronicler, he provided before his death not only all the materials and the craftsmen for Solomon to build the temple but its design as well (I Chron 22 2–19 28 11–21). Although this account cannot be taken at its face value, it, too, undoubtedly mirrors reality. Despite the elaborate preparations, David's plan was not carried out, because he was too preoccupied to deal with both external and domestic troubles. The main military engagements with the neighbouring peoples were concluded in the first half of his reign[72], but then, he had to face internal disturbances, such as Absalom's rebellion (II Sam 13–19), Sheba's revolt (20 1–2. 4–22), the national census and the plague (24 1–25). No wonder that he could not find intervals of uninterrupted peace long enough to build a temple before the end of his rule. In fact, Solomon devoted seven years to building the temple and thirteen years to the whole complex of its buildings (I Kings 6 38–7 1; cf. 9 10)[73].

Even so, David might have undertaken the building, had not Nathan imparted Yahweh's negative answer to the plan. David thought that his kingship was stable enough for the enterprise (II Sam 7 1). At first, Nathan also agreed (7 3), but, that very night, he announced Yahweh's dissent. Scholars have been mystified by Nathan's inconsistent attitude. S. Herrmann[74] has regarded it as one of the literary characteristics of the "Egyptian royal novel"; M. Noth[75] argued that it was a polite formality when facing royalty. It seems, however, that this baffling change resulted from antagonism at the royal court. Presumably, Nathan, at once, consulted the important courtiers and officials about the king's plan, and, quite simply, was unable to obtain a consensus on it. We can take it that the antagonism between Abiathar and Zadok, the chief priests of David[76], was already

---

[72] On the reconstruction of the chronological order of the events in the time of David, see Yeivin, in: EncBib, II 1954, 614f. (Hebrew).

[73] It is generally accepted that the words *kol-bêtô* in I Kings 7 1 denote the whole complex of buildings including the palace as well as the temple, though a total of twenty years is given in 9 10, see J. A. Montgomery & H. S. Gehman, The Books of Kings, 1951, 161; J. Gray, I & II Kings, 1970², 176f.

[74] WZ Leipzig 3, 58; cf. Weiser, ZAW 77, 157.

[75] David und Israel, in: Gesammelte Studien, I 343 (ET 257); cf. Cross, Canaanite Myth, 242. Against this view, Kutsch argues that Nathan was an outspoken prophet (ZThK 58, 138 n. 1).

[76] According to Cross, Zadok was an Aaronide priest from Hebron, while Abiathar was a

irreconcilable. Yet it is unlikely that it was a conflict between the Jebusite party represented by Nathan and Zadok and the Judahite-Yahwist group headed by Abiathar[77]. But the fact that Solomon's purge of all the opponents, including Abiathar, preceded his undertaking of the building of the temple (I Kings 2 13–46) shows that the struggle at David's court was the most serious hindrance to the plan proposed by David[78].

Remarkably, Yahweh's rejection of it (II Sam 7 5b–7) is communicated obliquely, sandwiched between two questions[79]: "Would you build me a house to dwell in?" (v. 5b) and "Did I speak a word with any of *šib̲ṭê yiśra'el*[80] . . . why have you not built me a house of cedar?" (v. 7). We do not find here the same straightforwardness with which the prophet condemned David for his affair with Bathsheba: "You are the man" (12 7). Had Yahweh, as many scholars think, rejected either a temple as such or the concept of the so-called Canaanite temple (see above p. 83), Nathan would have spoken more explicitly. The ambiguous expressions show that Yahweh dismissed David's plan with reluctance. In Mesopotamia, the god's disapproval of the king's plan was regarded as a sign of divine displeasure. Undoubtedly, the "temple episode" is conscious of this point. It has to explain a delicate situation, in which Yahweh sets David's plan aside, although the king enjoys divine grace.

Mushite from Shiloh, and David tried to keep a balance between the rival priestly families (Canaanite Myth 207ff.).

77 Against Ahlström, VT 11, 113ff.; H. Haag, Gad und Nathan, in: Galling Festschrift, 1970, 135–143.

78 Fretheim assumes that Abiathar and the Shilonite priests opposed the building of the temple on the grounds of keeping the tradition of a movable tent, that is, the moving Ark sanctuary (VT 18, 323ff.). But we cannot accept the view that the temple at Shiloh was not a "temple" in the true sense of the word, see below p. 96.

79 K. Koch observes that the Ziphites avoid a direct statement and address the king Saul in the form of a rhetorical question (I Sam 23 19 26 1), and he regards this polite formality as a reflection of the manner at the court in Jerusalem (Was ist Formgeschichte?, 1967², 172 [ET The Growth of the Biblical Tradition, 1969, 140]). About another use of rhetorical questions, see W. A. Brueggemann, Jeremiah's Use of Rhetorical Questions, JBL 92 (1973), 358–374.

80 The words *šib̲ṭê yiśra'el* in v. 7 are generally emended as *šop̲ṭê yiśra'el* according to I Chron 17 6, see S. R. Driver, Notes on the Hebrew Text and the Topography of the Books of Samuel, 1913², 274f. But Z. W. Falk holds that the emendation is not necessary, because the root *šbṭ* implies here "to rule" just like the root *špṭ* (*Šôp̲eṭ weševeṭ*, Lešonenu 30 [1966/67], 243–247 [Hebrew]); cf. S. E. Loewenstamm, Ruler and Judges, Reconsidered, Lešonenu 32 (1968/69), 272–274 (Hebrew). On the other hand, P. de Robert argues that the term *šib̲ṭê* originally stood here but the Chronicler changed it into *šop̲ṭê* (Judges ou Tribus en 2 Samuel VII 7?, VT 21 [1971], 116–118).

It is also striking that the "temple episode" ignores the existence of the temple at Shiloh, by saying that Yahweh had neither dwelt in a house since the day of Exodus nor had ever asked to have a house built for him. It is unlikely, however, that the temple at Shiloh was different in character from that of Solomon. Both are called *băyiṯ* (for Shiloh: Judg 18 31 I Sam 1 7. 24 3 15 Jer 7 14; for Jerusalem: I Kings 6 1ff. Is 2 2) or *hêḵăl* (for Shiloh: I Sam 1 9 3 3; for Jerusalem: II Kings 18 16 Jer 7 4)[81] and both held the Ark as the symbol of Yahweh's presence (for Shiloh: I Sam 3 3 4 3–4; for Jerusalem: I Kings 8 1–9). Therefore, both the suggestion that the shrine at Shiloh was not as permanent as that of Jerusalem because of its appellation *'ohœl* and *miškăn* in hendiadys (Ps 78 60; cf. II Sam 7 6) and the assumption that the description of the temple at Shiloh is an anachronism[82] are unacceptable. Nor is it easy to suppose that Nathan was not acquainted with the Shilonite tradition. It seems that the "temple episode" deliberately took no heed of the temple of Shiloh. Since the episode was composed to defend David's failure to build a temple, it had to emphasize that no one had ever been appointed by Yahweh to build a temple for him until the days of David[83]. A similar logic is found in a later development of the doctrine

[81] According to Schunck, the term *hêḵal* denotes the "central shrine" either of the tribal league (Shiloh) or of the kingdom (Jerusalem) (Zentralheiligtum, Grenzheiligtum und „Höhenheiligtum" in Israel, Numen 18 [1971], 132–140).

[82] On the thesis that the shrine at Shiloh was not "temple" but *miškan*, see de Vaux, RB 73, 487. It is generally held that the term *miškan* as the designation of the tent-sanctuary was brought into the religion of Israel together with the nomadic tradition of the ancestors of Israel, see Cross, The Priestly Tabernacle (1947), in: BAR 1, 1961, 224ff.; de Vaux, Les institutions, II 122ff. (ET 294ff.). Malamat assumes that this is an early West Semitic term mentioned in a Mari document as *maškanum* (History and Prophetic Vision in a Mari Letter, EI 5 [1958], 69 [Hebrew]; idem, Mari and the Bible, JAOS 82 [1962], 149); but see also W. L. Moran, in: ANET 625 n. 31; AHw 626. On the other hand, W. Schmidt argues that the term came from the Canaanites to Jerusalem, since it had already been used as an expression for the dwelling place of the gods in Ugarit (*Miškan* als Ausdruck jerusalemer Kultsprache, ZAW 75 [1963], 91–92). In addition, D. R. Hillers finds the term *mškn'* in the Aramaic inscriptions from Hatra from the first to the second century A. D., which implies not a tabernacle but a permanent temple (*Mškn'* "Temple" in Inscriptions from Hatra, BASOR 207 [1972], 54–56). After examining various interpretations of the nature of the shrine at Shiloh, Fretheim concludes that the temple of Shiloh was not a permanent temple because of the Ark which was moved from shrine to shrine of the tribal league (VT 18, 324ff.); cf. also Cross, Canaanite Myth, 231. 242f. – According to M. Haran, the descripton of the shrine at Shiloh as a temple is an anachronism (Shiloh and Jerusalem: the Origin of the Priestly Tradition in the Pentateuch, JBL 81, [1962], 14–24).

[83] Eissfeldt assumes that the tabernacle was actually kept in the temple at Shiloh as a sacred relic, so Nathan intentionally underlined the tradition of the tabernacle (Kultzelt und Tempel, in: K. Elliger Festschrift, 1973, 53f.).

of the exclusive election of Zion, in which the tradition of the Exodus is connected directly with Yahweh's choice of Zion without mentioning any other sanctuaries such as Shiloh and Bethel (see below pp. 148–149).

The "temple episode" is closely connected with the latter part of the prophecy (II Sam 7 8–16) in two statements which stand in contrast to the question: "Would you build me a house to dwell in?" (v. 5b). The first contrast is: "Yahweh will make you a house" (v. 11b), and the second: "He shall build a house for my name" (v. 13a). The first, by the word-play on *băyiṯ*, implies that David will not build a temple (*băyiṯ*) for Yahweh, but Yahweh will found a dynasty (*băyiṯ*) for David. The second refers to Solomon as the builder of the temple of Jerusalem instead of David. Commentators generally regard either the first or the second to be genuine, by eliminating one of them as a later interpolation[84]. But it must be pointed out that the both contrasts correspond exactly to the double theme of the royal-dynastic ideology in the ancient Near East, that is, the divine promise of a dynasty and the king's building of a temple[85]. This double theme is as a rule related to the same king, but owing to the special situation, in which the founder of the dynasty was not identical with the builder of the temple, it plays a twofold role in Nathan's prophecy – an apology for David's failure to carry out his plan of temple building and a legitimation of Solomon's throne and his temple. Moreover, it clearly corresponds to the doctrine of Yahweh's joint election of David's House and of Zion, the central doctrine of the royal-dynastic ideology of the House of David, with which we shall deal in the next chapter.

All the same, Nathan's prophecy, as a whole, does not treat the two themes equally. The theme of a temple only serves as an introduction to the theme of a dynasty. By a unique logic, Yahweh's promise of an eternal dynasty is drawn out of David's abortive plan. Clearly, this is not a simple divine promise but a strong legitimation of David's dynasty in Israel. Yahweh chose David as the *nagîḏ* over the people of Israel (II Sam 7 8), and his military success, vouchsafed by Yahweh, gave Israel a stable place to dwell in and secured it from attacks of enemies for ever (7 9–11a). In other words, the security and prosperity of Israel were finally established by the House of David. Moreover,

---

[84] The first contrast (between v. 5b and v. 11b) is held by Wellhausen, Die Composition, 254f.; Rost, Die Überlieferung von der Thronnachfolge, in: Das kleine Credo und andere Studien, 170; Kutsch, ZThK 58, 139, while the second (between v. 5b and v. 13a) is supported by W. Caspari, Die Samuelbücher, 1926, 482; Labuschagne, in: Studies on the Books of Samuel, 33; Carlson, David, the Chosen King, 109. On the other hand, Noth does not find any contrast in both cases (David und Israel, in: Gesammelte Studien, I 335f. [ET 251]).

[85] Cf. Caquot, SVT 9, 215; Gese, ZThK 61, 24.

Yahweh's choice of that House, which is unalterable, was made in rejection of the House of Saul (7 15). Thus, the House of David is incorporated as a new element into the inseparable relationship between Yahweh and Israel. We shall deal later with the implication of this triple nexus between Yahweh, Israel and the House of David. It thus becomes clear that the legitimation of the House of David towards the people of Israel is the climax of Nathan's prophecy.

We have shown that Nathan's prophecy has a literary unity. But it is also evident, from several traces of joins in it[86], that it was composed of various source materials, although all the elements are now organically bound together. The fact that unmistakable references to Solomon (7 12–14) are interwoven with the history of David indicates that it embraces material from at least two generations. From this observation we may assume the following course of development for Nathan's prophecy.

When David conceived the plan to build a royal sanctuary in his new capital, he consulted with Nathan to discover Yahweh's will. Nathan reluctantly delivered a prophecy to halt the plan, most probably because of the domestic antagonism between the two chief priests and perhaps because of the unstable situation in the kingdom. On another occasion, it is likely that Nathan prophesied as to Yahweh's promise concerning a stable dynasty, presumably in connection with the movement to help Solomon to the throne. Surprisingly, Nathan appears in biblical sources only in connection with the problems of Solomon's succession to the Davidic throne[87], apart from figuring in the narrative on the designation of Solomon through court intrigue (I Kings 1). He had taken a leading part in the denunciation of David's affair with Bathsheba (II Sam 12 1–25), whose main motif is simply the birth of Solomon as candidate for the succession. As soon as Solomon succeeded in seizing the throne with the help of Nathan and his party, he established a firm rule by ruthlessly purging all the anti-Solomonic factions (I Kings 1–2). Then he took up his father's old unfulfilled plan to build a royal sanctuary in Jerusalem and so complete his policy of absolute centralization. Undoubtedly, he had great need of legitimation

[86] Because of the abrupt change of the subject from the first person to the third, Rost singles out v. 11b. 16 as the oldest nucleus of the prophecy (in: Das kleine Credo und andere Studien 168ff.). Kutsch confines it to v. 11b only (ZThK 58, 144), while Coppens attributes v. 1–3, 11b. 16 to the original prophecy (L'union du trône et du temple d'après l'oracle de Nathan, EThL 44 [1968], 489–491). According to Cross, the chapter consists of the old oracle of Nathan (v. 1–7), the oracle of the eternal divine decree (v. 11b–16), the Deuteronomic linkage (v. 8–11a) and David's prayer (v. 18–29), which is a free Deuteronimic composition (Canaanite Myth 254).

[87] Cf. Gese, ZThK 61, 19f.

for both his throne and the building of the temple against the antagonism of the northern tribes, as well as against those who opposed his succession to David. At that time, either Nathan himself or his sons[88] met Solomon's requirements by composing "Nathan's prophecy" and "David's prayer". The source materials for the composition were Nathan's old prophetic sayings, delivered to David on several occasions. From the parallel of the collections of prophecies in the royal archives at Mari and Nineveh, we may infer that Nathan's prophecies were also preserved as a collection in the royal archive in Jerusalem. In this way, the prophecies which Nathan had made to David were reinterpreted for the legitimation of Solomon[89].

B. THE STRUCTURE OF THE ROYAL-DYNASTIC IDEOLOGY

Nathan's prophecy became the origin of the Judaean royal ideology and the messianism of later times[90]. It is not our purpose here to study this extensive ideological evolution. We will confine ourselves to examining the structure of the royal-dynastic ideology in II Sam 7 (cf. I Chron 17), and references will be made to subsequent developments only when they are required.

In II Sam 7, Yahweh's promise to establish David's dynasty is ex-

---

[88] In the list of Solomon's high officials there are two sons of a certain Nathan: Azariah over the officers and Zabud, priest and king's friend (I Kings 4 5). We do not know whether they were sons of the same person called Nathan, nor is it clear whether that person was identical with Nathan the prophet. But there is reason to assume that the sons of Nathan the prophet received high positions at Solomon's court, cf. Gray, I & II Kings, 133; Noth, Könige, I 64. If they were the sons of Nathan the prophet, Zabud could be the composer of II Samuel 7 owing to the nature of his office.

[89] One way or another, Nathan's prophecy is regarded as the Solomonic legitimation by many scholars, see Caquot, SVT 9, 215f.; Tsevat, HUCA 34, 71ff.; idem, Bib 46, 353ff.; Weiser, ZAW 77, 156ff.; Poulssen, König und Tempel, 43ff.; Seybold, Das davidische Königtum, 29. Recently, W. von Soden assumed that Nathan was the author of the J source in the primeval history (Gen 1–11), in which he implicitly criticized the deeds of Solomon (Verschlüsselte Kritik an Salomo in der Urgeschichte des Jahwisten?, WO 7/2 [1974], 238ff). But the suggestion seems highly hypothetical.

[90] Cf. G. von Rad, Das Geschichtsbild des chronistischen Werkes, 1930, 119ff.; Alt, Die Staatenbildung der Israeliten in Palästina (1930), in: Kleine Schriften, II 1953, 63f. (ET The Formation of the Israelite State in Palestine, in: Essays on Old Testament History and Religion, 1966, 235); Noth, Gott, König, Volk im Alten Testament (1950), in: Gesammelte Studien, I 224 (ET God, King, and Nation in the Old Testament, in: Essays, 174); Coppens, NRTh 90, 227; S. Japhet, The Ideology of the Book of Chronicles, 451ff. (Hebrew).

pressed in different forms respecting various subjects. That ideology consists of the following key-words under two categories:
I. Terms indicating the existence of a royal dynasty:
a) *băyiṯ* (v. 11. 16. 18. 19. 25. 26. 27);
b) *zæră‘* (v. 12);
c) *kisse’* (v. 13. 16);
d) *mămlaḵā* (v. 12. 16).
II. Terms representing the relationship between the king and God:
e) *’aḇ* and *ben* (v. 14);
f) *ḥæsæḏ* (v. 15);
g) *daḇar* (v. 21. 25. 28 ; cf. v. 17. 19. 29);
h) *ṭôḇā* (v. 28).

a) *băyiṯ* - Yahweh promised David that "he will make a *băyiṯ*" (v. 11) or "he will build a *băyiṯ*" (v. 27), and it "shall be made sure for ever" (v. 16). Reacting to the divine promise about his *băyiṯ* "for a great while to come" (v. 19), David entreated Yahweh that it "will be established" (v. 26) and "will be blessed for ever" (v. 29). Clear references to this divine promise are made in David's last words (II Sam 23 5), Abigail's words to David (I Sam 25 28), Solomon's oath (I Kings 2 24)[91] and Ahijah's oracle to Jeroboam (11 38). In all these examples, the term *băyiṯ* implies a "dynasty".

In the same way, the term בת or בית in West Semitic inscriptions means a "house", that is, a building as well as a dynasty[92]. כן. בת אבי. במתכת. מלכם. אדרם "My father's house was in the midst of mighty kings."[93] ומלכה. על. בית. אבה "And he made him king over his father's house."[94] A better translation for the expression "father's house" in these examples is "royal dynasty". But, owing to the double meaning of the term, its exact sense is sometimes ambiguous. For instance, in the building inscription of Barrakib, king of Y'dy-Sam'al, the term בית denotes both a dynasty and a palace[95]: ובית. אבי. [ע]מל. מן. כל (7–8) "The house of my father has profited more than anybody else." ואחזת. בית. אבי. והיטבתה. מן. בית. חד. מלכן. רברבן (11–14) "I took over the house of my father and made it more prosperous than the house of one of the mighty kings." והתנאבו. אחי. מלכיא. לכל. מה. טבת. ביתי (14–15) "My brethren, the kings are envious because of all the prosperity of my house." ובי. טב. לישה. לאבהי. מלכי.

[91] Sometimes the emendation of *lî* to *lô* is suggested, see Gray, I & II Kings, 106 note a. 107, but it is unnecessary, see Noth, Könige, I 34f.

[92] See C.-F. Jean & J. Hoftijzer, Dictionnaire des inscriptions sémitiques de l'ouest, 1965, 35f.; KAI III 5. 29.

[93] KAI § 24 5–6.

[94] KAI § 215 7.

[95] KAI § 216; ANET 655; cf. B. Landsberger, Sam'al, 1948, 71 n. 186.

שמאל. הא. בית. כלמו. להם. פהא. בית. שתוא. להם. והא. בית. כיצא. ואנה. בנית. ביתא. זנה. (15–20) "My fathers, the kings of Sam'al, had no good house. They had the house of Kilamuwa, which was their winter house and also their summer house. But I have built this house."
It appears that the term בית in lines 7–15 implies the "dynasty", while in lines 16–20 it denotes the "palace building". This twin usage of the term reminds us of the word-play on *băyiṯ* as a temple as well as a dynasty in Nathan's prophecy.

In Mesopotamia, there was a unique conception of a "dynasty" called *palû* (BALA), which groups the kings not by consanguineous bond but by geographical origin[96]. Accordingly, the Akkadian terms *bītu* and *bīt abi* originally had no sense of "dynasty"[97]. But under West Semitic influence, which is found mainly in the texts from Mari, Ugarit, Alalakh, El-Amarna and Neo-Assyria, they came to express a "dynasty"[98].
šanat Zimrilim ana giš*kussî bīt abīšu īrubū* "The year when Zimrilim ascended the throne of his father's house"[99]; *aššu ēpeš šarrūti bīt abīja* "In order to exercise the kingship of my father's house"[100]; *u liḫalliqu[šu] i[štu lib]bi bīt abīšu u ištu libbi māt abī[šu u] ištu* giš*kussî ša abīšu* "May they make him vanish from his father's house, from his father's land and from his father's throne."[101]
Evidently, the throne, the kingship and the land associated with *bīt abi* were the most important dynastic possessions.

In the second millennium B. C., the royal dynasty of a city-state was expressed by the formula: *bītu* + a city's name.
*ṣuḫārtam mārat Išḫi-Adad akkâsim eleqqē bīt Mari*ki *šumam išu u bīt Qatanim*ki *šumam išu* "The maiden daughter of Išḫi-Adad I will take for thee, for the House of Mari is renowned and the House of Qatna is renowned."[102]
amur bīt al Ṣurri iānu bīti ḫazāni kīma šuāta kīma bīt al Ugarita ibaši

---

[96] See T. Jacobsen, Primitive Democracy in Ancient Mesopotamia (1943), in: Toward the Image of Tammuz and Other Essays on Mesopotamian History and Culture, 1970, 406 n. 66; J. J. Finkelstein, The Genealogy of the Hammurapi Dynasty, JCS 20 (1966), 105f.; J. A. Brinkman, A Political History of Post Kassite Babylonia, 1968, 37f. n. 163.

[97] See AHw 132f.; CAD A 1 73ff.; CAD B 282ff.

[98] See W. F. Albright & W. L. Moran, Rib-Adda of Byblos and the Affairs of Tyre (EA 89), JCS 4 (1950), 167f.; CAD A 1 75.

[99] G. Dossin, Les noms d'années et d'éponymes dans les "Archives de Mari", in: Studia Mariana, 1950, 54.

[100] Borger, Asarh., § 27A I 58.

[101] PRU IV 1956, 137f. (18.06 + 17.365 13'–15').

[102] ARM I § 77 9–10; Albright & Moran, JCS 4, 167; cf. CAD B 293.

"Behold, the House of Tyre – there is no governor's house like it. It is like the House of Ugarit."[103]

On the other hand, the dynastic residence was called a "city of the father's house".

ina uru*Ḫalap*ki *bīt abīja* "In Aleppo, my father's house"[104]; . . . *ḫa-a-da-ra bīt abī-šú ša* m*Ra-ḫi-a-ni* kur*Šá-imeri-šú-a+a a-šar*(!) *i*ʾ*-al-du* ". . . hadara, his father's house, of Rezin of Damascus, where he was born."[105] The incomplete name of Rezin's birthplace may be reconstructed as kur*Bīt-Ḫadara* or the like. Although the name Hadara or Beth-Hadara is unknown, it is possible to assume that Rezin of Damascus came from Beth-Hadara where his dynasty had been established, just as Hadadezer, king of Zobah, came from Beth-Rehob (II Sam 8 3. 12; cf. 10 6)[106].

In the first millennium B. C., with the establishment of national kingdoms, the royal dynasty was expressed by the term *băyiṯ* in combination with the name of its founder. After Ishbaal became king over Israel in Mahanaim and David king over Judah in Hebron, "there was a long war between the House of Saul and the House of David" (II Sam 3 1. 6). In a fit of anger, Abner confirmed the end of the war: "to transfer the kingdom from the House of Saul, and set up the throne of David over Israel and over Judah" (3 10). His words show that this was a struggle for kingdom and throne between two dynasties. In the rebellion against the "House of David", the northern tribes said: "Look now to your own House, O David" (I Kings 12 16), and "there was none that followed the House of David, but the tribe of Judah only" (12 19–20). After that, the "House of David" became the dynasty of Judah alone, as the parallelism indicates: "And to the House of the king of Judah . . . O House of David" (Jer 21 11–12). In the same way, the dynasties of the Northern Kingdom were called by the names of the founders, that is, the "House of Jeroboam" (I Kings 13 34 14 10a. 10b. 13. 14 15 29 16 3. 7 21 22 II Kings 9 9 13 6), the "House of Baasha" (I Kings 16 11. 12 21 22 II Kings 9 9; cf. I Kings 16 7), and the "House of Jehu" (Hos 1 4). But, oddly enough, the dynasty of Omri is never called the "House of Omri" in biblical sources. Instead, it is called the "House of Ahab". However, the name Bīt-Humri is preserved in Assyrian sources

---

[103] EA § 89 48–51; cf. Albright & Moran, JCS 4, 164.

[104] S. Smith, The Statue of Idri-mi, 1949, 14 3; cf. CAD A 1 75.

[105] A. H. Layard, Inscriptions in the Cuneiform Character from Assyrian Monuments, 1851, 72b–73a 11–12; the transliteration is quoted from H. Tadmor, The Inscriptions of Tiglath-Pileser III, King of Assyria, (in preparation).

[106] Generally the name Hadara is assumed for this place, see ARAB I § 777; ANET 283. But Tadmor is of the opinion that several characters are missing before the sign *ḫa* and they must be a component of the place-name.

as the name of the Northern Kingdom[107]. In the Moabite inscription, the dynasty of Omri is mentioned as עמרי. מלך. ישראל ... בנה ... בתה "Omri, king of Israel ... his son ... his house"[108].

In Mesopotamia, many tribal lands were called Bīt-X, from the Kassite period onward. This nomenclature generally denotes the tribal name[109]. Only a few cases can be identified as the name of a dynasty: for example, Bīt-Bahiani for Gozan[110], [kurBīt]-mHa-za-ᵓa-i-li for Damascus[111] and Bīt-(A)gūsi for Arpad[112]. The name בת מפש in the inscriptions from Karatepe[113] is regarded as that of the dynasty which ruled over the Dannunites. But we do not know whether מפש is the founder's name or the eponym[114].

b) *zœrăʿ* – This term implies the direct offspring as well as the descendants in general. Clearly, *zărʿaḵa* whom Yahweh promised David to raise up after him (II Sam 7 12) refers to Solomon, since he would be the builder of the temple (v. 13a). The Chronicler brought this out by changing the wording from *ʾašœr yeṣeʾ mimmeʿǽḵa* "who shall come forth from you" (II Sam 7 12) to *ʾašœr yihyǽ mibbanǽḵa* "who will be one of your sons" (I Chron 17 11)[115]. Likewise, later references to this passage replaced *zărʿaḵa* by *binḵa* "your sons" (I Kings 5 19 8 19 II Chron 6 9). But in the Judaean royal-dynastic ideology the meaning of David's *zœrăʿ* in Nathan's prophecy was expanded to all the descendants of the House of David:

> "One of the sons of your body I will set on your throne. If your sons keep my covenant and my testimonies which I shall teach them, their sons also for ever shall sit upon your throne" (Ps 132 11–12; cf. Ps 89 5. 30. 37 Jer 33 22.26; Ps 18 51 = II Sam 22 51).

The expanded promise of *zœrăʿ* was expressed by other phraseologies as well: "There shall not fail you a man (*ʾîš*) on the throne of Israel" (I Kings 2 4 9 5; cf. 8 25 II Chron 6 16 7 18 Jer 33 17); "That David my servant may always have a lamp (*nîr*)[116] before me in Jerusalem" (I

---

[107] See S. Parpola, Neo-Assyrian Toponyms, 1970, 82f.; see below pp. 177–178.

[108] KAI § 181 4–7.

[109] RLA II 1938, 33ff.; cf. Oppenheim, Ancient Mesopotamia, 160; Brinkman, A Political History of Post-Kassite Babylonia, 158.

[110] See Parpola, Neo-Assyrian Toponyms, 78; S. Loewenstamm, in: EncBib, II 1954, 451.

[111] D. J. Wiseman, A Fragmentary Inscription of Tiglath-Pileser III from Nimrud, Iraq 18 (1956), 125 rev. 3; cf. ibid. 129.

[112] See above p. 22 n. 124.

[113] KAI § 26 A I 16. II 14–15. III 11. C IV 12.

[114] Cf. R. D. Barnett, Mopsos, JHS 73 (1953), 140–143.

[115] Cf. van den Bussche, EThL 24, 384ff.

[116] Since LXX rendered the term *nîr* by θέσις "thesis" (I Kings 11 36), κατάλειμμα

Kings 11 36; cf. I Kings 15 4 II Kings 8 19 II Chron 21 7); "I have prepared a lamp (*ner*) for my anointed" (Ps 132 17)[117].

The term *zæră'* also signifies a "family": "She arose and destroyed all the royal family (*kᵒl zæră' hămmămlakā*)" (II Kings 11 1; cf. II Chron 22 10); "Hadad the Edomite was of the royal family (*zæră' hămmælæk*) in Edom" (I Kings 11 14). Accordingly, the term also implies the pedigree, descent or lineage: "They could not prove their fathers' houses or their descent (*bêt 'ᵃbotam wᵉzăr'am*)" (Ezra 2 59 = Neh 7 61). In this usage, the cognate Akkadian term *zēru* implies the royal lineage (see above p. 13); clearly, it represents the conception of a dynasty in the West Semitic sense.

c) *kisse'* – The "throne" was the most important symbol of royal authority (cf. Solomon's throne in I Kings 10 18–20)[118]. The parallelism between "to transfer the kingdom" and "to set up the throne" (II Sam 3 10) indicates that the throne symbolized royal rule. Similarly, the expression "to sit on the throne" signifies "to become king": "Solomon your son shall reign after me, and he shall sit upon my throne" (I Kings 1 17; cf. 1 24). The same expression is used in the Phoenician, **ישב על כסא**[119], the Aramaic, **ישב על כרסא**[120] or **ישב על משב**[121], the Akkadian, *ina kussî ūšib*, (cf. *ana kussî ērub* and *kussâ iṣbat*)[122], and the Hittite, I.NA ᵍⁱˢGU.ZA *ešḫat*[123].

A myth from Ugarit vividly describes the significance of the throne

---

"remnant" (15 4) and λύχνος "lamp" (II Kings 8 19 II Chron 21 7), a meaning other than "lamp" for the term has been sometimes looked for. By assuming the Akkadian term *nēru* "yoke" as its cognate, J. W. Wevers argues that it means "royal prerogative" (Exegetical Principles underlying the Septuagint Text of I Kings II 12–XXI 43, OTS 8 [1950], 315). Similarly, P. D. Hanson maintains that the term is used in the metaphorical sense of "dominion" (The Song of Heshbon and David's *NÎR*, HThR 61 [1968], 310ff.). Noth once proposed that it implies a "new break" or "beginning" (Jerusalem und die israelitische Tradition [1950], in: Gesammelte Studien, I 179 [ET Jerusalem and the Israelite Tradition, in: Essays, 137f.]), but he later discarded the suggestion (Könige I 243f.). Although LXX did not understand the term correctly, it is most probable that the term is an archaic form connected with the Ugaritic word *nyr* "to shine", see R. H. Smith, The Household Lamps of Palestine in Old Testament Times, BA 27 (1964), 3. 21.

117 The extinguishing of lamps is a common metaphor for the misfortune of a person who died without offspring (Prov 13 9 24 20 Job 18 6 21 17; cf. Prov 20 20), see T. H. Gaster, Thespis, 1961², 335f.; Fretheim, Psalm 132: A Form-Critical Study, JBL 86 (1967), 299 n. 45; M. Dahood, Psalms, III 1970, 248.

118 Cf. M. Broshi, in: EncBib, IV 1962, 217f. (Hebrew); Noth, Könige, I 230ff.

119 KAI § 24 9. § 26 A I 11.

120 KAI § 216 5–7; cf. KAI § 224 17.

121 KAI § 214 8. 15. 20. 25.

122 CAD A 2 390ff.; CAD K 590f.; CAD Ṣ 28.

123 See above p. 16 n. 76.

as the centre of royal authority by telling that a king can rule only when his body fits the throne:

> „Straightway Aštar the Tyrant goes up to the Fastness of Zaphon (and) sits on Baal Puissant's throne (*yṯb. lkḥṯ*). (But) his feet reach not down to the footstool, nor his head reaches up to the top. So Aštar the Tyrant declares: 'I will not reign in Zaphon's Fastness!'"[124]

The throne, in its full form, is called the "royal throne" (*kisse' mămlăḵtô* Deut 17 18; *kisse' hămmᵉlûḵā* I Kings 1 46; cf. כסא מלכה KAI § 1 2), the "throne of Israel" (I Kings 2 4 8 20, etc.) or the "royal throne over Israel" (9 5). Moreover, the "father's throne" is the most important token of legitimate succession: "And Solomon sat upon the throne of David his father" (2 12; cf. 2 24); "I, Kilamuwa, son of Hayya, sat on my father's throne"[125]; "Since I sat upon my father's throne . . ."[126]. Thus, the expression "throne of David" always has a dynastic implication: "But king Solomon shall be blessed, and the throne of David shall be established before Yahweh for ever" (I Kings 2 45). In these words Solomon affirmed that the "throne of David" was not only his father's throne but also the dynastic symbol of the House of David. Therefore, the later kings of Judah were called "those who sit on the throne of David" (Jer 17 25 22 2, etc.).

When David gave the order to make Solomon king, Benaiah the son of Jehoiada answered him:

> "As Yahweh has been with my lord king, even so may he be with Solomon, and make his throne greater than the throne of my lord king David" (I Kings 1 37).

When Solomon sat on the royal throne, the servants came to congratulate David and said:

> "May your God make the name of Solomon more famous than yours, and make his throne greater than your throne" (1 47).

Be it noted that the congratulations were addressed not to Solomon but to David. Unless Solomon's name and throne, which the courtiers wished to become greater than those of David, are the dynastic symbols, we cannot understand the situation. Since an organic continuity of David's dynasty was recognized in the transfer of the kingship from David to Solomon, they regarded the growth of the throne and name of Solomon as Yahweh's blessing to David. Otherwise, their words would have offered an insult to David. In his testament, Arihalbu, king of Ugarit, attempted to attain dynastic stability and continuity by a levirate marriage after his death (see above p. 74). In cursing

---

[124] UT § 49 I 28–34; ANET 140.
[125] KAI § 24 9.
[126] EA § 17 11.

those who would break his testament, he invoked Baal: *kussâ lā urabbî* "May he not make great (his) throne!" (line 10). Since blessing and curse are the opposite sides of one and the same thing, Arihalbu's curse is exactly in reverse to what David's servants desired in their congratulations to David.

d) *mămlaḵā, (melûḵā, mălekûṯ)* – The term "kingdom" denotes the royal authority *per se*. The king "takes" (*laḵăd*) the kingdom (I Sam 14 47) and "exercises" (*ʿaśā*) it (I Kings 21 7). Then, it is "established" (*qûm* or *kûn*) in his hand (I Sam 24 21; I Kings 2 12. 46). According to the outlook of the biblical historiographers, however, it is Yahweh who "gives" (*naṯăn*) a kingdom to the king, "takes" (*laqăḥ*) it out of his hand or "tears" (*qarăʿ*) it away from him and gives it to another (I Sam 15 28 28 17 II Sam 16 8 I Kings 11 11, etc.). The transfer of the kingdom from one king to another is also expressed by the term "to transfer" (*lehăʿaḇîr*) (II Sam 3 10) and "to turn over" (*wăyyăsseḇ*) (I Chron 10 14 12 23; cf. I Kings 2 15). That is to say, the kingdom was a thing transferred from one to the other. The kingdom was transferred from the House of Saul (II Sam 3 10), or was torn away from the House of David (I Kings 14 8), but it would also be given back to the same House (12 26). This transference shows that the kingdom was a dynastic possession. Allegedly, Meribbaal said: "Today the house of Israel will give me back the kingdom of my father" (II Sam 16 3). It is also reported: "Jehoram stood on the kingdom of his father" (II Chron 21 4). From these examples we can learn that there was a claim that, to be legitimate, the transfer of the kingdom should be made from father to son.

Yet the term "kingdom" is seldom associated with the name of dynastic founders like the "House of Saul" (II Sam 3 1, etc.), the "descendants of David" (I Kings 11 39 Jer 33 22) or the "throne of David" (I Kings 2 12, etc.). Rather, it is generally connected with the names of reigning kings and implies their dominion (II Chron 12 1) or reign (Ezra 4 6); thus, the regnal year is indicated by the formula: "In the year x of the kingdom of king so-and-so", for instance, *bišenăṯ ha-ʾărbaʿîm lemălekûṯ dawîḏ* (I Chron 26 31); *bereʾšîṯ mămlœḵœṯ yehôyaqim* (Jer 27 1).

The term "kingdom", therefore, implies in the first place the royal authority of the reigning king. But when the dynastic problem makes itself felt, the dynastic character of the term emerges. This was the case in the above examples, that is, David against the House of Saul (II Sam 3 10), Meribbaal against the House of David (16 3), Jeroboam against the House of David (I Kings 12 26 14 8) and Jehoram towards his brothers (II Chron 21 4). In addition, the dynastic implication of the term is expressed both in Nathan's prophecy, where it is parallel to the "House" (II Sam 7 16), and in the prediction of the messianic king, who sits upon the "throne of David" and rules over "his kingdom" (Is 9 6).

So we may conclude that the terms *băyiṯ*, *zœră'*, *kisse'* and *mămlaḵā* are not synonymous but complement each other to express the existence of the royal dynasty. It is relevant that they are connected with the same verbs expressing "to make (firmly) exist", that is, *banā* or *'aśā* for *băyiṯ* (II Sam 7 21; cf. 7 11) and *kisse'* (Ps 89 5); *heqîm* for *zœră'* (II Sam 7 12) and *kisse'* (I Kings 9 5); *nœ'ᵉman* for *băyiṯ* and *mămlaḵā* (II Sam 7 16); and *naḵôn*, *heḵîn* and *kônen* for *băyiṯ* (7 26), *zœră'* (Ps 89 5), *kisse'* (II Sam 7 13. 16) and *mămlaḵā* (7 12). These four terms may be divided further into two categories: a) those for the royal lineage (*băyiṯ* and *zœră'*), and b) those for the royal authority (*kisse'* and *mămlaḵā*). The dynastic establishment is frequently expressed by a combination of the terms of both categories:
"I will raise up your *zœra'* (a) . . . and I will establish his *mămlaḵā* (b)" (II Sam 7 12); "And your *băyiṯ* (a) and your *mămlaḵā*(b) shall be made sure for ever" (7 16); "I will establish your *zœra'* (a) for ever, I will build your *kisse'* (b) for all generations" (Ps 89 5; cf. 89 30. 37).
This phenomenon corresponds to the basic structure of the royal-dynastic ideology, in which a royal dynasty is established when the royal authority (b) is succeeded by the same lineage (a).

It is worth noting that Yahweh's promise to establish a priestly dynasty in I Sam 2 35 is formulated in the same terminology, of course, except terms of the royal rule such as *kisse'* and *mămlaḵā*: "I will raise up (*wăhᵃqîmoṯî*) for myself a faithful priest who shall do according to what is in my heart and in my mind; and I will build him a sure house (*ûḇanîṯî lô băyiṯ nœ'ᵉman*) and he shall go in and out before my anointed for ever." Compare this with part of Nathan's prophecy: "I will raise up (*wăhᵃqîmoṯî*) your seed after you . . . he shall build a house for my name . . . your house . . . shall be made sure (*wᵉnœ'ᵉmăn bêṯḵa*) for ever before me (MT 'before you')" (II Sam 7 12aβ. 13a. 16a).

Now as to the terms representing the relationship between king and God. It has been recognized that Nathan's prophecy is a "covenant", despite the lack of the word *bᵉrîṯ* in it[127]. In fact, Yahweh's promise to David in the prophecy was referred to as a *bᵉrîṯ*, not only in its later development (I Kings 8 23 Is 55 3 Jer 33 20–21 Ps 89 4. 29. 35. 40 132 12 II Chron 6 14 7 18 13 5 21 7), but also, already, in the "last words of

[127] Cf. G. Widengren, King and Covenant, JSS 2 (1957), 22; J. Muilenburg, The Form and Structure of the Covenantal Formulations, VT 9 (1959), 356. R. de Vaux has made a comparison between Nathan's prophecy and the suzerain-vassal treaty in the ancient Near East (Le roi d'Israël, vassal de Yahvé [1964], in: Bible et Orient, 292ff. [ET King of Israel, Vassal of Yahweh, in: The Bible and the Ancient Near East, 157ff.]); cf. P. J. Calderone, Dynastic Oracle and Suzerainty Treaty – 2 Samuel 7, 8–16, 1966; D. J. McCarthy, Old Testament Covenant – A Survey of Current Opinions, 1972, 84f.

David" (II Sam 23 5), which appear to be derived from the Solomonic age[128]. Moreover, recent studies have shown that all the terms *'ab̲* and *ben*, *ḥæsæd̲*, *dab̲ar* and *ṭôb̲ā* belong to, or are associated with, the terminologies of treaty-covenant-making.

e) *'ab̲* and *ben* – In Nathan's prophecy, the relationship of *'ab̲* and *ben* between Yahweh and David's offspring is promised. The phrase formulating this relationship: "I will be his father and he shall be my son" (7 14) is regarded as an adoption formula in the ancient Near East (cf. Ex 4 22 Jer 3 4. 19 Ps 2 7 89 27f. I Chron 22 10 28 6)[129]. Although some scholars regard it as evidence of the mythological divine sonship of the Judaean kings[130], it appears that his adoptive relationship originated in a common metaphor in vassal treaties, in which the overlord is called *abu* "the father", while the vassal is granted *mārūtu* "sonship" (II Kings 16 7)[131]. The comparison between the unconditional promise to David's offspring (II Sam 7 14–15) and the vassal treaty between Tudhaliya IV, king of the Hittite Empire (1250–1220) and Ulmi-Tešub of ^{d}U-assa is instructive:

> "As for thee, Ulmi-Tešub, ... After thee thy son and thy grandson shall hold it, and no one shall take it from them. (But) if one of thy line sins (against Hatti), the king of Hatti will have him tried, and if he is condemned he will be sent to the king of Hatti where, if he merits it, he will be executed. Let no one take away Ulmi-Tešub's inheritance and country from his line to give to another line. Let it all remain the possession of Ulmi-Tešub and his line."[132]

---

[128] S. Mowinckel assumes the origin of the "last words of David" from the time of Hezekiah or Josiah (Die letzten Worte Davids. II Sam 23 1–7, ZAW 45 [1927], 57f.), while H. S. Nyberg maintains that the composition was related to the destruction of Samaria in 722 B. C. (Studien zum Religionskampf im Alten Testament, ARW 35 [1938], 384). E. Kutsch also holds that II Sam 23 5 was not earlier than the Deuteronomists (Verheißung und Gesetz. Untersuchungen zum sogenannten „Bund" im Alten Testament, 1973, 70f.). But A. R. Johnson contends against these arguments for the late date of the "last words of David" (Sacral Kingship in Ancient Israel, 1955, 15); cf. also O. Procksch, Die letzten Worte Davids, in: Kittel Festschrift, 1913, 112–125.

[129] See above p. 62 n. 30.

[130] J. Pedersen, Israel, III-IV 1940, 431f.; I. Engnell, Studies in Divine Kingship in the Ancient Near East, 1967², 175; about the critical remark on this assumption, see K.-H. Bernhardt, Das Problem der altorientalischen Königsideologie im Alten Testament, 1961, 74ff.

[131] See J. M. Munn-Rankin, Diplomacy in Western Asia in the Early Second Millennium B. C., Iraq 18 (1956), 76; cf. M. Weinfeld, The Covenant of Grant in the Old Testament and in the Ancient Near East, JAOS 90 (1970), 194.

[132] D. J. McCarthy, Treaty and Covenant, 1963, 183; KBo IV 10 obv. 4–11; cf. de Vaux, Le roi d'Israël, vassal de Yahvé, in: Bible et Orient, 293 (ET 158); Calderone, Dynastic Oracle and Suzerainty Treaty, 56.

In a later expansion this sonship became the primogeniture of the Davidic kings: "And I will make him the first-born" (Ps 89 28). It is likely that the custom of the father choosing a first-born stands behind the Davidic primogeniture[133]. This custom, attested in Mari, Nuzi, Alalakh, Ugarit and Israel (Gen 48 13–20; cf. Jer 31 9), was formulated either in an oath or in a contract[134].

f) *ḥæsæḏ* – F. C. Fensham[135] has argued that the *ḥæsæḏ* which the Kenites showed to the Israelites in the time of the Exodus (I Sam 15 6) is to be interpreted as a "covenant", which was in fact a "non-offensive alliance". Possibly, the same sort of *ḥæsæḏ* was made between Abraham and Abimelech (Gen 21 23) as well as between David and Nahash (II Sam 10 2 I Chron 19 2). But few think that the *ḥæsæḏ* in these passages implies a formal treaty[136]. It seems, however, that the servants of Benhadad, king of Damascus, refer to a treaty between the kings of Israel and the king of Damascus in their words: "The kings of the house of Israel are *mălḵê ḥæsæḏ*", that is, "the kings who are bound up (with us) by a treaty" (I Kings 20 31)[137].

On the other hand, N. Glueck[138] has defined that *ḥæsæḏ* is "a mutual relationship of rights and duties" and "constitutes the essence of a covenant." He has found this sort of *ḥæsæḏ* in the father-son relationship between Yahweh and David's descendants and has regarded it (Ps 89 50) as "the actual substance of the covenant"; therefore, *ḥăsḏê ḏawiḏ* (Is 55 3 II Chron 6 42), a later reference to Yahweh's promise to David, stands exactly for the "covenant of David"[139].

g) *daḇar* – This term, among other meanings, stands for a solemn promise. A promise made by Man to God is called *næḏær* "a vow" (Num 30 3)[140], but a sure promise made by God to a human being (Gen 15 1. 4

---

133 Cf. Weinfeld, JAOS 90, 193f.

134 See I. Mendelsohn, On the Preferential Status of the Eldest Son, BASOR 156 (1959), 38–40.

135 Did a Treaty between the Israelites and the Kenites exist?, BASOR 175 (1964), 51–54.

136 See N. Glueck, Das Wort *ḥesed*, 1927, 1. 10f. 16 (ET *Ḥesed* in the Bible, 1967, 35. 45. 50); H. J. Stoebe, in: Theologisches Handwörterbuch zum Alten Testament, ed. E. Jenni, I 1971, 605.

137 Cf. Gray, I & II Kings, 429.

138 Das Wort *ḥesed* 20 f. (ET 55); cf. Weinfeld, הברית והחסד – Bond and Grace – Covenantal Expressions in the Ancient World – A Common Heritage, Lešonenu 36 (1971/72), 91ff. (Hebrew).

139 Glueck, Das Wort *ḥesed*, 40ff. (ET 75ff.); cf. Eissfeldt, The Promise of Grace to David in Isaiah 55:1–5, in: Muilenburg Festschrift, 1962, 196–207; Caquot, Les "grâce de David". À propos d'Isaie 55/3b, Semitica 15 (1965), 45–59.

140 See J. Pedersen, Der Eid bei den Semiten in seinem Verhältnis zu Verwandten Erscheinungen sowie die Stellung des Eides im Islam, 1914, 119ff.; de Vaux, Les institutions, II 360f. (ET 465f.).

17 22–23 Deut 9 5 II Sam 7 21. 25. 28) can legitimately be considered a covenant[141]. In later times, Nathan's prophecy was frequently referred to as what Yahweh promised (I Kings 2 24 5 19 6 12 8 15–26 II Chron 1 9 6 4–17 23 3) and swore to David (Ps 89 4. 36. 50 132 11). G. E. Mendenhall[142] rightly gives a definition of "covenant" as "a solemn promise made binding by an oath".

h) *ṭôḇā* – W. L. Moran[143] has suggested that the Aramaic word טבת and its Akkadian cognates *ṭābūtu, ṭūbtu* and *ṭūbu* often refer to "a friendly relationship effected through treaty". Then, A. Malamat[144] has pointed out that the *ṭôḇā* which Yahweh promised David (II Sam 7 28) implies Yahweh's covenant with him. M. Weinfeld[145] has also remarked that the same covenant is meant by the *ṭôḇā* that Yahweh promised concerning David's future in Abigail's words (I Sam 25 30). It seems, in our opinion, that "*kᵊl hăṭṭôḇā* which Yahweh had done to David his servant and to his people Israel" (I Kings 8 66) also indicates the "covenant of David".

From the foregoing inquiries into eight key-words in II Sam 7 it transpires that Yahweh's promise (*daḇar*), which was made about the establishment of David's dynasty (*băyiṯ, zœră', kisse', mămlaḵā*) and about the special relationship between Yahweh and David's House (*'aḇ* and *ben*), is to be regarded as a covenant (*ḥœsœḏ, ṭôḇā*)[146]. G. E. Mendenhall[147] has shown that the Davidic covenant, together with the Abrahamic (Gen 15 17 1–14) and the Noachite (9 8–17) covenants, belongs to a promissory type of covenant, whose characteristic feature is found in an unconditional divine promise for the future in contrast to the obligatory nature of the Sinaitic covenant. M. Weinfeld[148] has pointed out that the promissory covenant resembles the royal grant, while the obligatory covenant is comparable to the vassal treaty. Since a sharp contrast has become clear between the Sinaitic and the Abrahamic-Davidic covenants in both style and character, the question has been posed about the relationship between them. As for the origin of

---

[141] Cf. McCarthy, Old Testament Covenant, 81.

[142] In: The Interpreter's Dictionary of the Bible, I 1962, 714.

[143] A Note on the Treaty Terminology of the Sefîre Stelas, JNES 22 (1963), 173–176.

[144] Organs of Statecraft in the Israelite Monarchy (1965), in: BAR 3, 1970, 197; cf. D. R. Hillers, Covenant. The History of a Biblical Idea, 1969, 113.

[145] King-People Relationship in the Light of I Kings 12:7, Lešonenu 36 (1970/71), 10ff. (Hebrew).

[146] H. Gottlieb finds a similar covenantal relationship between El and Keret, king of Ugarit, in the Canaanite epic (El und Krt – Jahwe und David, VT 24 [1974], 159–167).

[147] Covenant Forms in Israelite Tradition (1954), in: BAR 3, 1970, 25–53; idem, in: The Interpreter's Dictionary of the Bible, I 714–723.

[148] JAOS 90, 184–203.

the two covenants, it has been suggested that the tradition of the Sinaitic covenant stemmed from the northern tribes, whereas the Abrahamic-Davidic covenants had their origin in the south[149]. L. Rost[150] has maintained that both covenantal traditions continued alongside each other in the north and in the south until their fusion during the Deuteronomic reform under Josiah. Although this thesis was criticized as too simple a separation of the traditions[151], scholars have generally remarked that there always existed a certain degree of tension between them[152]. It seems, however, that the Sinaitic and the Davidic covenants were not in opposition to each other, at least for those who promulgated the Davidic one.

When David was elevated to the throne over Israel by the elders of Israel, he made a covenant with them (II Sam 5 3). Although the details of it are unknown to us, we may assume that it was bilateral[153]. From the political point of view, the people of Israel were the weaker partner, but David had reason to make his identification with "greater Israel" conspicuous. Therefore, the rights and duties of both parties must have been regulated in the covenant. On the one hand, the people of Israel swore allegiance to the House of David. Manifestly, on the basis of this covenant, a Judaean historian saw the separation of the northern tribes from the Davidic rule as their rebellion (*wayyipšeʿû*) against the House of David (I Kings 12 19 II Chron 10 19; cf. 13 5–7)[154]. On the other hand,

---

149 See M. Newman, The People of the Covenant, 1962; R. E. Clements, Abraham and David, 1967, 47ff.; cf. McCarthy, Old Testament Covenant, 73ff. 82ff.

150 Sinaibund und Davidsbund, ThLZ 72 (1947), 129–234.

151 Noth, Gott, König, Volk im Alten Testament, in: Gesammelte Studien, I 224f. (ET 174); A. H. J. Gunneweg, Sinaibund und Davidsbund, VT 10 (1960), 335–341; cf. Clements, Prophecy and Covenant, 1965, 62ff.

152 Alt, Das Königtum in den Reichen Israel und Judah (1951), in: Kleine Schriften, II 132f. (ET The Monarchy in the Kingdoms of Israel and Judah, in: Essays, 256f.); Mendenhall, in: BAR 3, 46ff.; M. Sekine, Davidsbund und Sinaibund bei Jeremia, VT 9 (1959), 47–57; Bright, A History of Israel, 221; McCarthy, Old Testament Covenant, 58.

153 G. Fohrer assumes that it was a unilateral covenant imposed by David (Der Vertrag zwischen König und Volk in Israel [1959], in: Studien zur alttestamentlichen Theologie und Geschichte, 1969, 331f.). But A. Malamat argues that the Davidic kings could begin their rule over the northern tribes only upon a covenantal agreement between themselves and their future subject (in: BAR 3, 165); cf. also B. Mazar, The Kingship in Israel, in: Types of Leadership in the Biblical Period, 1973, 32f. (Hebrew).

154 Tadmor demonstrates that the term *pašoʿa* is equevalent to the Akkadian *ḫaṭû* in the sense "denoting the violation of a loyalty-oath on the part of a vassal" ("The People" and the Kingship in Ancient Israel: The Role of Political Institutions in the Biblical Period, JWH 11 [1968], 61f.).

the king's duties were prescribed, presumably, in something like the "law of the king" (Deut 17 14–20), in which the House of David expressed its fidelity to Yahweh, the national God of Israel, to whom the people of Israel had been bound by the Sinaitic covenant. In so doing, the House of David was involved in a Yahweh-Israel relationship. We may assume that, at this juncture, it became a matter of grave concern for the House of David how to deal with the Sinaitic covenant. For had the situation been left as it was, Davidic authority over Israel would have been precarious from the ideological point of view, since the people of Israel had had a covenant with Yahweh over which the House of David had no power of control. This ideological problem was solved by Nathan's prophecy, maintaining that, since Yahweh made a new covenant with David, the old Sinaitic covenant could be valid, from now on, only in accordance with the new one. Thus a decisive change took place in the people's relation to Yahweh. While they were directly connected with Yahweh in the Sinaitic covenant (Ex 19 3–6 24 3–11), the Davidic kings now stood between them and Yahweh as mediators[155].

This unique triple relationship between Yahweh, the House of David and the people of Israel is expressed in II Sam 7 as follows: Yahweh is God, who "brought up the people of Israel from Egypt" (v. 6), who "went to redeem Israel to be his people" (v. 23) and who "became their God" (v. 24). Needless to say, this is a restatement of the Exodus tradition with which the Sinaitic covenant is closely connected. But the main theme of the chapter is the manifesto that the covenant of David realized the ideal of the Sinaitic covenant. Entirely thanks to David, the people of Israel finally received a stable place to live (v. 10) and eternal peace (v. 11). Only through the establishment of the House of David, the name of "Yahweh *ṣᵉḇa'ôṯ*, God over Israel will be magnified for ever" (v. 26). Yahweh's sonship was now given to the descendants of David (v. 14) instead of to the people of Israel (Ex 4 22)[156].

In the Davidic covenant, Yahweh is addressed as "David's lord" (II Sam 7 18–20. 28. 29), and David is called "Yahweh's servant" (7 5. 8. 19–21. 26–29). R. de Vaux[157] has suggested that this lord-servant relationship is the suzerain-vassal relationship. Analogically speaking, his

---

[155] Cf. J. Scharbert, Heilsmittler im Alten Testament und im Alten Orient, 1964, 130ff.; Poulssen, König und Tempel, 43f.; Seybold, Das davidische Königtum im Zeugnis der Propheten, 34. 43.

[156] On Israel's sonship of Yahweh, see McCarthy, Notes on the Love of God in Deuteronomy and the Father-Son Relationship between Yahweh and Israel, CBQ 27 (1965), 144–147.

[157] Le roi d'Israël, vassal de Yahvé, in: Bible et Orient, 287–301 (ET 152–166); cf. Seybold, Das davidische Königtum im Zeugnis der Propheten, 40ff.

suggestion seems right, but in reality it is the relationship between a tutelary deity and his dynasty. Barrakib, king of Y'dy-Sam'al, called both Rakibel and Tiglath-Pileser מראי "my lord"[158]. From other inscriptions from Y'dy-Sam'al, we learn that Rakibel was the tutelary deity of the dynasty called בעל בת[159] or בעל בית[160] "the lord of the house", אלהי בית אבי "the god of my father's house"[161], and אלהי אבה "the god of his father"[162]. B. Landsberger[163] has made it clear that בעל צמד אש לגבר "Baal-Ṣamad who belongs to Gabbar", and בעל חמן אש לבמה "Baal-Hamman who belongs to BMH"[164] were the tutelary deities of Gabbar and BMH, respectively; and this points to dynastic changes from Gabbar to BMH and from BMH to Hayya, who was Kilamuwa's father and the founder of the dynasty to which Barrakib belonged (cf. also his mention of "Kilamuwa's palace", KAI § 216 17–18). When Rakibel is called "the god of my father's house" or "the god of his father", the implication of "the father" or "the father's house" is undoubtedly dynastic[165]. Evidently, each dynasty had its own patron deity. Likewise, the patron deity of the dynasty of Qatna was called *ilim ša abīja* "the god of my father"[166], *ilī*^{meš} *ša abi* "the god(s) of the father"[167], *ilī*^{meš} *šarri* "the god(s) of the king"[168] and ^{d}*Šamaš il abīja* "Šamaš, the god of my father"[169].

We will not deal here with the vexed problem of "the god of the father"[170]. We only observe that each royal dynasty in Syria-Palestine

---

[158] KAI § 216 5–7.

[159] KAI § 24 16.

[160] KAI § 215 22.

[161] KAI § 217 3.

[162] KAI § 214 29.

[163] Sam'al, 1948, 48f.

[164] KAI § 24 15–16.

[165] Cf. H. Donner, apud W. Röllig, KAI II 222; Cross, Canaanite Myth, 10.

[166] ARM V § 20 16.

[167] J. Bottéro, Les inventaires de Qatna, RA 43 (1949), 178 II 43; cf. II 44.

[168] Ibid. 174 II 1. 176 II 31.

[169] EA § 55 53. 56. 59. 63. About the "god of the king" called the "god of the father" in Qatna, see Bottéro, RA 43, 33ff.

[170] Alt has advanced the theory that each of the patriarchs was a founder of the cult of a nameless patron deity called the "god of X" who was worshipped by his descendants (Der Gott der Väter [1929], in: Kleine Schriften, I 1953, 1–78 [ET The God of the Fathers, in: Essays, 3–77]). Against this thesis, J. Lewy has argued that the Amorites in the Assyrian colonies in the early second millennium B. C. called a family's patron deity by the formula of his proper name and the "god of the father" (Les textes paléo-assyriens et l'Ancien Testament, RHR 110 [1934], 29–65). For the further discussions, see M. Haran, The Religion of the Patriarchs, in: WHJP, II 1970, 299ff.; de Vaux, Histoire ancienne d'Israël, 1971, 424ff.; Cross, Canaanite

had its own tutelary deity or deities called "the god(s) of the father" or "the god of the father's house". To this category belong *ilāni*^{meš} *bīt abīšu* "the gods of his father's house" of the king of Ashkelon, whom Sennacherib deported to Assyria[171]. But we are not sure whether *bēl Ḫa[labi] u ilim ša abī[ka]* "Lord of Aleppo and the god of your father" mentioned in a Mari letter[172] was a dynastic tutelary deity. It seems that this deity should rather be compared with the "God of the Fathers" of the Hebrew patriarchs[173]. From the above analysis it is patent that, when Yahweh was called "God of David your/his father" (II Kings 20 5 = Is 38 5 I Chron 28 9 II Chron 17 3–4 21 12 34 3; cf. I Kings 15 3), the implication was clearly Yahweh as the tutelary God of the dynasty of David. It seems that the same relationship is expressed by the words "My house is with God" in the "last words of David" (II Sam 23 5). By establishing the special relationship with Yahweh, the national God of Israel, the House of David firmly incorporated the Davidic monarchy into the ancient tradition of Israel[174].

This threefold relationship between Yahweh, the House of David and the people of Israel was confirmed by a twofold covenant which the House of David made with Yahweh on the one side and with the people on the other. It is true that neither David nor Solomon actually made such a double covenant. But it is likely that, when the Davidic covenant was established, the one made between David and the people at Hebron (II Sam 5 3; cf. 2 4) was re-interpreted in the new framework of the double covenant. Without this assumption, it is extremely difficult to find the origin of the double covenant which Jehoiada made at the restoration of the dynasty of David (II Kings 11 17). Opinions are divided on the parties between whom Jehoiada made the covenant. G. von Rad[175] and M. Noth[176] have argued for a single covenant

---

Myth, 3ff.; H. Vorländer, Mein Gott. Die Vorstellungen vom persönlichen Gott im Alten Orient und im Alten Testament, 1975.

[171] D. D. Luckenbill, The Annals of Sennacherib, 1924, 30 II 62.

[172] ARM X § 156 10–11; cf. P. Artzi & A. Malamat, The Correspondence of Šibtu, Queen of Mari in *ARM* X, Or NS 40 (1971), 89 n. 37.

[173] See Malamat, BA 34, 20.

[174] H. Vorländer maintains that Yahweh stood to the House of David in the relationship of a personal patron deity (Mein Gott 232ff.). But it seems problematic to deal, as he does, with the relationship between a king and his tutelary god on a level with the relationship between a private person and his patron deity. Mazar has underlined that in every national kingdoms established in the 11th century B. C. the king ruled over his kingdom by the grace of the national god (in: Types of Leadership in the Biblical Period 30f. [Hebrew]).

[175] Deuteronomiumstudien (1948), in: Gesammelte Studien, II 1973, 146 (ET Studies in Deuteronomy, 1953, 63f.); cf. Kutsch, Verheißung und Gesetz, 164.

[176] Das alttestamentliche Bundschließen im Lichte eines Mari-Textes (1955), in:

either between Yahweh on the one side and the king and the people on the other, or between the king and the people only. According to D. J. McCarthy[177], the covenant was twofold, but the twofold relations existed between God and the people on the one hand and between the king and the people on the other. J. Gray and B. Mazar maintained that it was a threefold covenant, that is, between God and the king, between God and the people and between the king and the people[178]. It is most plausible, however, that, as. K. Baltzer[179] and A. Malamat[180] have held, Jehoiada made a double covenant between Yahweh and the king on the one side and between the king and the people on the other. It seems to me that "a covenant between Yahweh and the king and the people, that they should be the people of Yahweh" (11 17a), in effect, implies the Davidic covenant, in which a Davidic king serves as mediator between Yahweh and the people.

It is far from easy to find any parallel example for this sort of double covenant in the ancient Near East. However, J. A. Montgomery[181] has mentioned a triple relationship between the god, the king and the nation in a constitution for the State of Kataban written in South Arabic, while K. Baltzer[182] has pointed out that the investiture of a Hittite vassal involved his oath to the overlord on the one side and the oath of the "land", namely, the people of the vassal state, to the vassal himself on the other. As another example, we may mention an interesting ritual of the covenant which Esarhaddon, king of Assyria, made. (The following Akkadian transliteration is quoted from K. Deller & S. Parpola, Neuassyrische Prophetensprüche, [unpublished manuscript], see above p. 90)[183].

ṭup-pi a-de-e an-ni-u šá ^{d}*Aš+šur ina* UGU *ḫa-ʾu-u-ti ina* IGI LUGAL *e-rab* Ì DÙG.GA *i-za-ar-ri-qu* UDU.SISKUR^{meš} *ep-pu-šú* ŠIM$^{ḫi.a}$ *il-lu-ku a-na* IGI LUGAL *i-sa-as-si-u*

a-bat ^{d}15 *šá* ^{uru}*Arba-ìl a-na* ^{I}*Aš+šur*-PAP-AŠ MAN KUR *Aš+šur* DINGIR^{meš} AD^{me}*-ja* ⌜ŠEŠ^{me}*-ja*⌝ ⌜*ak*⌝*-an-ni ina* ŠÀ *a-d[e-e*. . . (four lines are missing).

A^{meš} *zar-za-ri ta-si-qi-šú-*⌜*nu*⌝ DUG *ma-si-tú ša* 1 BÁN A^{meš} *zar-za-ri tu-um-ta-al-*

Gesammelte Studien, I 151f. (ET Old Testament Covenant-Making in the Light of a Text from Mari, in: Essays, 115f.).

177 Treaty and Covenant 142f. n. 4.

178 Gray, I & II Kings, 579f.; Mazar, in: Types of Leadership in the Biblical Period, 32 (Hebrew).

179 Das Bundesformular, 1960, 85ff. (ET The Covenant Formulary in Old Testament, Jewish, and Early Christian Writings, 1971, 78ff.).

180 In: BAR 3, 166.

181 The Books of Kings 423.

182 Das Bundesformular 85ff. (ET 78ff.).

183 Craig, Assyrian and Babylonian Religious Texts, I 23f. II 27–III 14'; cf. CAD A 1 132f.; CAD Ṣ 115.

li ta-at-ta-an-na-šú-nu ma-a ta-qab-bi-a ina ŠÀ-*ku-nu ma-a* d15 *PA-aq-tú ši-i ma-a tal-la-ka ina* URUmeš *-ku-nu na-gi-a-ni-ku-nu* NINDAmeš *ta-ka-la ta-maš-ši-a a-de-e an-nu-ti ma-a* TA ŠÀ Ameš *an-nu-ti ta-šat-ti-a ta-ḫa-sa-sa-ni ta-na-ṣa-ra a-de-e an-nu-ti ša ina* UGU I*Aš+šur*-PAP-AŠ *áš-kun-u-ni*

"This tablet of the covenant of Aššur enters upon (a kind of cloth) to the king. They sprinkle sweet oil, make sacrifices, burn incense and read it to the king. The word of Ištar of Arbela to Esarhaddon, king of Assyria.

The gods of my fathers and my brothers here in the covenant . . .

You gave them water of a jar. You have filled a cup of 1 *seah* with water from a jar and given it to them.

You will say in your mind: 'Ištar is a caretaker.'

You will go to your towns and your districts and you will eat bread. Then, you will forget this covenant. But whenever you will drink this water, you will remember and will keep this covenant which I established in favour of Esarhaddon."

Although we cannot understand all the details of the ritual, it is possible to interpret it as follows: this covenant was made "in favour of Esarhaddon", most probably to secure his throne, or, perhaps, as his vassal-treaty[184], to ensure the dynastic succession. It seems that "the covenant of Aššur", which was brought in and read to the king, was one between the god Aššur and the king[185]. Then, it appears that "the gods of my fathers and my brothers", perhaps the patron deities of the dynasty, were called as witnesses to the other covenant-making, for which Ištar acted as mediator. This other covenant was made between the king and the people. At the ceremony, the king gave them a cup of water from a jar. While drinking it, they pledged allegiance to the king. After going back to their home towns, they had to perform the ceremony repeatedly to renew the covenant by drinking "this water".

As mentioned, the similarity between the Davidic and the Abrahamic covenants is remarkable in style as well as in content. Yahweh promised the unconditional prosperity of their descendants both to the patriarch and to the king. It has been suggested that the Abrahamic covenant influenced the formation of the Davidic, or *vice versa*[186]. Al-

184 ANET 534–541. About *adê*, see I. J. Gelb, BiOr 19 (1962), 161–162; Tadmor, JWH 11, 61f.

185 Our interpretation has some difficulty, since the covenant between god Aššur and the Assyrian kings has not been attested in any other inscriptions; but it is worth mentioning that we do have *šá a-di-e* LUGAL DINGIR.MEŠ *el*[*i* . . . "that the covenant of the king of the gods . . ." in K 4730 (Tadmor, The "Sin of Sargon", EI 5 [1958], 155 obv. 19); in spite of the broken context, it is likely that this is the *adê* which had been established between the "king of the gods" (i. e. Aššur) and Sargon II but was violated by the king. Prof. H. Tadmor informed me that the interpretation of this passage would be discussed in the forthcoming article by B. Landsberger & H. Tadmor, Sargon's Sin and Sennacherib's Testament, (see JCS 26 [1974], 192 no. 114).

186 Mendenhall holds that "in the time of David, the tradition of the covenant with

though the originality of the Abrahamic covenant seems certain[187], the land promised to Abraham in all likelihood reflects the boundaries of the Davidic empire (Gen 15 18–21). Moreover, the future kings promised to Abraham as his descendants (17 6) indicate, most probably, the dynasty of David[188]. It is conceivable, therefore, that the present shape of the Abrahamic covenant was moulded in the Davidic-Solomonic period by re-interpreting the ancient tradition of the patriarch to show that, "in David, the promise to the patriarchs is fulfilled, and renewed"[189]. Needless to say, this was another effort to promote the legitimation of Davidic rule over Israel.

Naturally, then, the ideology of the Davidic covenant was ultimately rejected by the northern tribes. When they dissolved the covenant with the House of David, Jeroboam, whom they made king over Israel, declared that "God who brought up Israel out of the land of Egypt"[190] should be worshipped in the newly established royal sanctuaries at Bethel and Dan (I Kings 12 28f.). The course of events compelled Jeroboam to return to the old Sinaitic covenant. But his failure to replace the Davidic covenant by one of his own became an ideological weakness militating against the establishment of stable dynastic rule in the Northern Kingdom.

Abraham became the pattern of a covenant between Yahweh and David" (in: BAR 3, 47). According to Newman, Yahweh's covenant with the priestly dynasty of Aaron centred in Hebron was the model of the Davidic covenant (The People of the Covenant 160ff.). Clements also assumes that David was associated with the Abrahamic tradition while he was still in Hebron (Abraham and David 56ff.). On the other hand, the dependence of the Abrahamic covenant on the Davidic covenant is maintained by Caquot, L'alliance avec Abram (Genèse 15), Semitica 12 (1962), 51–66; cf. H. Cazelles, Connexions et structure de Gen. XV, RB 69 (1962), 321–349.

[187] Cf. von Rad, Das erste Buch Mose. Genesis, 1972[9], 146f. (ET Genesis, 1961, 184f.).

[188] Cf. Mendenhall, in: The Interpreter's Dictionary of the Bible, I 718; Clements, Abraham and David, 55ff.; Mazar, The Historical Background of the Book of Genesis, JNES 28 (1969), 75.

[189] Mendenhall, in: The Interpreter's Dictionary of the Bible, I 718.

[190] The MT: "Behold, thy *gods*, O Israel, who *brought* thee *up* (*hæʿælûḵa*) . . .", clearly underwent a polemical distortion, see Montgomery & Gehman, The Books of Kings, 255; Gray, I & II Kings, 315f.; Noth, Könige, I 282f. Some scholars interpret the plural verb here as the plural of excellence with "Elohim", see de Vaux, Le schisme religieux de Jéroboam Ier (1943), in: Bible et Orient, 154 (ET The Religious Schism of Jeroboam I, in: The Bible and the Ancient Near East, 100); Soggin, Das Königtum in Israel, 1967, 96. But Donner argues that we can find here a Deuteronomic polemic against Yahweh of Bethel and Yahweh of Dan („Hier sind deine Götter, Israel!", in: K. Elliger Festschrift, 1973, 45–50).

Chapter 6: The House of David and Jerusalem

A. THE CAPTURE OF JERUSALEM

As we have demonstrated in the previous chapter, the royal-dynastic ideology of the House of David was crystallized in Jerusalem in the days of David and Solomon. In the formation of this ideology, Jerusalem figured centrally. It was not merely the place where the dynasty was established but one of the basic elements of Davidic ideology. The indivisible relation of the House of David to Jerusalem, which was created in this period, is one of the most characteristic features of the dynasty.

Jerusalem had been the most important political point in the central mountains of southern Palestine since the beginning of the second millennium B. C. Archaeological explorations have shown that the south-eastern spur of Jerusalem, generally accepted as the site of the City of David, was occupied as early as the third millennium B. C. The information found in the Execration texts (18th century B. C.) and in the El-Amarna letters (14th century B. C.), together with the archaeological finds, shows that Jerusalem was a flourishing city-state in the Judaean hills from the 19th to the 14th century B. C.[1], but its significance declined during the period of turmoil caused by the conquest and settlement of the Israelite tribes in the last centuries of the same millennium. From biblical sources we can surmise that Jerusalem fell from power when Adonizedek, its king and leader of the Amorite coalition in the Judaean hills and in the southern and eastern Shephelah, was defeated by Joshua (Josh 10; cf. Judg 1 5–7). The Jebusites apparently came from elsewhere and took possession of Jerusalem after the tribe of Judah had destroyed it and left it in ruins (Judg 1 8)[2]. Mainly owing to its natural impregnability, Jebusite Jerusalem remained independent until the coming of David. It is listed as one of the unconquered Canaanite cities (Judg 1 21; cf. Josh 15 63)[3].

---

[1] See B. Maisler (Mazar), Das vordavidische Jerusalem, JPOS 10 (1930), 181–191; idem, in: EncBib, III 1958, 795f. (Hebrew); Y. Aharoni, From Shiloh to Jerusalem, in: Jerusalem through the Ages, 1968, 85ff. (Hebrew).

[2] Cf. Maisler (Mazar), JPOS 10, 184ff.; Aharoni, The Land of the Bible, 1966, 195ff.

[3] A. Alt has pointed out that Jerusalem, together with other Canaanite city-states like

Moreover, its position held no threat and its value was not mighty enough for the Israelite tribes. Although it was situated on the major route along the north-south mountain ridge between Shechem and Hebron, the Jebusites had little control over that highway in the pre-monarchical period (Judg 19 10–12). The absence of any mention of Jerusalem in the days of Samuel and Saul also testifies to its unimpressive position in that period[4].

It was David who changed this humble city-state into the mightiest city in Palestine. A. Alt[5] has rightly remarked that David's capture of Jerusalem (II Sam 5 6–9 I Chron 11 4–8) was not a mere military operation but a highly political action in the context of the formation of his empire. It was an attempt to build a new capital, from which he would exercise kingship over the double kingdoms of Judah and Israel. On the one hand, it stood on the border between the northern and the southern tribes. On the other, it had been unrelated to any tribe of Israel until David captured it[6]. This twofold neutrality fitted the capital of the Davidic kingdom, based, as that kingdom was, on the balance of power between north and south[7]. We may compare this conjuncture with the foundation by Menes, first king of the First dynasty of Egypt (c. 3100 B. C.), of the White Wall, later called Memphis, as his capital at the junction of Upper and Lower Egypt, which were, for the first time, united under him[8]. Y. Aharoni[9] has argued that the same political considerations were instrumental in Saul's choice of Gibeah of Saul for his capital, because it stood near the border between the northern and the southern tribes, over whom he

---

Gezer and Aijalon, formed the dividing line between the northern tribes and the tribe of Judah (Die Landnahme der Israeliten in Palästina [1925], in: Kleine Schriften, I 1953, 123 [ET The Settlement of the Israelites in Palestine, in: Essays on Old Testament History and Religion, 1966, 167]).

[4] Cf. Alt, Jerusalems Aufstieg (1925), in: Kleine Schriften, III 1959, 252f.; Aharoni, in: Jerusalem through the Ages, 93f. (Hebrew).

[5] Jerusalems Aufstieg, in: Kleine Schriften, III 253.

[6] According to the boundary description of the tribes (Josh 15 8 18 16) and the town list (18 28), Jerusalem belonged to the tribe of Benjamin, but Benjamin was unable to capture it (Judg 1 21). About the claim of Judah to Jerusalem (Josh 15 63), see Z. Kallai-Kleinman, Jerusalem – in Judah or in Benjamin?, in: Judah and Jerusalem, 1957, 34–36 (Hebrew).

[7] Cf. Alt, Jerusalems Aufstieg, in: Kleine Schriften, III 253f.; idem, Die Staatenbildung der Israeliten in Palästina (1930), in: Kleine Schriften, II 1953, 45 (ET The Formation of the Israelite State in Palestine, in: Essays, 217); M. Noth, Geschichte Israels, 1954², 175 (ET The History of Israel, 1960², 190).

[8] See I. E. S. Edwards, The Early Dynastic Period in Egypt, CAH I ch. XI, 1964, 11f.

[9] In: Jerusalem through the Ages, 93 (Hebrew).

exercised his kingship. But if Gibeah of Saul was his home town, as is generally agreed (I Sam 10 5. 26 11 4)[10], it corresponds rather to David's Bethlehem (16 1–5. 18 17 12. 15. 58 20 6. 28–29, etc.; cf. Lk 2 3–4) than to Jerusalem. Moreover, we are dubious of the administrative establishment of Saul's rule over the southern tribes (see above p. 66–67).

A. Alt[11] has maintained that Jerusalem owed its ascendancy not to natural conditions but exclusively to David's personal decision, based on the above-mentioned political considerations. The thesis has been widely accepted[12]. Nevertheless, it seems that other material aspects were also involved. Although it was, as saw, a minor city-state on the eve of David's capture of it, Jerusalem had had its days of glory up to the El-Amarna period[13]. In other words, its potentialities as a political metropolis were simply latent before David made himself its master. It is likely that he took account of all its advantageous features in planning the site and construction of his future capital, and first of all, of its strategic values. Though straddling the vital north-south route along the backbone of Palestine, Jerusalem was not well placed for the east-west routes connecting the Judaean hills with the coastal plain and the Jordan valley, which ran some ten kilometres either north or south of it[14]. It is improbable, however, that this geographical setting, as is often suggested, was a disadvantage for Jerusalem as the natural political focus of this area[15]. On the contrary, it is precisely because of it that Jerusalem was chosen by the pre-Davidic rulers as well as by David to be their royal residence. The short distance from Jerusalem to the road junctions did not prevent its rulers from controlling the cross-

---

[10] See Mazar, in: EncBib, II 1954, 413 (Hebrew); Aharoni, The Land of the Bible, 254. But in the genealogical lists in I Chron 8 29–40 9 35–44, the House of Saul is connected with Gibeon, see A. Demsky, The Genealogy of Gibeon (I Chronicles 9:35–44): Biblical and Epigraphic Considerations, BASOR 202 (1971), 16–23.

[11] Jerusalems Aufstieg, in: Kleine Schriften, III 243ff.

[12] For instance, Noth, Geschichte, 175 (ET 190); K.-H. Bernhardt, Das Problem der altorientalischen Königsideologie im Alten Testament, 1961, 101f.; G. Fohrer, Zion-Jerusalem im Alten Testament (1964), in: Studien zur alttestamentlichen Theologie und Geschichte (1949–1966), 1969, 205f. (ET in: Theological Dictionary of the New Testament, VII 1971, 300f.).

[13] See Maisler (Mazar), JPOS 10, 181ff.; Aharoni, in: Jerusalem through the Ages, 85ff. (Hebrew); cf. F. Stolz, Strukturen und Figuren im Kult von Jerusalem, 1970, 7.

[14] Y. Karmon has made it clear that the natural ganglion of the Judaean road network was Gibeon and the another focus was Bethlehem (Topographical Influences on the Judaean Roads, in: Judah and Jerusalem, 1957, 144–150 [Hebrew]).

[15] Against Alt, Jerusalems Aufstieg, in: Kleine Schriften, III 243ff.; Noth, Geschichte, 175 (ET 190); cf. D. R. Ap-Thomas, in: Archaeology and Old Testament Study, ed. D. W. Thomas, 1967, 278.

roads[16]. The kingdom of Jerusalem in the 14th century B. C. had governance over Beth-horon, a key-point at the entrance to the "way of Beth-horon", which was the main ascent from the coastal plain to the central mountains[17]. In the 13th century, it seems, Adonizedek, king of Jerusalem, held sway over Gibeon, situate on another key-point of the same route (Josh 10 1–5)[18]. At the same time, owing to its distance from the cross-roads, Jerusalem was sheltered from the direct attack of enemies coming up from the coastal plain. For instance, Shishak, king of Egypt (945–925), came up against Jerusalem by way of Beth-horon and Beth-shemesh up to Gibeon; but, after agreeing to accept a heavy tribute from the king of Judah in one of the cities to the west or north of Jerusalem, such as Aijalon or Gibeon, he continued his campaign to the north without assaulting Jerusalem[19]. This strategic consideration can also be discerned in Omri's choice of a royal residence of Samaria, which lies a few kilometres north-west of the principal road junction in central Palestine, where Shechem stands. It is possible, therefore, as B. Mazar[20] has suggested, that David was quick to exploit the vital geography of Zion for undertaking military operations against Ishbaal.

Secondly, David's capture of Jerusalem was motivated by his plan to set up the City of David. We will examine the implications of the name and nature of the City in the next section of this chapter. Thirdly, it is likely that the elevation of Jerusalem to be the pivot of the national-religious tradition of Israel was envisaged from the start. It is true that all the Yahwistic traditions of Jerusalem were created by David, who brought in the Ark of Yahweh, and by Solomon, builder of the temple for Yahweh there. Pre-Davidic Jerusalem, it is plain, had nothing to do with Yahwism except in mysterious traditions of Abraham (Gen 14 18–20 22 1–14). But it is hardly plausible that David and Solomon could change Jerusalem into the holiest city in Israel solely by their own initiative and actions. In the ancient Near East, the choice of holy places was not left to human arbitrariness but was determined by a manifestation of the god's presence, generally at a certain site with special natural conditions, such as springs, sacred trees, mountains, and

[16] Cf. Karmon, in: Judah and Jerusalem, 150 (Hebrew).

[17] See Z. Kallai & H. Tadmor, Bīt Ninurta = Beth Horon – On the History of the Kingdom of Jerusalem in the Amarna Period, EI 9 (1969), 138–147 (Hebrew).

[18] Cf. Mazar, Jerusalem before the Reign of David, in: Sepher Yerushalayim, ed. M. Avi-Yonah, 1956, 107 (Hebrew).

[19] See Mazar, The Campaign of Pharaoh Shishak to Palestine, SVT 4 (1957), 61; Aharoni, The Land of the Bible, 283ff.

[20] David's Reign in Hebron and the Conquest of Jerusalem, in: Silver Festschrift, 1963, 235–244.

so forth[21]. It is thus legitimate to suppose that David intended to utilize the ancient religious traditions of Jerusalem for the creation of the new Yahwistic traditions in the city. This subject will be discussed in detail in section C of this chapter.

B. THE CITY OF DAVID

After David took the city-fortress of Jebusite Jerusalem, called the "stronghold of Zion" (II Sam 5 7 I Chron 11 5), it was renamed the "City of David" (II Sam 5 9; cf. 5 7 I Chron 11 5. 7). Archaeologists have identified it with the eastern spur projecting southwards from the Old City of today[22]. Both in Israel and in the ancient Near East, places were renamed to mark a change of ownership[23], and there is no doubt that the change of ownership coincided with David's renaming of the stronghold of Zion. The question is what sort of ownership was established.

In the period of the Israelite conquest, several cities were renamed by the conquerors, for instance, Laish became Dan (Judg 18 29; cf. Josh 19 47)[24], Havvoth-ham[25] became Havvoth-jair (Num 32 41; cf. Deut 3 14 Josh 13 30 Judg 10 4), and Kenath became Nabah (Num 32 42). Since these new names are made out of the eponyms of a tribe or clan, the renaming shows that ownership was established there by the tribe or clan in question (cf. also Gen 4 17). These examples, to be sure, are irrelevant in illustrating the nature of ownership of the City of David. A pertinent example must be sought among cities in whose designation a king's name is a constituent. Only three such cities in biblical sources can be considered: they are Raamses (Ex 1 11), the City of Sihon, that is, Heshbon (Num 21 26–28) and Gibeah of Saul, that is, Gibeah of Benjamin (Gibeah of Benjamin: Judg 19 14 20 4 I Sam 13 2. 15 14 16 II Sam 23 29 I Chron 11 31; Gibeah of Saul: I Sam 11 4 15 34 II Sam 21 6 Is

---

[21] See R. de Vaux, Les institutions de l'Ancien Testament, II 1960, 95ff. (ET Ancient Israel, 1961, 276ff.).

[22] See J. Simons, Jerusalem in the Old Testament, 1952, 35ff.; K. Kenyon, Excavations in Jerusalem, 1965, PEQ 98 (1966), 77f.

[23] See O. Eissfeldt, Renaming in the Old Testament, in: D. W. Thomas Festschrift, 1968, 71f.; cf. Alt, Ägyptische Tempel in Palästina und die Landnahme der Philister (1944), in: Kleine Schriften, I 223.

[24] On the renaming of places in the period of the conquest, see A. Malamat, The Danite Migration and the Israelite Exodus-Conquest: A Biblical Narrative Pattern, Bib 51 (1970), 14f.

[25] The emendation of *ḥăwwoṭehæm* into Havvoth-ham was suggested by A. Bergman (Biran), The Israelite Occupation of Eastern Palestine in the Light of Territorial History, JAOS 54 (1934), 176.

10 29). Biblical Raamses was Per-Ramses Meri-Amon, built by Ramses II (1290–1224) to dwell in on the site of the ancient Hyksos city of Avaris in the north-eastern Delta[26], but, apart from the long continuity of both as dynastic residences, there was little resemblance between Per-Ramses and the City of David.

As for Heshbon and Gibeah of Benjamin, we may postulate a situation similar to the change of name from the stronghold of Zion to the City of David. It seems that the beginning of the ancient poem of the ballad singers (Num 21 27b) recounts how Heshbon was destroyed when seized by Sihon but rebuilt and renamed the City of Sihon[27]. Although there is obscurity owing to the confusion between Gibeah, Gibeah of Benjamin, Gibeah of Saul, Gibeath Haelohim, Geba and Gibeon[28], it is generally accepted that Gibeah of Benjamin (Tell el-Ful), sometimes simply styled Gibeah, was the capital city of Saul's kingdom, and as such called Gibeah of Saul. B. Mazar[29] has suggested that Gibeah of Benjamin is to be identified also with Gibeath Haelohim, where a stronghold of the Philistines stood (I Sam 10 5), although this is disputed by some scholars[30]. If we follow Mazar's suggestion, we may take it that Saul renamed the place Gibeah of Saul when he conquered

---

26 See A. Gardiner, The Delta Residence of the Ramessides, JEA 5 (1918), 127–138. 179–200. 242–271; idem, Egypt of the Pharaohs, 1961, 258; B. Couroyer, La résidence ramasside du Delta et la Ramses biblique, RB 53 (1946), 75–98.

27 Cf. A. H. van Zyl, The Moabites, 1960, 10. 114f.; but M. Noth maintains that those who issued a summons to rebuild Heshbon were the Israelites that had conquered and destroyed it (Das vierte Buch Mose. Numeri, 1966, 144f. [ET Numbers, 1968, 164f.]); cf. de Vaux, Histoire ancienne d'Israël. Des origines à l'installation en Canaan, 1971, 522ff. J. R. Bartlett argues that the name "City of Sihon" does not necessarily mean that Sihon was the king at the time of the destruction of Heshbon, and he concludes that the campaign may refer to the Davidic conquest of Moab (The Historical Reference of Num XXI 21–30, PEQ 101 [1969], 94–100); but see also idem, Sihon and Og, Kings of the Amorites, VT 20 (1970), 258. On the other hand, according to J. van Seters, the original poem was a song of taunt against Moab, from which Jer 48 45–46 also derived, and had nothing to do with Sihon, the Amorite king (The Conquest of Sihon's Kingdom: A Literary Examination, JBL 91 [1972], 192ff.). As a result of excavations, a long-standing identification of Heshbon with Tell Hesbân to the north of Medeba seems problematic now, see R. S. Boraas & S. H. Horn, Heshbon 1971. The Second Campaign at *Tell Ḥesbân*. A Preliminary Report, 1973.

28 Cf. Mazar, in: EncBib, II 411–416 (Hebrew); A. Demsky, Geba, Gibeah and Gibeon – A Historico-Geographic Riddle, BASOR 212 (1973), 26–31.

29 In: EncBib, II 413. 415 (Hebrew); cf. K.-D. Schunck, Benjamin, 1963, 89f. n. 57.

30 Aharoni, The Land of the Bible, 254. Some archaeologists maintain that there was no Philistine presence at Tell el-Ful, see L. A. Sinclair, in: Encyclopaedia of Archaeological Excavations in the Holy Land, II 1976, 444ff. The identification of Gibeath Haelohim with Gibeon (el-Jib) is held by some scholars, see J. Blenkinsopp, Gibeon and Israel, 1972, 59; Demsky, BASOR 212, 27f.

the Philistine fortress on the summit of Gibeah of Benjamin and rebuilt it. It is by no means clear, however, whether Saul could establish his absolute ownership over Gibeah of Benjamin[31], since it was an old Israelite settlement[32]. Moreover, we are not sure whether any renaming really took place either at Heshbon or at Gibeah of Benjamin. The parallelism between Heshbon and the City of Sihon (Num 21 27b. 28a) seems to show that the City of Sihon was not the new name of Heshbon but another appellation for it, or an epithet. Similarly, Gibeah of Saul seems to have been just another name for Gibeah of Benjamin, both names being used side by side in biblical sources.

W. F. Albright[33] has suggested that Bīt-Humri was the official name of the capital city of the Northern Kingdom and that Samaria was the old name of the hill. If this were correct, Samaria, that is, Bīt-Humri, should be added to the example of cities renamed after a king, although the name Bīt-Humri is not preserved in biblical sources. But the suggestion is hardly tenable, because the name Bīt-Humri always refers to the land of Israel and never to the city of Samaria[34], and the names Samaria and Bīt-Humri are sometimes juxtaposed[35], clearly indicating two different geographical areas. Nor have we any evidence that Bīt-Humri, as the official name of the capital city, began to be applied at an early stage to the whole country[36]. If that had been the official name of Samaria, it would have been altered when Jehu overthrew the dynasty of Omri and made Samaria his residence. But it persisted as the name of the Northern Kingdom of Israel in Assyrian sources until the end. It should be regarded as a designation of the land, after the name of the dynasty which reigned when the Assyrians first became acquainted with it[37].

When Egypt ruled over Syria and Palestine in the period of the New Kingdom, military and administrative centres were established in the chief cities of each district[38], cities under the direct control of the

---

[31] Against Aharoni, in: Jerusalem through the Ages, 93 n. 22 (Hebrew).

[32] In Gibeah, there were Saul's house (I Sam 10 26 15 34), his field (11 4–5; cf. II Sam 9 7) and his palace (I Sam 13 2 14 2. 16 22 6 23 19 26 1; cf. 13 16), but his ancestral tomb was at Zela (II Sam 21 14). Blenkinsopp assumes that Zela (Josh 18 28) was Saul's place of origin (Gibeon and Israel 58f.).

[33] JBL 71 (1952), 251.

[34] See S. Parpola, Neo-Assyrian Toponyms, 1970, 82f.

[35] "Conqueror of Samaria and of the entire (country of) Bīt-Humria", H. Winckler, Die Keilschrifttexte Sargons, I 1889, 148 31–32; ANET 284. "Šinuhtu, Samaria and entire (country of) Bīt-Humria", F. H. Weissbach, ZDMG 72 (1918), 178 15; ANET 285.

[36] Against M. F. Unger, Israel and the Aramaeans of Damascus, 1957, 64. 159 n. 12.

[37] Cf. B. Landsberger, Sam'al, 1948, 19.

[38] See W. Helck, Die ägyptische Verwaltung in den syrischen Besitzungen, MDOG 92

Egyptian kings and called by new names expressive of their ownership. For instance, Gaza, the capital city of the Egyptian province of Canaan, was called "That-Which-the-Ruler-Seized" by Thut-mose III[39] and perhaps "the City of Ramses-Meri-Amon, the city which is in [Canaan]" by Ramses II[40]. Other cities of Ramses II were called "Ramses-Meri-Amon, the city which is in Upe"[41], "Ramses-Meri-Amon, the city which is in the Valley of the Cedar"[42], and "Simyra of Sessi"[43]. According to W. Helck[44], Mer-ne-Ptah, successor to Ramses II, called Simyra "the City Mer-ne-Ptah Hotep-hir-Maat, which is in the district of 'á-r-m()"[45]. As the last example shows, the cities were generally renamed again every time a new king ascended the throne[46].

In Mesopotamia, there were place-names of the type Dūr-RN or Kār-RN "Fortress or Harbour of RN"[47]. Both were originally built as strongholds in unruly areas to defend the border or to establish the king's rule[48]. Sometimes they were newly built in occupied areas like Dūr-Samsuiluna[49], Dūr-Tukulti-apil-Ešarra[50], or Kār-Aššur-aḫu-iddina[51]. But, more often, conquered cities were changed into centres of provinces or strongholds by a renaming after the king. Til-Barsip of Bīt-Adini was renamed Kār-Šulmānu-ašarīdu[52], the city of Harhar was

(1960), 11f.; idem, Die Beziehungen Ägyptens zu Vorderasien im 3. und 2. Jahrtausend v. Chr., 1962, 256ff.

39 ANET 235.

40 E. Edel, Weitere Briefe aus der Heiratskorrespondenz Ramses II. KUB III 37 + KBo I 17 und KUB III 57, in: Alt Festschrift, 1953, 32. 50f.

41 Ibid. 32. Edel holds that this was an official Egyptian name for Damascus (ibid. 44ff.), while Helck is of the opinion that it is identified with Kumidi (Die Beziehungen Ägyptens 258. 276).

42 Gardiner, The Ḳadesh Inscriptions of Ramesses II, 1960, 8.

43 "Sessi" was a nickname of Ramses II, see J. A. Wilson, in: ANET 477 n. 30.

44 Die Beziehungen Ägyptens 262.

45 ANET 258f. 'Á-r-m() is generally emended to Amurru, see Wilson, in: ANET 259a n. 11; Helck, Die Beziehungen Ägyptens, 262.

46 See Gardiner, JEA 5, 136; Helck, Die Beziehungen Ägyptens, 262.

47 See RLA II 241ff.; CAD D 196; CAD K 233.

48 A. L. Oppenheim, Ancient Mesopotamia, 1964, 119.

49 A. Poebel, Eine sumerische Inschrift Samusuilunas über die Erbauung der Festung Dur-Samusuiluna, AfO 9 (1933/34), 241–292.

50 P. Rost, Die Keilschrifttexte Tiglat-Pilesers III, 1893, 64 40; ARAB I § 795; cf. ibid. § 765. The location of the city is unclear, see J. A. Brinkman, A Political History of Post-Kassite Babylonia, 1968, 230 n. 1447.

51 Borger, Asarh., § 27 A II 82; ANET 290. This city was built at a site near Sidon, after Sidon was completely destroyed in order to establish the centre of the Assyrian trade in Phoenicia, see H. Tadmor, Philistia under Assyrian Rule, BA 29 (1966), 98.

52 Parpola, Neo-Assyrian Toponyms, 199; cf. ARAB I § 602.

called Kār-Šarrukîn[53], Elenzaš of Bīt-Barrū was changed into Kār-Sin-aḫḫe-erība[54]. A. Finet[55] has suggested that the name Dūr-Yaḫdun-Lim, a fortress in the district of Sagaratim, was changed Dūr-Yasmaḫ-Adad by the Assyrian usurper of Mari, but was revived by Zimrilim on his restoration of the dynasty of Mari. In contrast to these fortresses in outlying areas, both Kār-Tukulti-Ninurta[56] and Dūr-Šarrukîn[57] were new capitals built on virgin soil by Tukulti-Ninurta I (1244–1208) and Sargon II (721–705), respectively. To this category also belonged Azitawaddiya, built by Azitawadda, king of the Dannunites, in c. 800 B. C.[58].

Our examples testify to a custom common in the ancient Near East, that is, the founder gave his name to a city which he built, or a conqueror gave his to a taken city (cf. II Sam 12 28). But one cannot facilely draw conclusions from them about any common nature of ownership of cities named or renamed after kings. It must have been as diversified as the regimes in the region. Moreover, the longevity of the City of David as a dynastic residence was exceptional. No capital city named after a king served as the seat of his dynasty for more than a generation. Admittedly, Per-Ramses remained as the residential city throughout the whole Ramesside period, from its foundation by Ramses II until the kings of the 21st dynasty moved to Tanis[59]. But the epithet of the city, "Great of Victories", was changed to "The Great Spirit of the Sun Horus of the Horizon" after the death of Ramses II, merely to commemorate the founder, who was now one with the sun-god[60]. This unusual phenomenon in Egypt reflects the special situation

---

[53] Parpola, Neo-Assyrian Toponyms, 198f.; cf. ARAB II § 57–58.

[54] Parpola, Neo-Assyrian Toponyms, 198; cf. ARAB II § 237. 307.

[55] In: ARM XV 123 n. 1.

[56] Parpola, Neo-Assyrian Toponyms, 199; cf. ARAB I § 167–168. 173. 175. 177–178. About the founding of the city, see J. M. Munn-Rankin, Assyrian Military Power, 1300–1200 B. C., CAH II ch. XXV, 1967, 29f.

[57] Parpola, Neo-Assyrian Toponyms, 112f.; cf. ARAB II § 72–75; see also A. T. Olmstead, History of Assyria, 1923, 268ff.; E. Unger, in: RLA II 249ff.; Tadmor, Temple City and Royal City in Babylonia and Assyria, in: City and Community, 1966, 200ff. (Hebrew).

[58] KAI § 26 A II 10. 18.

[59] There is an opinion that Per-Ramses was situated on the same site as the later city of Tanis, see P. Montet, Tanis, Avaris et Pi-Ramses, RB 39 (1930), 1–28; Gardiner, Tanis and Pi-Ramesses: A Retraction, JEA 19 (1933), 122–128; idem, Ancient Egyptian Onomastica, II 1947, 171*ff. In that case, we must conclude that Per-Ramses was renamed as Tanis by the kings of the 21st dynasty. But scholars have tended to discard that identification, see J. van Seters, The Hyksos, 1966, 127ff.; cf. also Gardiner, Egypt of the Pharaohs, 1961, 258.

[60] Gardiner, JEA 5, 136f.

of the Ramesside period, when the weak kings of the later 19th and the 20th dynasties were very conscious of the greatness of their predecessors, especially of Ramses II. However, Ramses III, the strongest of the successors of Ramses II (1195–1164), could not refrain from taking credit of founding the city according to true Egyptian fashion. So he changed its epithet from that of Ramses II to his own: "Per-Ramses, Prince of Heliopolis Great of Victories"[61].

The foregoing survey shows that a simple comparison with other cities royally called or renamed sheds little light on the nature of David's ownership over the City of David[62]. In this respect, G. Buccellati[63] has correctly argued against the thesis of A. Alt and others, that the expression "City of David" is evidence that Jerusalem was a city-state, private property of the House of David, a feudal possession of the crown, and the like[64]. Still and all, his conclusion that there was no difference between Jerusalem and the rest of the territory from the viewpoint of royal possession[65] is hard to accept. The House of David doubtless had a special relation to the City of David. The nature of this relationship can be clarified only by a careful analysis of the biblical sources.

To begin with, the problem of the identification of the City of David must be solved; it is not as self-evident as is often supposed. The two versions of the narrative of David's capture of Jerusalem offer involved informations on the topography:

> "And the king and his men went to Jerusalem, against the Jebusites, the inhabitants of the land, . . . David took the stronghold of Zion, that is, the City of David . . . And David dwelt in the stronghold, and called it the City of David" (II Sam 5 6a. 7. 9a).
>
> "And David and all Israel went to Jerusalem, that is Jebus, where the Jebusites were, the inhabitants of the land . . . David took the stronghold of Zion, that is, the City of David . . . And David dwelt in the stronghold; therefore it was called the City of David" (I Chron 11 4. 5b. 7).

Out of this narrative and other biblical sources, we can safely equate Jerusalem with Jebus (Josh 15 8 18 16. 28 Judg 19 10 I Chron 11 4; cf. Josh 15 63 Judg 1 21)[66] and the City of David with the stronghold of

---

[61] Ibid. 136. 192ff.

[62] Cf. M. Weippert, ZDPV 89 (1973), 96.

[63] Cities and Nations of Ancient Syria, 1967, 217f.

[64] For instance, Alt argues that Jerusalem was, as the "City of David", "his (i. e. David's) own personal estate, existing . . . outside the twin kingdoms of Israel and Judah" (Die Staatenbildung, in: Kleine Schriften, II 46 [ET 217f.]); cf. Noth, Geschichte, 176 (ET 191); J. Bright, A History of Israel, 1972², 195.

[65] Cities and Nations 221ff.

[66] M. Miller maintains that Jebus was originally the name of a village located near to

Zion (I Chron 11 5. 7 I Kings 8 1 II Chron 5 2). L.-H. Vincent[67] has maintained that the name Jebus was only that of a Canaanite clan, and that Jerusalem was never thus called in reality. But his view falls away in the light of the biblical sources. The problem is – how were these two sets of topographical names related to each other? A. Alt[68] held that the City of David was only another name for Jerusalem. L.-H. Vincent[69] has argued that the stronghold of Zion was a fortified building or citadel called Zion or Jerusalem. J. Simons[70] has demonstrated that the stronghold of Zion was the fortified residence of the Jebusite ruler on the south-eastern hill, while Jerusalem or Jebus was the name of a larger settlement, including both the south-eastern and the south-western hills. It is awkward to concede the first view, for the biblical sources sometimes imply that the City of David was an area different from Jerusalem:

> "He (i. e. Solomon) took the daughter of Pharaoh, and brought her into the City of David, until he had finished building his own house and the house of Yahweh and the wall around Jerusalem" (I Kings 3 1; cf. 9 24 II Chron 8 11). "Then Solomon assembled the elders of Israel . . . in Jerusalem, to bring up the Ark of the covenant of Yahweh out of the City of David, which is Zion" (I Kings 8 1 II Chron 5 2).

If we endorse the equation of the City of David with the stronghold of Zion, the second view cannot be supported. An individual building was never called a "city". The third argument, the so-called "two-hills theory", is suspect from the archaeological point of view: so far, no remains of settlement prior to the seventh or eighth century have been discovered on the western hill[71].

In our view, "Jebus = Jerusalem" and "the stronghold of Zion = the City of David" stood for the territory and its centre, respectively[72].

Jerusalem, and the equation of this Jebus with Jerusalem is "a case of mistaken identity" (Jebus and Jerusalem: A Case of Mistaken Identity, ZDPV 90 [1974], 115–127). But his thesis is unconvincing.

[67] In: Dictionnaire de la Bible supplément, IV 1949, 898f.; idem, Jérusalem de l'Ancien Testament, II 1956, 612. 631.

[68] Jerusalems Aufstieg, in: Kleine Schriften, III 254.

[69] Jérusalem, I 1912, 142ff.; cf. idem, in: Dictionnaire de la Bible supplément, IV 914. In the latter article, he has widened a little the area called "Zion" from a fortified building to the rocky ridge on the scarp on which a stronghold stood.

[70] Jerusalem in the Old Testament 243ff.

[71] See N. Avigad, Excavations in the Jewish Quarter of the Old City of Jerusalem, 1969–1970. Preliminary Report, IEJ 20 (1970), 8; R. Amiran & A. Eitan, Excavations in the Courtyard of the Citadel, Jerusalem, 1968–1969. Preliminary Report, IEJ 20 (1970), 9f.; cf. also K. Kenyon, Excavations in Jerusalem, 1961, PEQ 94 (1962), 85; idem, Excavations in Jerusalem, 1962, PEQ 95 (1963), 18.

[72] Cf. T. A. Busink, Der Tempel von Jerusalem. Von Salomo bis Herodes, I 1970, 98.

The beginning of the narrative of David's capture of Jerusalem reads: "... to Jerusalem, against the Jebusites, the inhabitants of *the land*" (II Sam 5 6a). "... to Jerusalem, that is Jebus, where the Jebusites were, the inhabitants of *the land*" (I Chron 11 4).
The term *ha'aræṣ* "the land" cannot here be the designation of Canaan. Accordingly, W. G. E. Watson[73] tried to explain it as the designation of "the city", but his argument is unconvincing. It seems that it implies "the land of the Jebusites", that is, "Jebus". Moreover, the Jebusites were also called "the inhabitants of Jerusalem" (Josh 15 63 Judg 1 21). If "the land" here corresponds to "Jerusalem", its implication must be *mātu* in *māt* uru*Urusalim* in the El-Amarna letters[74], the territory of the city-state of Jebusite Jerusalem. Evidently, that territory was much smaller than the territory of Jerusalem under Abdi-heba[75]. Still, Jebusite Jerusalem must have had a certain area. If the name "Jerusalem = Jebus" stands for the whole territory of the city-state, it is to be assumed that "the stronghold of Zion" was the residence of the ruler. Indeed, if the name "Jerusalem" had signified a stronghold of about four hectares only, how could the Jebusites, whom the Israelite tribes could not drive out, "dwell with the people of Judah (or Benjamin) at Jerusalem to this day" (Josh 15 63 Judg 1 21)? This, too, shows that Jerusalem was an area more extensive than a stronghold.

From this appraisal of the topography we can learn the nature of David's ownership over the City of David. It is clear that the ownership of the stronghold of Zion was transferred from the Jebusite ruler to David when he took and renamed it. After that, however, he purchased a threshing-floor from Araunah, most probably the last ruler of Jebusite Jerusalem (II Sam 24 18–25)[76]; this reveals that his original ownership

---

[73] David ousts the City Ruler of Jebus, VT 20 (1970), 501f.

[74] EA § 287 25. 46. 61. 63. § 289 14. 29. § 290 15.

[75] The description of the border between the tribes of Benjamin and Judah around Jerusalem (Josh 15 8 18 16) shows that Jebusite Jerusalem was squeezed between the Israelite tribes. About the extent of Abdi-heba's Jerusalem, see Kallai & Tadmor, EI 9, 143ff. (Hebrew).

[76] It has been assumed that the name Araunah-Awarna-Ornan was derived from the Hurrian word *ewri* or *ewar* "lord", see J. A. Montgomery, Ras Shamra Notes III, JAOS 55 (1935), 94; Maisler (Mazar), The Scribe of King David and the Problem of the High Officials in the Ancient Kingdom of Israel (1946/47), in: Canaan and Israel, 1974, 219f. (Hebrew); J. Gray, Canaanite Kingship in Theory and Practice, VT 2 (1952), 212. On the other hand, H. B. Rosén assumes the Hittite word *arawanni* „free" as the origin of the name (Arawna – nom hittite?, VT 5 [1955], 318–320). G. W. Ahlström argues that the expression *'aᵃrăwnā hămmælæḵ* in II Sam 24 23 implies "Araunah the king" (Der Prophet Nathan und der Tempelbau, VT 11 [1961], 117f.). Against this view, F. M. Cross contends that the text in question is corrupted (Canaanite Myth and Hebrew Epic, 1973, 210 n. 58). According to Stolz, the name

did not extend over the threshing-floor adjacent to the stronghold; in other words, the threshing-floor was administratively separate from the stronghold. This situation corresponds to the structure of the city-state in Syria-Palestine, which included numerous settlements outside the capital city as independent administrative units[77]. Therefore, in the beginning David's "private" ownership was limited to the stronghold. Then he added the threshing-floor of Araunah by purchase[78], but the whole territory of the ex-city-state Jerusalem was never incorporated into his property. In fact, the extent of the area called the City of David was never changed substantially from the time of David down to the day of Nehemiah. G. Fohrer[79] has held that the expression "places about Jerusalem" (Jer 17 26 32 44 33 13) means the old territory of the city-state. But we have no evidence for the assumption that the administrative division of the Jebusite city-state was preserved in the kingdom of Judah. The name Jerusalem appears to have become the designation of the area including the City of David and its suburb, after the old territory of the city-state was merged into the Israelite tribal boundaries[80].

The nature of David's ownership over the City of David can be further illuminated by a demographic inquiry into Davidic Jerusalem. Although the source material provides only meagre information about those who lived with David in Jerusalem, it is not impossible to calculate the size of that population[81]. First of all, David had a large harem, including eight wives: Michal (I Sam 18 27 II Sam 3 13–16 6 20–23 I Chron 15 29), Ahinoam, Abigail (I Sam 25 42–43 27 3 30 5 II Sam 3 2–3 I Chron 3 1), Maacah, Haggith, Abital, Eglah (II Sam 3 3–5 I Chron 3 2–3) and Bathsheba (or Bathshua) (II Sam 11 2–27 12 24 I Kings 1 11–31 2 13–22 I Chron 3 5), and ten concubines (II Sam 15 16 20 3; cf. 16 21–22)[82]. These eighteen wives and concubines bore him about twenty children: Amnon, Chileab (or Daniel), Absalom, Adonijah, Shephatijah, Ithream (II Sam 3 2–5 I Chron 3 1–3), Shammua (or

---

Araunah indicates Uruwna-Varuna-Uranos, i. e. the Indo-European sky god (Strukturen und Figuren 10).

77 Cf. Buccellati, Cities and Nations, 40ff.

78 Some scholars are of the opinion that the story of Araunah cannot be utilized as historical evidence, see W. Fuss, II Sam 24, ZAW 74 (1962), 164; Stolz, Strukturen und Figuren, 9f.

79 Zion-Jerusalem im Alten Testament, in: Studien, 198. 219 (ET 296. 307).

80 Cf. Kallai-Kleinman, in: Judah and Jerusalem, 36 (Hebrew).

81 E. Auerbach figures out 23,000 souls for the total population of Jerusalem in the time of the kingdom of Judah (Wüste und gelobtes Land, II 1936, 57ff.).

82 Besides, we have informations about the wives and concubines whom David took in Jerusalem (II Sam 5 13 I Chron 14 3) and about Saul's wives whom David took over (II Sam 12 8).

Shimea), Shobab, Nathan, Solomon, Ibhar, Elishua, Nepheg, Japhia, Elishama, Eliada (or Beeliada), Eliphelet (or Elpelet), Noga (II Sam 5 14–15 I Chron 3 5–9 14 3–6) and Tamar (II Sam 13 1–22 I Chron 3 9). Accordingly, the royal family alone numbered about forty souls. They were surely surrounded by officials in charge of the harem and the royal children as well as household servants. Unfortunately, we have no information about them with the exception of Jonathan, David's uncle and Jehiel, the son of Hachmoni, who were, it seems, the guardians of the children (I Chron 27 32). To reckon the probable census of David's household, we can refer to the following two data: a) when Absalom and Adonijah prepared for the *coup d'état*, they provided themselves with fifty runners (II Sam 15 1 I Kings 1 5); b) Ziba, Saul's servant, had fifteen sons and twenty servants (II Sam 9 10 19 18). In the light of these numbers of servants in private households, it seems justifiable to suppose that the royal harem had a hundred officials and household servants – twice as many as Absalom's and Adonijah's households and five times as many as Ziba's.

David was assisted in the administration of the kingdom and of his estate by ministers and other personnel. In two lists of high-ranking officials (II Sam 8 15–18 = I Chron 18 14–17 II Sam 20 23–26) and in another list (I Chron 27 25–34) we find the following: a commander of the army, a commander of the Cherethites and the Pelethites, a secretary, a herald, a minister in charge of forced labour, two counsellors, a king's friend, two attendants of the king's sons, twelve overseers of the royal property, and several priests. They fall into three categories: a) military men, b) civil administrators and c) clerics. As for the military staff, we have some reliable numbers. Under Joab, commander of the army, there was the supreme army council called "the thirty" or "heroes", which was the nucleus of the standing army (II Sam 23 8–39 I Kings 1 8. 10, etc.; I Chron 11 10–47)[83]. This troop had had six hundred members ever since the days of David's wanderings in the wilderness of Judah (I Sam 22 1–2 23 13 25 13 27 2 30 10). Under Benaiah, commander of the guard, there were six hundred foreign mercenaries called the Cherethites, the Pelethites or Gittites (II Sam 15 18): these were David's bodyguards[84].

---

[83] On the standing army of David, see A. van Selms, The Armed Forces of Israel under Saul and David, in: Studies on the Books of Samuel, ed. van Zyl, 1960, 55–66; Mazar, The Military Élite of King David, VT 13 (1963), 310–320; Y. Yadin, The Art of Warfare in Biblical Lands, II 1963. 275ff.

[84] Cf. Yadin, The Art of Warfare, II 277ff. According to van Selms, the total of David's standing army, his bodyguards and other military persons was about 2,000 men (in: Studies on the Books of Samuel 61f.). About the Cherethites and the Pelethites, see L. M. Muntingh, The Cherethites and the Pelethites. A Historical and Sociological

From these echelons in charge of the civil administration[85] we must subtract the counsellors, the attendants of the king's sons, and the overseers of the royal property, since one counsellor was the same Jonathan who was counted as a guardian of the king's sons, while the other counsellor, Ahithopel, lived in his home-town Gilo (II Sam 15 12); the attendants of the king's sons were counted among the officials of the harem; and the overseers of the royal property remained in the country-side. However, we may add a considerable number of subordinates, at least to the secretary, the herald and the minister in charge of forced labour. If we conjecture twenty officials to each minister, the total establishment in the three ministries becomes sixty.

Clerics also played an active part at David's court. Zadok and Abiathar were the two chief priests. Ira the Jairite was David's personal chaplain (II Sam 20 26). Some of David's sons were priests as well (8 18). Nathan and Gad were court prophets. The Levites were the keepers of the Ark (15 24). Many other personal names and censuses of people who were responsible for various religious offices are mentioned in I Chron 15–16 and 23–26. It is true that we can hardly take this tradition at its face value, since the Chronicler attributed to David the role of cult founder of the temple of Jerusalem *a priori*[86]. We would rather rely on the account that there were eighty-five priests at Nob in the days of Saul (I Sam 22 18). From this we can infer that about a hundred persons served as priests, prophets, seers, Levites and other clerics both at court and in the sanctuary of Jerusalem.

Other classes of people lived around David in Jerusalem, too. They were his kinsmen, like Jonadab (II Sam 13 3. 32), royal pensioners, like Meribbaal (9 7. 13 19 29) and the children of Barzillai (I Kings 2 7; cf. II Sam 19 32–41), Jebusite aristocrats, like Araunah (24 16–24 I Chron 21 15–28), male and female singers (II Sam 19 36), the craftsmen from Tyre (5 11 I Chron 14 1), and others. Although we have no clue to the exact size of this retinue, a hundred as a round number seems likely guess.

Thus, the total reaches sixteen hundred. To this figure we must add the numbers of their households. It is reasonable to assume that at least half of them had their own households, like Amnon (II Sam 13 7ff.), Absalom (13 20ff. 14 24. 30f.; cf. 15 1), Joab (14 29–31), Uriah the Hittite (11 2ff.), Meribbaal (9 12–13) and Araunah. Presuming five

Discussion, in: Studies on the Books of Samuel, 43–54; H. Schult, Ein inschriftlicher Beleg für „Plethi"?, ZDPV 81 (1965), 74–79.

[85] On the officials of David, see above p. 68 n. 56.

[86] Cf. R. E. Clements, God and Temple, 1965, 128f.; S. Japhet, The Ideology of the Book of Chronicles and its Place in Biblical Thought, Diss. Jerusalem, 1973, 236ff. (Hebrew).

persons to each household (for instance, Araunah had four sons: I Chron 21 20), they numbered four thousand (= 1,600 × 1/2 × 5).

So we may conclude that the total population of Jerusalem in the time of David was at least five thousand six hundred (= 1,600 + 4,000). These persons were called "all his house" and "all his servants who were with him in Jerusalem" at the time of Absalom's rebellion (II Sam 15 16 15 14).

Table of the Population of Jerusalem in the Time of David

Royal family	40
Officials and household servants of the harem	100
Standing army	600
Foreign mercenaries	600
Civil officials	60
Clerics	100
Others	100
Household members of the above personnel	4,000
Total	5,600

Where did these people live? After the capture of the stronghold of Zion, David strengthened its fortifications and built his palace in it (II Sam 5 9. 11 7 1 I Chron 11 8 15 1). But he did not extend its area[87]. Archaeological surveys have shown that the City of David extended over an area of about four hectares[88]. But we cannot allocate more than three hectares to the dwelling quarters, since the palace and the royal necropolis (I Kings 2 10 11 43, etc.) must have occupied considerable space. In the estimation of J. Garstang[89], Jerusalem had from ten to twelve acres (that is, about 4 to 4.8 hectares) and from two thousand five hundred to three thousand souls in the Canaanite period. His calculation of the population is based on an estimated density of about six hundred persons to the hectare[90]. If we accept that density, the population of an area of three hectares would be eighteen hundred.

Although a direct comparison between the number of inhabitants of ancient towns and that of modern cities may be misleading, it is still possible to utilize twentieth-century statistics to shed light on conditions in antiquity, if our treatment of data is right[91]. Thus, we shall

[87] Cf. Kenyon, PEQ 98, 78.

[88] Kenyon assumes 10.87 acres (= 4.38 hectares) for the area of the town (Jerusalem. Excavating 3000 Years of History, 1967, 30); cf. Aharoni, in: Jerusalem through the Ages, 85 (Hebrew); Busink, Der Tempel von Jerusalem, I 82 n. 16.

[89] Joshua, Judges, 1931, 170.

[90] Ibid. 121. 166; cf. Avi-Yonah, in: EncBib, I 1950, 146 (Hebrew).

[91] For instance, R. M. Adams, Land behind Baghdad, 1965.

refer to the provisional data from the census of population and housing made by the Central Bureau of Statistics of Israel in 1972[92]. First of all, the data show that there are 118 households with 753 persons on the hill (district number 619) which roughly covers the ancient City of David. These figures are not directly comparable to conditions in the days of David, since houses were densely crowded together in the City of David (cf. II Sam 11 2), while this area is now comparatively sparsely peopled. Therefore, it will be better to refer to the data about the population of the Old City of Jerusalem within the walls. The area of the Old City is 0.85287 sq. kms and its population was 36,801 in 1961, 23,675 in 1967, and 22,163 in 1972[93]. But we cannot obtain the real density of population from these figures, since the Temple area occupies more than a sixth (0.137 sq. kms) of the Old City and the density varies greatly from district to district. Accordingly, the situation of each district must be examined.

Table of the Population of the Old City of Jerusalem in 1972

District	Quarter	Area (sq. kms)	Population	Density/sq. km
611	Christian	0.173	3,847	22,200
612	Armenian	0.131	1,667	12,710
231	Jewish	0.114	1,498	13,120
641	Moslem	0.0925	6,142	66,400
642	Moslem	0.0746	3,777	50,510
643	Moslem	0.26777	5,232	19,520

We see that the population density of the Old City within the walls ranges from 127 to 664 persons to the hectare. Thus the density of the most crowded district is approximately as high as that estimated by Garstang for Canaanite settlements. Accordingly, we may accept the view that ancient towns in Palestine had a density of about six hundred to seven hundred persons to the hectare, and thence conclude that the City of David in the time of David had a maximum capacity of about two thousand inhabitants[94].

This figure, roughly, is only a third of the number of people in David's entourage, compelling us to assume that the rest of the courtiers and their families lived in settlements outside the walls of the

---

[92] I received the following data from Mr. R. Tsameret, Central Bureau of Statistics, Jerusalem. I wish to thank him for his kind help.

[93] Census of Population and Housing 1967 – East Jerusalem, 1968, XIf.

[94] J. Wilkinson calculates the population of Jerusalem by his estimate of the quantity of the water-supply and assumes 2,500 inhabitants in the time of David (Ancient Jerusalem – its Water Supply and Population, PEQ 106 [1974], 50).

City of David, together with Jebusites who had been driven out (cf. Josh 15 63 Judg 1 21) and probably some other Israelites[95]. In fact, the City of David had suburbs like the threshing-floor of Nacon (II Sam 6 6) or Chidon (I Chron 13 9) called Perez-uzzah, where Obed-edom the Gittite lived, the threshing-floor of Araunah (II Sam 24 16. 18–25 I Chron 21 15. 18–28), En-rogel (II Sam 17 17 I Kings 1 9), and so forth[96]. In later days these were called "the places about Jerusalem" (Jer 17 26 32 44 33 13) and formed "greater Jerusalem"; an indication that only the royal family and part of the courtiers lived in the City of David itself. In other words, the City of David was the royal court in the broad sense of the term. It is interesting to note that the royal palace of Mari in the time of Zimrilim occupied an area of a little more than two and half hectares with three hundred rooms and courts[97], a space more than half of that of the City of David. If the whole City of David was the royal palace in the broad sense of the term, we can regard it as the estate of the House of David[98].

Moreover, we must not forget that the necropolis of the House of David lay in the City of David[99]. S. Yeivin[100] has shown that it was the current custom in the whole ancient Near East to bury the kings in the inner citadels of their capital cities. But it seems that the necropolis in the City of David served not only the Judaean kings but also the members of the royal family[101]. Since in ancient Israel the family tombs

---

[95] Alt maintains that no free population of the Israelite tribes came to Jerusalem with David (Die Staatenbildung, in: Kleine Schriften, II 47 [ET 219]). But it is possible to assume that some Israelites already began to settle in Jerusalem in the time of David (cf. I Chron 9 3. 38), see S. Talmon, The Judaean *ʿAm Haʾareṣ* in Historical Perspective, in: Fourth World Congress of Jewish Studies, I 1967, 76; H. Schmid, Der Tempelbau Salomos in religionsgeschichtlicher Sicht, in: Galling Festschrift, 1970, 241.

[96] About the suburbs of Jerusalem, see Mazar, in: EncBib, III 822ff. (Hebrew); Busink, Der Tempel von Jerusalem, I 98.

[97] See A. Parrot, Mission archéologique de Mari, II 1958, 5; cf. Malamat, Mari, BA 34 (1971), 5ff.

[98] Noth argues that David established rulership over Jerusalem but had no ownership over the lands in Jerusalem (Das Krongut der israelitischen Könige und seine Verwaltung, ZDPV 50 [1927], 214f.). His argument is based on the equation of Jerusalem with the City of David.

[99] I Kings 2 10 11 43 14 31 15 8. 24 22 51 II Kings 8 24 9 28 12 22 14 20 15 7. 38 16 20 II Chron 9 31 12 16 13 23 16 14 21 1. 20 24 16. 25 27 9; cf. Yeivin, The Sepulchres of the Kings of the House of David, JNES 7 (1948), 30–45; Simons, Jerusalem in the Old Testament, 194ff.; D. Ussishkin, The Necropolis from the Time of the Kingdom of Judah at Silwan, Jerusalem, BA 33 (1970), 46.

[100] JNES 7, 30ff.

[101] Cf. "the tombs of the sons of David" (II Chron 32 33), see Simons, Jerusalem in the Old Testament, 208 n. 1.

stood on land belonging to the family, the City of David must have been the property of the House of David.

C. THE CONCENTRATION OF THE RELIGIO-NATIONAL TRADITIONS

While setting up his royal court in the City of David as the administrative centre of the kingdom, David carried out another important project, namely, the concentration of the religio-national traditions in Jerusalem. The project was consummated by Solomon with the building of the temple on Mount Zion. It was a highly political operation, intended by David and Solomon to establish the central position of Jerusalem, the new political heart of the united kingdom, in the religio-traditional sphere as well. In other words, it was an attempt to create, out of the earlier traditions, a new tradition with its core in Jerusalem and the House of David, designed to be the common tradition of the people made one under the rule of that dynasty. In this process, the earlier traditions associated with Mount Zion, which had been the central holy place in Jerusalem ever since the pre-Davidic period and now belonged to the House of David as its property, were reinterpreted to validate the rule of the House of David over Israel. Out of this ideological effort grew the doctrine of Yahweh's double election of Zion and of the House of David, upon which rested the dynastic stability of the House of David.

To begin with, it is very likely that the regime of David and Solomon attempted to furnish Jerusalem with a legitimate position in the ancient traditions of Israel. Since the religious traditions of pre-Davidic Jerusalem were alien to the Israelite tribes, the city was, originally, not mentioned in their traditions. But when the ancient patriarchal traditions were put together as a great epic at the Davidic-Solomonic court[102], Jerusalem was linked with them. It may be assumed, therefore, that some allusions to Jerusalem and Mount Zion were incorporated into the narrative of the sacrifice of Isaac (Gen 22 1–14) in this period. Although the name of the place disappears at the end of the narrative (v. 14), the "mount of Yahweh" must be Mount Zion (cf. Is 2 3 30 29 Mic 4 2 Ps 24 3), and a word-play on ראה seemingly points to "jeru", the first component part of the name Jerusalem[103]. We do not

[102] Cf. Mazar, The Historical Background of the Book of Genesis, JNES 28 (1969), 73–83.

[103] See Mazar, "King's Chapel" and "Royal City", in: Judah and Jerusalem, 1957, 28 (Hebrew); Stolz, Strukturen und Figuren, 207f. But M. D. U. Cassuto finds in the stem ראה an allusion to the name Moriah (Jerusalem in the Pentateuch [1951], in: Biblical & Oriental Studies, I 1973, 75f.).

know for certain where "the land of Moriah" (Gen 22 2) was. But it seems probable that the Chronicler's identification of the mountain with "Mount Moriah where Yahweh appeared unto David" (II Chron 3 1), and on which the temple stood, breathes an old tradition[104].

The situation is clearer in the account of Abram and Melchizedek, king of Salem and priest of El Elyon (Gen 14 18–20). Recently, J. A. Emerton[105] has assessed various opinions about the much discussed problems of this enigmatic chapter. We can agree with his conclusion that the episode reflects conditions under David[106]. But we can hardly grant the view that one of the purposes of the episode was "to encourage Israelites to accept the fusion of the worship of Yahweh with the cult of El Elyon"[107]. Many scholars assume that El Elyon was the chief god of the pantheon of pre-Davidic Jerusalem[108]. However, it seems more probable that this divine name originally indicated one of the manifestations of El, the principal god of the Canaanite pantheon[109]. As. O. Eissfeldt[110] has convincingly demonstrated, the cult of El was assimilated into the worship of Yahweh in the pre-monarchical period. That is to say, for the Israelites in the days of David, El Elyon was no longer the name of a Canaanite deity but one of Yahweh's epithets, such as El Olam, El Shadday, El Bethel, and so forth[111]. On the

---

[104] Cf. Mazar, in: Judah and Jerusalem, 27f. (Hebrew).

[105] Some False Clues in the Study of Genesis XIV, VT 21 (1971), 24–47; idem, The Riddle of Genesis XIV, VT 21 (1971), 403–439; cf. I. Hunt, Recent Melchisedek Study, in: The Bible in Current Catholic Thought, ed. J. L. McKenzie, 1962, 21–33; W. Schatz, Genesis 14, 1972.

[106] VT 21, 426; cf. Mazar, JNES 28, 74; Schatz, Genesis 14, 280. 320. About various theses on the evaluation of the chapter from a historical document to a later legend, see ibid. 41ff.

[107] Emerton, VT 21, 437.

[108] H. S. Nyberg, Studien zum Religionskampf im Alten Testament, ARW 35 (1938), 356; G. Widengren, Sakrales Königtum im Alten Testament und in Judentum, 1955, 47; A. R. Johnson, Sacral Kingship in Ancient Israel, 1955, 43ff.; H. Schmid, Jahwe und die Kulttraditionen von Jerusalem, ZAW 67 (1955), 168–197; Clements, God and Temple, 43f.; Stolz, Strukturen und Figuren, 149ff.

[109] Cf. Cross, Yahweh and the God of the Patriarchs, HThR 55 (1962), 241ff.; idem, Canaanite Myth and Hebrew Epic, 1973, 46ff.; R. Lack, Les origines de ʿELYON, le Très-haut, dans la tradition cultuelle d'Israël, CBQ 24 (1962), 44–64; J. J. M. Roberts, The Davidic Origin of the Zion Tradition, JBL 92 (1973), 331f. On the other hand, Schatz argues that El and Elyon were originally distinct gods, the god of earth and the god of heaven (Genesis 14, 207ff.); cf. G. Levi della Vida, El Elyon in Gen 14:18–20, JBL 63 (1944), 1–9; M. Pope, El in the Ugaritic Pantheon, 1955, 55ff. According to R. Rendtorff, El Elyon is a combined designation of God which unites the features of various deities (El, Baʿal und Jahwe, ZAW 78 [1966], 277–292).

[110] El und Yahweh (1956), in: Kleine Schriften, III 1966, 386–397.

[111] Cf. Eissfeldt, Jahwes Verhältnis zu Eljon und Schaddaj nach Psalm 91 (1957), in:

other hand, Melchizedek was a traditional figure important enough to be exploited by David. Undoubtedly, he was the priest of El Elyon in pre-Davidic Jerusalem, before the fusion of El Elyon with Yahweh took place. But we must pay attention to the fact that, in this episode, he is regarded no longer as a priest of a Canaanite god but of Yahweh whose epithet is El Elyon[112]. Had Melchizedek still been a representative of a Canaanite cult, the episode would have been of no use to David in his purpose of authenticating the position of Jerusalem in the ancient traditions of Israel. By making Melchizedek the priest of Yahweh anachronistically, he sought to show the patriarch's acceptance of Jerusalem as a sanctuary of Yahweh styled El Elyon (cf. 14 22).

David appears to have applied his general policy of assimilating conquered peoples to the Jebusites in Jerusalem as well. Not only Araunah, the last Jebusite ruler, but also the rest of the people were left alive (I Chron 11 8b)[113]. The fact that David took wives "from Jerusalem" (II Sam 5 13) clearly attests that a peaceful agreement came into existence between him and the Jebusites[114]. Presumably, Bathsheba (or Bathshua), the mother of Solomon, came from a Jebusite family[115]. Some Jebusite noblemen, such as Uriah the Hittite, became high-ranking courtiers[116]. Nonetheless, we are sceptical of the view that the religious traditions of pre-Davidic Jerusalem were brought directly into the cult of Yahweh in Davidic-Solomonic Jerusalem through these assimilated Jebusites[117]. The patriarchal traditions preserved in the

---

Kleine Schriften, III 446f. Mazar finds a cosmic character in the epithet Elyon as the spirit of the age which corresponds to the political development in the national kingdoms in Syria-Palestine in the tenth century B. C. (JNES 28, 75; idem, The Philistines and the Rise of Israel and Tyre, 1964, 19f.).

112 Cf. G. von Rad, Das erste Buch Mose. Genesis, 1972⁹, 138 (ET Genesis, 1961, 175). W. Zimmerli maintains that a post-exilic editor, who was responsible for the Melkizedek episode, must have regarded Melkizedek as the ancestor of the Israelite royal high priesthood (Abraham und Melchisedek, in: Rost Festschrift, 1967, 264).

113 Cf. Mazar, in: Jerusalem through the Ages, 5 (Hebrew); cf. also Hertzberg, Die Samuelbücher, 1960², 221 (ET I & II Samuel, 1964, 270).

114 J. Maier assumes that David as the conqueror of the city took over the harem of the Jebusite ruler of Jerusalem (Vom Kultus zur Gnosis, 1964, 36); cf. also H. Schmid, in: Galling Festschrift, 241.

115 See Yeivin, The Beginning of the Davidids (1944/45), in: Studies in the History of Israel and His Country, 1959/60, 198ff. (Hebrew).

116 Cf. Maisler (Mazar), The Scribe of King David, in: Canaan and Israel, 208ff. (Hebrew); Yeivin, Social, Religious and Cultural Trends in Jerusalem under the Davidic Dynasty, VT 3 (1953), 149ff.

117 The so-called "Jebusite hypothesis" is advocated by those who regard El Elyon as the chief god of the Jebusite pantheon, see above p. 137 n. 108; see also H. H. Rowley, Zadok and Nehushtan, JBL 58 (1939), 113–141; idem, Melchizedek and Zadok (Gen. 14 and Psalm 110), in: Bertholet Festschrift, 1950, 461–472; idem,

Book of Genesis testify to the aspirations of the Davidic-Solomonic period that Israel should occupy a central position ethnically as well as politically among all the nations of the world under the guidance of Yahweh, the national God of Israel[118]. It is more plausible, therefore, that the conquered people accepted the cult of the conqueror, and not *vice versa*. We must conclude that David exploited the religious traditions of pre-Davidic Jerusalem, but his objective was not appeasement of the conquered people but legitimation of Jerusalem in the Yahwistic tradition of Israel.

It is only against this background that we can understand correctly the implications of God's promise of the priesthood to the Davidic kings "according to the order of Melchizedek" (Ps 110 4). Of course, Melchizedek represents the prototype of the priest-king of Jerusalem in this psalm. But, at the same time, he no longer has any thing to do with the historical or traditional figure in pre-Davidic Jerusalem. By a twist of chronology, he is made an ancient priest of Yahweh who has dwelt on Mount Zion (v. 2). Accordingly, in the view of the psalmist, it was Yahweh who designated him as a priest-king of Jerusalem in the past, and now Yahweh will give the same position to the Davidic kings who are ruling in Jerusalem as successors to him. If our interpretation is correct, it is self-evident that this divine promise cannot be regarded as the legitimation of the Canaanite type of sacral kingship[119] for the Davidides[120], let alone as the legitimation of the Zadokite priesthood[121]. The purpose of the psalm is twofold. On the one hand, by mentioning "the order of Melchizedek" as Yahweh's designation, it shows that the kingship and the priesthood of Jerusalem have been associated with Yahweh since the days of Melchizedek, who was contemporaneous with Abraham. On the other, it serves to justify the priestly function of the

---

Melchizedek and David, VT 17 (1967), 485; Ahlström, VT 11, 113ff. On the critical remarks on this thesis, see Cross, Canaanite Myth, 209ff.; Roberts, JBL 92, 329ff.

118 Cf. Mazar, JNES 28, 74f.

119 Against Johnson, Sacral Kingship, 46; Widengren, Sakrales Königtum, 10ff.; cf. also von Rad, Das judäische Königsritual (1947), in: Gesammelte Studien, I 1971⁴, 206 (ET The Royal Ritual in Judah, in: The Problem of the Hexateuch and Other Essays, 1966, 223).

120 For critical remarks on the theory of the Israelite sacral kingship, see Noth, Gott, König, Volk im Alten Testament (1950), in: Gesammelte Studien, I 1960², 188–229 (ET God, King, and Nation in the Old Testament, in: The Laws in the Pentateuch and Other Essays, 1966, 145–178); Bernhardt, Das Problem der altorientalischen Königsideologie, 91ff.

121 Against Rowley, JBL 58, 125; idem, in: Bertholet Festschrift, 469ff.; idem, VT 17, 485; H. Schmid, Melchisedek und Abraham, Zadok und David, Kairos 7 (1965), 148–151. For critical remarks on this view, see J. W. Bowker, Psalm CX, VT 17 (1967), 31–41.

Davidic kings. Although we have no information on conflicts between the secular and the sacerdotal authorities in the period of David and Solomon, it can be assumed that the high-handed policy of these kings in religious matters incurred the resistance of priestly circles[122]. It is only because David and Solomon kept a tight rein on them that the fatal conflict did not come to the surface then, as it did in the time of Saul (I Sam 13 8–15 15 1–35 22 11–19) or in the period of the later kings of Judah (II Chron 24 20–22. 25 26 16–20). It appears that David tried to defend his priestly authority by claiming his succession to "the order of Melchizedek", a mysterious priest-king of Jerusalem in the past[123].

David's great achievement in his religious policy was the transfer of the Ark to the City of David (II Sam 6 1–19 I Chron 13 5ff). Despite its great importance in the cult of the temple of Jerusalem (I Kings 8 1–9 II Chron 5 2–10), the origin and the original significance of the Ark are, oddly enough, very obscure, as well as its final destination[124]. Since the inquiry into all these questions is beyond the scope of the present study, we shall confine ourselves to the problems in the period of the early monarchies. M. Noth[125] has maintained that, by transferring the Ark to the City of David, David aimed to bring over the old traditions of the Israelite amphictyony to his new capital and so establish the legitimation and pre-eminence of Jerusalem among the other sanctuaries in Israel. It seems, however, that this theory fails to explain the complexity of the situation surrounding the transfer. To begin with, it is remarkable that no mention at all is made of the Ark in Saul's period[126]. If the Ark had really been of importance for the

---

[122] Mazar assumes that the conflict between the royal and sacerdotal authorities began at the end of Solomon's reign and as a result of the conflict the house of Zadok lost the office of the chief priest (in: Judah and Jerusalem, 30f. [Hebrew]); cf. also J. de Fraine, L'aspect religieux de la royauté israélite, 1954, 314; A. Weiser, Die Psalmen, II 1950, 460f. (ET The Psalms, 1962, 695). L. Rost underlines the subordinate status of the priests under the king and *śarîm* in the kingdom of Judah (Der Status des Priesters in der Königszeit, in: K. Elliger Festschrift, 1973, 151–156).

[123] About the priestly office of the Judaean kings, see de Fraine, L'aspect religieux, 309ff.; de Vaux, Les institutions, II 239f. (ET 376f.); A. Cody, A History of Old Testament Priesthood, 1969, 98ff.

[124] On the problems of the Ark, see de Vaux, Les institutions, II 127ff. (ET 297ff.); Clements, God and Temple, 28ff.; Maier, Das altisraelitische Ladeheiligtum, 1965; H. Davies, The Ark of the Covenant, ASTI 5 (1966/67), 30–47; Busink, Der Tempel von Jerusalem, I 276ff.; Fohrer, Die alttestamentliche Ladeerzählung, JNSL 1 (1971), 23–31.

[125] Jerusalem und die israelitische Tradition (1950), in: Gesammelte Studien, I 172ff. (ET Jerusalem and the Israelite Tradition, in: Essays, 132ff.); idem, David und Israel in 2 Sam 7 (1957), in: Gesammelte Studien, I 341ff. (ET David and Israel in II Samuel VII, in: Essays, 255ff.).

[126] The "Ark of God" in I Sam 14 18 must be emended as "ephod" with LXX, see Maier,

Israelite tribes[127], Saul would have taken it back at all costs. The view that it was still under Philistine control in that period[128] is unacceptable, since Saul, after his first victory over the Philistines (cf. I Sam 14 31), held sway over the region of Kiriath-jearim where the Ark was kept. We must, therefore, conclude that Saul was not interested in the Ark (cf. I Chron 13 3).

Recently, J. Blenkinsopp[129] has suggested that Saul actually established the ark-sanctuary in the region of Gibeon, but that the Judaean historiographer blurred the fact. Although Blenkinsopp's painstaking treatment of the source materials is impressive, the suggestion remains highly hypothetical, as he himself admits. It is more likely that Saul's disregard of the Ark reflects the historical situation. Setting aside the question of origin, the Ark was the war palladium of the tribal confederation of Shiloh (I Sam 4 3–18)[130]. With the collapse of the Shilonite confederation, it passed into Philistine hands and remained under Philistine control, regardless of its removal from the Philistine cities to Bethshemesh and finally to Kiriath-jearim (5 1–7 2). Although Samuel restored the confederation, his authority was confined to some areas of Ephraim and Benjamin (cf. 7 16–17). As is generally accepted, his recorded recapture of all the territories of Israel from the Philistines (7 14) cannot be regarded as a historical fact. In other words, he was not capable of taking the Ark back from the Philistines, even though he wanted to do so. When the impotence of his regime became palpable, Saul was elevated to be the first king, thanks to co-operation between Samuel and the people of Israel (see above pp. 31 ff.). Although Saul's kingdom included "all the territory of Israel", the centre of gravity was still in central Palestine. It is clear, therefore, that the kingdom was established on the basis of the tradition of the Shiloh-Samuel tribal confederation. But Saul never attempted to renew the tradition of the confederation. Instead, he based his regime on the tribe of Benjamin, from which he came. He set up his capital at Gibeah of Benjamin called

---

Das altisraelitische Ladeheiligtum, 42f. But Hertzberg is of the opinion that there were distinct traditions reflected in MT and LXX (Die Samuelbücher 89f. [ET 113f.]).

127 Albright maintains that Samuel's silence about the Ark shows his rejection of the cult and ritual (Samuel and the Beginning of the Prophetic Movement, 1961, 16ff.); but this view is hardly acceptable.

128 Eissfeldt, Silo und Jerusalem (1957), in: Kleine Schriften, III 420; H.-J. Kraus, Gottesdienst in Israel, 1962², 208f. (ET Worship in Israel, 1966, 178).

129 Gibeon and Israel 65ff.

130 Fohrer argues that the Ark was neither Yahweh's representation nor war palladium but only a pledge of divine help (JNSL 1, 30); but see R. Smend, Jahwekrieg und Stämmebund, 1963, 56ff. (ET Yahweh War & Tribal Confederation, 1970, 76ff.); P. D. Miller, The Divine Warrior in Early Israel, 1973, 145ff.

Gibeah of Saul[131]. His court was formed mainly of Benjaminites (I Sam 22 7). In the same way, the servants of Ishbaal were called Benjaminites (II Sam 2 15. 25. 31; cf. 3 19). It is likely that this heavy leaning on the tribe of Benjamin was a corollary of Saul's hasty policy of centralization. It seems that it was owing to this policy that Saul finally clashed disastrously with the sacerdotal authorities. We have suggested that the co-operation between Saul and Samuel came into being when Saul tried to exploit Samuel's authority so as to provide the ideological foundation of his kingship (see above p. 49). But these good relations were instantly upset when Saul disobeyed Samuel's command to wage a Holy War on the Amalekites (I Sam 15). Likewise, despite the service of Ahijah, son of Ahitub, in Saul's camp in the early days (14 3. 18), Saul was enraged with the priests of Nob and massacred them (22 11–19). Both Samuel and the priests of Nob were direct successors of the Shilonite tradition. It follows that Saul's rupture with Samuel and the priests of Nob was a mark of his hostility towards the Shilonite tradition. No wonder that Saul did not show any interest in the Ark, the symbol of the Shilonite confederation. The words of David: "We neglected it (i. e. the Ark) in the days of Saul" (I Chron 13 3), exactly reflect this situation. The tradition of the Ark became so obsolete in the time of Saul that David, it seems, had to look for the place where it was kept (Ps 132 6). It was David who renewed the Shilonite tradition of the Ark, which had sunk into oblivion[132].

Things were quite different for David, who badly needed the legitimation of his rule over the northern tribes. By defeating the Philistines, he accomplished the long-thwarted purpose of both the Shilonite confederation and Saul. At this stage, by renewing the Shilonite tradition of the Ark, he skilfully demonstrated the double aspect of the matter at once. On the one hand, the removal showed that his rule was the rightful successor of the confederation, which had been the authentic organization of the northern tribes in the pre-monarchical period. On the other, it recalled Saul's failure as the liberator of Israel from the Philistines. It is not incidental, therefore, that "all the house of Israel" took part in the transfer of the Ark to the City of David (II

---

[131] Blenkinsopp argues that Saul's capital was at Gibeon (Did Saul make Gibeon his Capital?, VT 24 [1974], 1–7); cf. I. Hylander, Der literarische Samuel-Saul-Komplex (I Sam I-XV), 1932, 262; K.-D. Schunck, Benjamin, 1963, 132f.

[132] Cf. H. Gese, Der Davidsbund und die Zionserwählung, ZThK 61 (1964), 13f.; Maier, Vom Kultus zur Gnosis, 60f.; S. Herrmann, Autonome Entwicklungen in den Königreichen Israel und Juda, SVT 17 (1968), 154. According to Fohrer, David changed the name of the Ark from the "Ark of Elohim" to the "Ark of Yahweh" (JNSL 1, 24f.).

Sam 6 1. 5. 15. 19), and that the sterility of Michal, Saul's daughter, is related later on in the same narrative (6 20–23)[133].

The theology of the Ark developed in Jerusalem after the Ark was transferred thither. This theology held that "where the Ark is, there is Yahweh"[134]. Hence, by telling how the Ark came from Shiloh to Jerusalem, it represented Yahweh's migration from Shiloh to Jerusalem. This highly ideological claim developed further into the doctrine of Yahweh's election of Zion and his abandonment of Shiloh (Ps 78 60–69; cf. 132 13–14 Jer 7 12. 14 26 6. 9) [135]. All the same, the Jerusalem regime could not, by the presence of the Ark, convince the people straightway of Yahweh's new abode in Zion. Accordingly, Solomon had to visit Gibeon after his accession to seek the word of Yahweh (I Kings 3 3–14 II Chron 1 2–13), although the Ark had already been installed in the City of David. It seems that the high place of Gibeon was the royal-national sanctuary at that time[136]. Only after the building of the temple in Jerusalem as "the royal sanctuary and the temple of the kingdom", was the religious authority of Gibeon also absorbed by Jerusalem.

The concentration of the religio-national traditions in Jerusalem came to a climax in the construction of the temple on Mount Zion. Admittedly, it seems difficult to extract contemporaneous information from the detailed descriptions of David's preparation for the work in I Chron 22–29, since they came from the Chronicler's own material[137]. Still, judging from the fact that Solomon started to build the temple in his fourth year (I Kings 6 1 II Chron 3 2), that is, in the first year of his sole reign after three years of co-regency[138], we can hardly doubt that some preparations had been made in David's last years, and David's purchase of Araunah's threshing-floor (II Sam 24 18–25 I Chron 21 18–22 1) was doubtless related to those preparations[139], for there, presumably,

---

[133] Cf. Maier, Das altisraelitische Ladeheiligtum, 64; J. Gutmann, The History of the Ark, ZAW 83 (1971), 25.

[134] G. von Rad, Zelt und Lade (1931), in: Gesammelte Studien, I 1971^4, 115 (ET The Tent and the Ark, in: Essays 109).

[135] Eissfeldt holds that the position of Shiloh was as important as that of Jerusalem for Israel (Silo und Jerusalem, in: Kleine Schriften, III 418). But it seems that the concept of Yahweh's election of Shiloh was formed secondarily as a projection of the election of Zion.

[136] Cf. Mazar, in: Judah and Jerusalem, 27 (Hebrew); Ahlström, Aspects of Syncretism in Israelite Religion, 1963, 27; Schunck, Benjamin, 132ff.; Blenkinsopp, Gibeon and Israel, 96.

[137] See Noth, ÜSt, 112f.; Eissfeldt, Einleitung in das Alte Testament, 1964^3, 728f. (ET The Old Testament, 1965, 537).

[138] See Yeivin, in: EncBib, II 1954, 637 (Hebrew); Tadmor, in: EncBib, IV 1962, 300ff. (Hebrew).

[139] Cf. Mazar, in: Judah and Jerusalem, 27 (Hebrew); but some scholars argue against

stood the ancient sanctuary of pre-Davidic Jerusalem[140]. We can thus discern, behind the present aetiological narrative of the altar, David's calculated acquisition of the ancient holy place as well as his consecration of the altar of the future temple (cf. I Chron 22 1).

The temple of Solomon was one of the buildings of that king's great citadel complex, whose main edifice was his palace (I Kings 6–7 II Chron 3–4). Most certainly, the House of David possessed absolute ownership over the temple from the beginning until its destruction in 586 B. C. The ground on which it stood was the possession of the House of David (cf. II Chron 3 1), its founder was Solomon (cf. I Kings 8 13. 20. 27. 43 II Chron 6 2. 10. 18. 38), and the Davidic kings had control over its administration – appointment of its priests (II Sam 8 17–18 20 25–26 I Kings 2 26–27. 35 4 2. 4–5 II Kings 23 5), the disposal of its revenues (I Kings 15 18 II Kings 12 19 18 15; cf. I Kings 14 26 II Kings 14 14), repairs and modifications (II Kings 12 5–17 15 35 16 10–18 18 16 21 4–5. 7 23 4. 6–7. 11–12)[141]. But this does not mean, as some scholars maintain[142], that the temple of Solomon was a mere royal chapel attached to the palace. It is clear that the intention of David and Solomon was the founding of the central national sanctuary in Jerusalem. We can learn the national character of the temple not only from the narrative about its dedication (I Kings 8 II Chron 5 2–7 10) but also from the episode of Jeroboam's foundation of rival sanctuaries at Bethel and Dan (I Kings 12 26–33)[143]. M. Noth[144] has argued that this national character was given by the Ark installed in it. But J. Maier[145] has contended against the view that the temple was built for the Ark. It seems that, regardless of the Ark, it drew its

---

this view, see Fuss, ZAW 74, 160; N. Poulssen, König und Tempel im Glaubenszeugnis des Alten Testamentes, 1967, 175.

[140] See Mazar, in: Judah and Jerusalem, 28 (Hebrew); Ahlström, VT 11, 115f.; Fuss, ZAW 74, 164. But Hertzberg holds that the narrative affirms that the site became sacred for the first time on the appearance of the angel to David (Die Samuelbücher 341 [ET 414]); cf. de Vaux, Les institutions, II 145 (ET 310).

[141] Cf. de Vaux, Les institutions, II 158f. (ET 320); Poulssen, König und Tempel, 11ff.

[142] Alt, Die Staatenbildung, in: Kleine Schriften, II 46 (ET 218); K. Möhlenbrink, Der Tempel Salomos, 1932, 52; K. Galling, Königliche und nichtkönigliche Stifter beim Tempel von Jerusalem, ZDPV 68 (1951), 135ff.; Albright, Archaeology and the Religion of Israel, 1956⁴, 139; Ussishkin, Building IV in Hamath and the Temples of Solomon and Tell Tayanat, IEJ 16 (1966), 110. About the discussion on the "private temple and the royal chapel", see Busink, Der Tempel von Jerusalem, I 618ff.

[143] Cf. H. Vincent, Le caractère du temple solomonien, in: Mélanges Robert, [1957], 141ff.

[144] Geschichte Israels 191 (ET 209); cf. Bernhardt, Das Problem der altorientalischen Königsideologie, 167; Bright, A History, 214.

[145] Das altisraelitische Ladeheiligtum 69; cf. Busink, Der Tempel von Jerusalem, I 642ff.

national character from the covenant of David. As we have shown, through the covenant with David, Yahweh, the national God of Israel, became the patron deity of the House of David (see above pp. 112–114). Owing to this special relationship with Yahweh, Solomon could invite Yahweh to the temple on Mount Zion, the estate of the House of David. The same relationship enabled him to clothe the royal sanctuary with a national character. In short, this temple was the embodiment of the covenant of David, in which the triple relationship between Yahweh, the House of David and the people of Israel was established (see above pp. 111 ff.).

This view is reflected in Solomon's address to the people at the ceremony of dedication (I Kings 8 14–21) and in the beginning of his dedicatory prayer (8 22–26). Although many scholars assume the Deuteronomistic origin of these passages[146], we need not dismiss any possibility of detecting Solomonic echoes in them[147]. In any case, the building of the temple is regarded here as the fulfilment of the Davidic covenant. The remarkable expansion of the original covenant in II Sam 7 can be found in the explicit mention of the election of Jerusalem in addition to David's election (I Kings 8 16), and in the overt association of the Davidic with the Sinaitic covenant (8 21)[148]. Moreover, the foundation of the temple is taken as a sign of the perpetuity of the House of David (8 23–26). Indeed, it was a common conception in the ancient Near East that an enduring temple building shows the prosperity of the dynasty. For instance, at the dedication of repaired Esagila, the temple of Marduk in Babylon, Esarhaddon, king of Assyria (680–669), prayed:

> "May Marduk and Sarpanit, the gods who are my support, look with favour upon the pious deeds of my hand, and in the steadfastness of their hearts may they bless my kingship. My priestly seed, may it endure, together with the foundation platform of Esagila and Babylon, for all time to come."[149]

Similarly, at the restoration of Etemenanki, the ziggurat of Esagila, Nabopolassar, king of Babylonia (625–605), prayed:

> "O Marduk, my lord, look at my pious deeds graciously and by your exalted command, which is unchangeable, may the work, the deeds of my hands, be strong for ever! As the bricks of Etemenanki are firmly established, build up the foundation of my throne until the distant day!"[150]

---

[146] Noth, ÜSt, 5f. 70; idem, Könige, I 1968, 173ff.; Montgomery & Gehman, The Books of Kings, 1951, 193; Gray, I & II Kings, 1970², 215.

[147] See Y. Kaufmann, The History of the Religion of Israel, II 1953, 206ff. (Hebrew); Mazar, The Philistines and the Rise of Israel and Tyre, 20.

[148] Cf. Gray, I & II Kings, 220.

[149] ARAB II § 659 E; Borger, Asarh., § 11 Episode 39 VII 42b–VIII 9.

[150] NBKI 64 31–49.

According to R. B. Y. Scott[151], the names of the two columns Jachin and Bóaz, which stood before the temple (I Kings 7 15–22 II Chron 3 15–17), represent the first words of the dynastic oracle: "Yahweh will establish (*yakîn*) the throne of David and his kingdom to his seed for ever!" and "In the strength (*beʿoz*) of Yahweh shall the king rejoice." S. Yeivin[152] has, however, argued that the names of Solomon's ancestors might be found in those of the columns. It is difficult to determine the real implications of the names owing to lack of evidence, but it seems that they had dynastic connotations one way or another.

More explicitly, the Ark in the temple played the role of a dynastic symbol for the House of David. After David transferred the Ark to the City of David, it became the war palladium of the militia of Israel and Judah (II Sam 11 11; cf. 15 24–29). When it was put in the *debîr* of the temple, its significance changed again (I Kings 8 1–11 II Chron 5 2–14)[153]; it was no longer the war palladium, but the holiest symbol of the temple, whatever its real function may have been. Thus, it had a multi-symbolic purport, and every symbolism was focussed on the legitimation of the House of David as the royal dynasty ruling over Israel. First of all, the Ark stood for the valid successorship of the House of David to the tribal confederation of Shiloh. Secondly, it testified to Yahweh's choice of Mount Zion instead of Shiloh. Thirdly, it was a token of the unification of Israel and Judah under the House of David[154].

From the narrative of Jeroboam's foundation of rival sanctuaries at Bethel and Dan (I Kings 12 26–33), it is apparent that the temple of Jerusalem was also recognized as the central national shrine by the northern tribes in the time of Solomon. But it can be assumed that the separatist movement against the religious centralization in Jerusalem had already begun alongside the rebellion of Jeroboam under Solomon (11 26–40). It should be noted that the prophet Ahijah, who played an important part in that rebellion, came from Shiloh, which had been the centre of the confederation of the northern tribes, and that Solomon expelled Abiathar, a descendant of the priests of Shiloh. To judge from these facts, it is very likely that hostility to Solomon's religious policy

[151] The Pillars Jachin and Boaz, JBL 58 (1939), 143–149.

[152] Jachin and Boaz, PEQ 91 (1957), 6–22.

[153] Gutmann argues that the Ark in the temple of Solomon is simply the projection into the text of the Ark which Josiah introduced into the temple (ZAW 83, 22ff.). The suggestion is unacceptable.

[154] Some scholars assume that the Ark might be the container for the documents of the covenant of David as the names "Ark of the covenant" and "Ark of the testimony" show, E. Nielsen, Some Reflections on the History of the Ark, SVT 7 (1960), 74; Maier, Das altisraelitische Ladeheiligtum, 70f.; idem, Urim und Tummim, Kairos 11 (1969), 26. But this is a hypothetical assumption.

crystallized in the Shilonite circle[155]. More evidence of the challenge of that circle to Jerusalem can be found in the sharp self-justification of Jerusalem against the northern tribes (Ps 78; especially v. 59–69) and in the claim of the House of Zadok upon the House of Eli for the legitimate priesthood in Israel (I Sam 2 30–36). Therefore, we must discard the view that Ahijah condemned Jeroboam for his schism from Jerusalem but regarded the political separation from the House of David as justified[156]. Ahijah's accusation of Jeroboam (I Kings 14 7–9) simply shows his disappointment with Jeroboam's syncretic policy[157].

After their separation from the rule of the House of David, the northern tribes rejected its claim that Yahweh had chosen Mount Zion as his dwelling-place. Elijah did not come to Jerusalem but made a pilgrimage to Mount Horeb to meet Yahweh (I Kings 19 8). But the Judaean prophets in the period of the divided monarchy took it for granted that Yahweh dwelt on Mount Zion (Am 1 2 Mic 1 2–3 4 1–2. 7 Is 2 2–3 6 1–13 8 18, etc.). After the downfall of Samaria in 722 B. C., the situation changed, owing to the lack of a national centre for the northern tribes. Especially when Josiah achieved national re-unification and the absolute cult-centrality of Jerusalem, Jerusalem became the only national shrine in Israel again, though Josiah's reign was short-lived (Jer 41 5 Ps 122 4). We must conclude that the temple of Jerusalem was only recognized as the national shrine by the northern tribes when the House of David ruled over them[158].

The policy of concentrating the religio-national traditions in Jerusalem had its zenith in the building of the temple on Mount Zion. As the completion of a plan which had been suspended since the days of David, it was naturally regarded as the fulfilment of Yahweh's promise to him. Reinforcing the covenant of David, which formulated Yahweh's election of him, the temple now testified to Yahweh's election of

---

155 A. Caquot has suggested that the prophet Ahijah was a descendant of the priests of Shiloh (Aḥiyya de Silo et Jéroboam 1er, Semitica 11 [1961], 17–27). Although we cannot accept his equation of the prophet Ahijah with Ahijah, the priest of Saul (I Sam 14 3), Caquot is right in pointing out the Shilonite rivalry of Jerusalem. According to M. A. Cohen, the Shilonite priesthood played the leading role in the political changes from Saul to David and from Solomon to Jeroboam (The Role of the Shilonite Priesthood in the United Monarchy of Ancient Israel, HUCA 36 [1965], 59–98). His argument is unconvincing.

156 Against Noth, Jerusalem und die israelitische Tradition, in: Gesammelte Studien, I 177ff. (ET 136ff.); idem, Jerusalem and the Northern Kingdom, in: Jerusalem through the Ages, 1968, 33*–38*; de Vaux, Jérusalem et les prophètes, RB 73 (1966), 491.

157 Cf. Poulssen, König und Tempel, 84ff.

158 Against Noth, de Vaux, see above n. 156; cf. also P. Welten, Kulthöhe und Jahwetempel, ZDPV 88 (1972), 33ff.

Mount Zion as his eternal dwelling-place. Evidently, both elections were inseparably interrelated. The election of David was materialized by the election of Zion, the election of Zion could stand so long as the election of David was valid. Thus, the royal-dynastic ideology of the House of David was brought to finality in this doctrine of the joint election of David and of Zion. Not surprisingly, the doctrine served as the foundation of ideological creation throughout the long history of the House of David. We can find it in at least three traditions: a) the new tradition of the United Kingdom, b) the polemics against the northern tribes, and c) the royal ideology of the kingdom of Judah.

David's formation of a United Kingdom, which controlled virtually all Palestine and Syria, doubtless inspired the people of Israel to a re-interpretation of their ancient traditions into a great synthesis. It is widely recognized that, in the Davidic-Solomonic age, the traditions of the patriarchs, the Exodus, the wilderness and the conquest of Canaan were put together into a monumental, consecutive epic in the frame-work of Yahweh's promise of the land to the patriarchs and its fulfilment in the conquest of Canaan[159]. In a similar spirit, the "Song of the Sea" (Ex 15 1–18) joins the tradition of the Exodus to that of the conquest, which reflects David's empire (v. 14–15). But it expands the theme to the establishment of Yahweh's dwelling on the "mountain" and his ever-lasting reign there (v. 17–18). Although it is disputed[160], we are inclined to accept the view that the "mountain" implies Mout Zion[161]. Ps 114[162] describes in the most concise way Yahweh's dwelling in Judah and the establishment of the United Kingdom as the direct consequence of the Exodus: "When Israel went forth from Egypt . . . Judah became his sanctuary and Israel his dominion" (v. 1–2). The characteristic feature of this tradition is to be seen in the direct relation of the Exodus to Yahweh's election of Zion as the centre of the United Kingdom. Therefore, in this tradition, Yahweh came directly from Sinai

---

[159] See von Rad, Das formgeschichtliche Problem des Hexateuch (1938), in: Gesammelte Studien, I 58ff. (ET The Form-Critical Problem of the Hexateuch, in: Essays, 50ff.); Mazar, JNES 28, 73ff.

[160] Albright attributes it to the 13th century B. C. (The Archaeology of Palestine, 1949, 232f.); cf. F. M. Cross & D. N. Freedman, The Song of Miriam, JNES 14 (1955), 237–250; Cross, Canaanite Myth, 121ff.

[161] See Fohrer, Überlieferung und Geschichte des Exodus, 1964, 115; Clements, God and Temple, 52ff.; Muilenburg, A Liturgy on the Triumphs of Yahweh, in: Vriezen Festschrift, 1966, 249; B. S. Childs, A Traditio-Historical Study of the Reed Sea Tradition, VT 20 (1970), 410ff.

[162] Cross dates Ps 114 to the pre-monarchical period, and assumes the ritual procession of the Gilgal cult as *Sitz im Leben* for both the Song of the Sea and Ps 114 (Canaanite Myth 138f.). But the mention of Judah and Israel side by side (v. 2) clearly shows the post-Davidic situation, cf. Weiser, Psalmen, II 470 (ET 709).

to Zion (Ps 68 18). Moreover, the election of David is not mentioned explicitly, since the existence of the United Kingdom was in itself the proof of his election.

The polemics against the northern tribes can be divided into two categories: against the Shilonite circle in particular and against the northern tribes in general. The first polemic is crystallized in Ps 78[163], in which the traditions of Exodus and the wilderness are utilized as evidence of the stubbornness of the northern tribes, and it culminates in Yahweh's election of Zion instead of Shiloh (v. 60. 67–69) and his election of David as the shepherd of Israel, as king over the northern tribes (v. 70–72). Although the same themes are treated in this psalm and in the "Song of the Sea", the tone of treatment, as well as Yahweh's itinerary, is entirely different in the two traditions. In the "Song of the Sea", the unity of Israel, that is, of the United Kingdom, is presupposed, in Ps 78 there is a sharp polemic against the separatists. In the former, Yahweh came from Sinai to Zion directly, in the latter, he chose Zion after his rejection of Shiloh where he had once dwelt.

The second polemic, that is, against the northern tribes in general, is formulated in I Kings 8 16 LXX:

> "Since the day that I brought my people Israel out of Egypt, I chose no city in all the tribes of Israel in which to build a house, that my name might be there; but I chose Jerusalem that my name should be there, and I chose David to be over my people Israel."

As in the new tradition of the United Kingdom, the Exodus is directly related to Jerusalem, but the emphasis is laid here on the exclusive election of David and of Jerusalem, with a strong polemical accent. The present formula is generally regarded as Deuteronomistic, but this sort of polemic was not necessarily a Deuteronomistic invention[164]. It can be regarded as the direct development of the "temple episode" and David's election in Nathan's prophecy (II Sam 7 6–8 I Chron 17 5–7) (see above pp. 96–97).

In the Judaean royal ideology, it is taken for granted that every king is a descendant of David and that Yahweh dwells on Mount Zion. For the Judaean kings, it was of fundamental importance that they were the successors to David and that their kingship was validated

---

[163] Some scholars argue for the Deuteronomic influence on Ps 78, see H. Junker, Die Entstehungszeit des Ps 78 und des Deuteronomiums, Bib 34 (1953), 487–500; R. P. Carroll, Psalm LXXVIII: Vestiges of a Tribal Polemic, VT 21 (1971), 133–150. But others attribute it to the time of the united monarchy, see Eissfeldt, Das Lied Moses Deuteronomium 32, 1–43 und das Lehrgedicht Asaphs Psalm 78 samt einer Analyse der Umgebung des Mose-Liedes, 1958, 41ff.; Albright, Yahweh and the Gods of Canaan, 1968, 17 n. 41. 25 n. 56. 212.

[164] See above p. 145 n. 146 n. 147.

by Yahweh who dwelt in the temple of Jerusalem. Thus, the royal ideology asserts that Yahweh sets the king on Zion as his son (Ps 2 6–7; cf. 89 27–28 II Sam 7 14 I Chron 17 13), sends him help, support and protection from Zion (Ps 20 2–3), gives him justice and righteousness (72 1–2; cf. Ps 101), makes him victorious over his enemies (Ps 2 9 18 51 = II Sam 22 51 Ps 20 10 21 9ff. 28 8 60 110 144 1–10), and promises him a long reign (21 5 45 7 61 7) and an everlasting dynasty (45 17–18 89 30. 37–38 132 11–12).

The long history of the House of David teaches us that this royal ideology was accepted by the people of Judah. Despite a fair number of *coups d'état*, in which Judaean kings were killed (II Kings 12 21 14 19 21 23 II Chron 24 25 25 27 33 24; cf. II Kings 11 1 II Chron 22 10), the covenant of David never lost its validity in Judah. This is shown by the words of Jehoiada the priest and of Jeremiah the prophet:

> "The son of the king shall reign as Yahweh spoke concerning the sons of David" (II Chron 23 3).
>
> "If you can break my covenant with the day and my covenant with the night, so that day and night will not come at their appointed time, then also my covenant with David my servant may be broken, so that he shall not have a son to reign on his throne" (Jer 33 20–21).

Chapter 7: The Problems at the Passing of the Royal Throne

A. THE DYNASTIC SUCCESSION

In ancient Near Eastern monarchies, the death of a king was a highly critical moment. From the ideological point of view, in Egypt it implied a temporal victory of hostile powers which caused cosmic chaos[1]. In Mesopotamia, as the institution of the substitute king shows, the country's welfare was dependent on the king's well-being, since he was considered to be a divine pledge in human hands[2]. In the political sphere, the interregnum almost always brought about turmoil, which provided an excellent opportunity for the conquered to revolt against the ruling power (cf. Ps 2). Moreover, several pretenders to the throne usually rose up and struggled until one gained the upper hand. The monarchies in ancient Israel were no exception. In this respect, however, there was a sharp contrast between the Northern Kingdom and Judah. In the former, pretenders to the throne frequently came from outside the reigning royal house. As a result, nine usurpers arose one after another in the space of two centuries. But Judah was ruled by the House of David as its only dynasty throughout its existence, that is, for about three hundred and fifty years. This does not mean that Judah escaped such troubles, since members of the royal family occasionally fought each other for succession to the throne.

Twenty kings, with an interruption during Athaliah's usurpation, succeeded each other on the Davidic throne. It was transferred from father to son except twice, Jehoahaz being succeeded by Jehoiakim, his brother (II Kings 23 34 II Chron 36 4), and Jehoiachin by Zedekiah, his uncle (II Kings 24 17 Jer 37 1)[3]. As both irregular successions were enforced by the Egyptian and the Babylonian kings, respectively, after they had conquered Judah, it is clear that the normal succession invariably went from father to son. Some scholars argue that Asa was not the son of Abijah but his brother, since the name of the mother of

---

[1] See H. Frankfort, Kingship and the Gods, 1948, 101.

[2] See ibid. 262ff.; A. L. Oppenheim, Ancient Mesopotamia, 1964, 100.

[3] According to II Chron 36 10, Zedekiah was Jehoiachin's brother, but see I Chron 3 15-16.

both of those two is the same (I Kings 15 2. 10)[4]. But, in the light of the principle of succession, this suggestion cannot be sustained. Except for the succession from Jehoahaz to Jehoiakim, imposed by the Egyptian king, we have no example of brother succeeding brother in the monarchies of Israel and Judah in biblical times, with one exception – Jehoram of the Omri dynasty succeeded Ahaziah, his brother. But this took place "because Ahaziah had no son" (II Kings 1 17). Since Abijah had twenty-two sons (II Chron 13 21), there is no reason to doubt that Asa was, indeed, one of them.

As for the order of succession, primogeniture was the basic principle: "But he (i. e. Jehoshaphat) gave the kingdom to Jehoram, because he was the first-born" (II Chron 21 3). When the first-born was dead, the surviving eldest son had priority. Therefore, after the death of Amnon and Absalom, Adonijah was regarded as David's successor by himself as well as by others, as both he and Solomon admitted: "You know that the kingdom was mine (i. e. Adonijah's), and that all Israel fully expected me to reign" (I Kings 2 15); "Ask for him (i. e. Adonijah) the kingdom also; for he is my elder brother" (2 22). But the principle of primogeniture and that of the surviving eldest son's priority were sometimes overruled. In that event, we almost always have an additional explanation of the new king's enthronement despite his inferior rank in the order of succession. The most expanded story of this kind is that of Solomon's succession to David (II Sam 9–20 I Kings 1–2)[5]. Short, much less elaborate, notes are added to the information on the succession of the following kings: Abijah (II Chron 11 21–22), Ahaziah (= Jehoahaz) (21 17 22 1), Joash (II Kings 11 1–2 II Chron 22 10–11), Azariah (II Kings 14 21 II Chron 26 1), Jehoahaz (II Kings 23 30 II Chron 36 1) and Zedekiah (II Kings 24 17). In this connection, the note on Jehoram's accession (II Chron 21 3) is exceptional, since it relates that he was designated as successor on the basis of primogeniture. But, since he purged his brothers (21 4), we can assume that he had special cause to defend his legitimacy as the first-born against the opposition party. We will deal with this question later.

The stereotyped chronological note for the kings of Judah in the First and Second Books of the Kings includes, *inter alia*, the king's age at succession and the length of his reign. By adding up the two figures we arrive at his age at death. Then, by subtracting the next king's age at accession from his predecessor's age at death, we obtain the age of the

[4] J. Wellhausen, Israelitische und jüdische Geschichte, 1914[7], 69; E. Meyer, Geschichte des Altertums, II/2 1931[4], 273 n. 1. But, according to II Chron 13 2, Abijah's mother was Micaiah, the daughter of Uriel of Gibeah.

[5] Cf. L. Rost, Die Überlieferung von der Thronnachfolge Davids (1926), in: Das kleine Credo und andere Studien zum Alten Testament, 1965, 191ff.

reigning king when his son and heir was born. When the co-regency of the next king is assumed, we must subtract the length of the co-regency as well, to get the age of the royal father at his successor's birth.

Table of the Ages of the Kings of Judah[6]

King's name	Age at accession	Regnal years	Years of co-regency[i]	Age at death	Age at the heir's birth
David[ii]	30	40		70	50?
Solomon[iii]	17?	40	3?	57?	16?
Rehoboam[iv]	41	17		58	
Abijah[v]		3			
Asa[vi]		41			
Jehoshaphat[vii]	35	25	3?	60	24?
Jehoram[viii]	32	8	4?	40	18
Ahaziah[ix]	22	1		23	22
Athaliah[x]		6			
Joash[xi]	7	40		47	22
Amaziah[xii]	25	29		54	22?
Azariah[xiii]	16	52	16?	68	18?

Notes to the Table

i For the number of years of co-regency we follow the suggestion of H. Tadmor, in EncBib, IV 269. 300ff. (Hebrew).

ii II Sam 5 4–5 I Kings 2 11 I Chron 29 27.

iii I Kings 11 42 II Chron 9 30. On the year of his birth and the age at accession, see S. Yeivin, EncBib, II 641f. (Hebrew).

iv I Kings 14 21 II Chron 12 13.

v I Kings 15 2 II Chron 13 2.

vi I Kings 15 10 II Chron 16 13.

vii I Kings 22 42 II Chron 20 31.

viii II Kings 8 17 II Chron 21 5.

ix II Kings 8 26. According to II Chron 22 2, he was enthroned at the age of forty-two. But this figure is corrupt.

x II Kings 11 3 II Chron 22 12.

xi II Kings 12 1–2 II Chron 24 1.

xii II Kings 14 2 II Chron 25 1.

xiii II Kings 15 2 II Chron 26 3.

---

[6] Cf. H. Tadmor, in: EncBib, IV 1962, 303f. (Hebrew); A. Jepsen, apud R. Hanhart, Untersuchungen zur israelitisch-jüdischen Chronologie, 1964, 43; E. R. Thiele, The Mysterious Numbers of the Hebrew Kings, 1965², 206.

Jotham[xiv]	25	16	16?	41	21
Ahaz[xv]	20	16	9?	36	11
Hezekiah[xvi]	25	29		54	42
Manasseh[xvii]	12	55		67	45
Amon[xviii]	22	2		24	16
Josiah[xix]	8	31		39	16, 14, 29[xx]
Jehoahaz[xxi]	23	3 months			
Jehoiakim[xxii]	25	11		36	18
Jehoiachin[xxiii]	18	3 months			
Zedekiah[xxiv]	21	11			

xiv II Kings **15** 33 II Chron **27** 1. The nine years of Ahaz's co-regency are included in Azariah's regnal years. Accordingly, we must subtract from Azariah's age at his death not only Jotham's age at accession and sixteen years of his co-regency, but also nine years of Ahaz's co-regency, to obtain Azariah's age at Jotham's birth.

xv II Kings **16** 2 II Chron **28** 1.

xvi II Kings **18** 2 II Chron **29** 1.

xvii II Kings **21** 1 II Chron **33** 1.

xviii II Kings **21** 19 II Chron **33** 21.

xix II Kings **22** 1 II Chron **34** 1.

xx The figures 16,14, 29 indicate Josiah's age at the birth of Jehoahaz, Jehoiakim and Zedekiah, respectively.

xxi II Kings **23** 31 II Chron **36** 2.

xxii II Kings **23** 36 II Chron **36** 5.

xxiii II Kings **24** 8. According to II Chron **36** 9, he was enthroned at the age of eight. Then, Jehoiakim was twenty-eight years old when his heir was born.

xxiv II Kings **24** 18 II Chron **36** 11.

The table shows that, with the exception of Solomon, Manasseh, Amon and Zedekiah, all the kings were born when their fathers' ages were between eleven and twenty-four, that is, around twenty. On the other hand, as we have mentioned, special information is provided about the accession of the following kings: Solomon was one of David's minor sons; Abijah was not the first-born; Ahaziah was the last and only surviving son of Jehoram; Joash was also the only surviving son of Ahaziah; Azariah was "chosen"; Jehoahaz and Zedekiah were Josiah's younger sons. Accordingly, judging from their fathers' ages, it is very likely that all the kings, with the exception of Solomon, Abijah, Azariah, Jehoahaz and Zedekiah as well as Manasseh and Amon, were the first-born or the eldest or only surviving sons. Although data for Asa and Jehoshaphat are lacking, they also seem to be the first-born or the eldest surviving sons. Pay attention to Abijah's very short reign of three years, to Asa's long reign of forty-one years, and to Jehoshaphat's advanced age at accession, thirty-five years. These statistics show that ten out of eighteen kings succeeded to the throne of David on the basis of the principle of primogeniture or the priority of the surviving eldest son. Manasseh and Amon were hardly first-born or surviving eldest sons, since they were born when their fathers were aged forty-two and forty-five, respectively. Although we have no specific details on their succession, both must have contrived to ascend the throne by some irregular procedure.

Thus it becomes clear that the principle of primogeniture was not decisive, even if it was fundamental. In reality, multiple factors contributed to determining the succession. First of all, the reigning king possessed the prerogative of designating the heir-apparent. Thus David appointed Solomon (I Kings 1 30. 33–35), and Abijah was named by Rehoboam (II Chron 11 22). Both Adonijah's failure and Jehoram's designation show that the first-born or the eldest surviving son was not recognized as the legitimate successor save by official nomination of the reigning king.

In the designations of Solomon and Abijah alike, their mothers had great influence on the royal decisions. Bathsheba made a special petition to David (I Kings 1 11–21), Maacah was the most beloved among Rehoboam's ladies in the harem (II Chron 11 21). The queen-mother's part in king's choice of his heir-apparent is also attested in other kingdoms in Syria-Palestine. Ammitaqum, the prince of Alalakh (c. 1700 B.C.), mentioned it in his will: *kīma abūšu u ummāšu ana šarrim uwiddīšu* "Just as his father and his mother had appointed him to king"[7]. In an indirect way, the same procedure was described by Abdi-heba, the ruler of Jerusalem (c. 1400 B.C.): *lā abīja u lā ummīja šaknāni ina ašri annie zuruḫ šarri dannu ušeribāni ana bīt abīja* "It was neither my father nor my mother who set me in this place; the arm of the mighty king brought me into the house of my father."[8] The words imply that the Egyptian overlord intervened in the strife for the succession in the kingdom of Jerusalem. As a result, the normal practice that the king and the queen-mother designated the heir-apparent was overridden, and the Egyptian king appointed Abdi-heba to be king. It is clear that he was a member of the royal family of Jerusalem but his parents did not want to choose him as the successor, presumably because of his inferior rank in the order of succession. In the kingdom of Ugarit, Ahatmilku, queen-consort of king Niqmepa (c. 1300 B.C.), played an important role after the death of her spouse in settling a dispute about the succession[9]. This activity of the queen in designating the heir-

[7] D. J. Wiseman, The Alalakh Tablets, 1953, 33 ATT/39/81 9–10.

[8] EA § 286 9–13; ANET 487; cf. EA § 287 25–28.

[9] See PRU IV 121ff. (RS.17.352); cf. H. Donner, Art und Herkunft des Amtes der Königinmutter im Alten Testament, in: Friedrich Festschrift, 1959, 116ff.; A. R. Rainey, The Kingdom of Ugarit (1965), in: BAR 3, 1970, 84f.; M. S. Drower, Ugarit, CAH II ch. XXI (b), 1968, 14.

apparent is regarded as a "Western custom"[10], and, indeed, we can find a clear Western influence on the Assyrian court in the role of Naqia-Zakutu, queen-consort of Sennacherib (704–681): she intervened not only in Esarhaddon's succession but also in Aššurbanipal's nomination as crown prince[11].

The queen-mother's authority in this matter stemmed from her official rank at the court. In Judah, she possessed the title of *g^e^ḇîrā*, the "Great Lady"[12]. It appears that this was conferred upon her at her son's designation as heir-apparent or at his accession, and retained by her for life. We can assume that, after surviving her son Abijah, Maacah was still the Great Lady under Asa, her grandson; she is, therefore, attested to as the queen-mother of both Abijah and Asa, his son (I Kings 15 2. 10)[13]. It is likely that the name of the king's mother mentioned in the introductory formula of the kings of Judah is that of the Great Lady in that reign, who was not always identical with his real mother. This supposition is supported by the fact that the name of the queen-mother is missing for Jehoram (II Kings 8 16–19) and Ahaz (16 1–2): the reasonable assumption is that the office of the Great Lady was vacant under both those kings, because their mothers died before their accessions. Asa's degradation of Maacah (I Kings 15 13 II Chron 15 16), as well as Athaliah's usurpation (II Kings 11 1–3 II Chron 22 10–12), bears witness to the power wielded by the Great Lady at court. But her position was evidently dependent on her son: for example, it appears that Hamtal, the queen-mother of Jehoahaz (II Kings 23 31), was deprived of the rank of Great Lady during the reigns of Jehoiakim and Jehoiachin, but it was restored to her when Zedekiah, her other son, was enthroned (24 18)[14].

It is generally assumed that the office did not exist in the Northern Kingdom[15]. But Jezebel, the queen-consort of Ahab, doubtless played the role. Apart from her intervention in domestic politics under Ahab

---

[10] Oppenheim, Ancient Mesopotamia, 358 n. 33.

[11] See H. Lewy, Nitokris-Naqîʾa, JNES 11 (1952), 264–286; Donner, in: Friedrich Festschrift, 111f.; W. Röllig, Politische Heiraten im Alten Orient, Saeculum 25 (1974), 22f.

[12] About the office of *g^e^ḇîrā*, see G. Molin, Die Stellung der Gebira im Staate Juda, ThZ 10 (1954), 161–175; R. de Vaux, Les institutions de l'Ancien Testament, I 1958, 180ff. (ET Ancient Israel, 1961, 117ff.); Donner, in: Friedrich Festschrift, 105ff.; G. W. Ahlström, Aspects of Syncretism in Israelite Religion, 1963, 57ff.

[13] Cf. Molin, ThZ 10, 163ff.; W. F. Albright, Archaeology and the Religion of Israel, 1956^4, 158; M. Noth, Könige, I 1968, 335f.

[14] Cf. Molin, ThZ 10, 164.

[15] Donner maintains that the office of Great Lady was related to dynastic monarchies (in: Friedrich Festschrift 106f.). On the other hand, Ahlström argues that it was associated with the *hieros gamos* ritual (Aspects of Syncretism 75ff.).

as the queen-consort (I Kings 21 5–16), she had much influence over Ahaziah, her son, as the queen-mother (22 53), and became the cause of Jehu's revolt (II Kings 9 22). In effect, she is called, though implicitly, *hăggᵉḇîrā* (10 13). In the light of the cited instances of the prominence of the queen-mother in western countries, it is unlikely that it was only in the Northern Kingdom that she held aloof from politics. The absence of the name of the queen-mother from the introductory formula of the kings of Israel is, it seems, due to the shortcomings of the source material rather than to non-existence of the office of Great Lady[16].

But neither in Judah nor in Israel have we any evidence of the queen-mother's official voice in the naming of the heir-apparent. This may have to do with the fact that there was no official rank of queen-consort at the court of Judah. A principal lady had a different status among ladies in a harem in other countries[17], but, at the court of Judah, all the wives of the king theoretically held the same rank, a situation that was liable to provoke palace intrigues in connection with the designation of the heir-apparent. The contest for succession between Adonijah and Solomon (I Kings 1–2) should be regarded as one of these intrigues. At that time, the leading courtiers were divided into two groups revolving about the two rival princes. Adonijah was followed by Joab and Abiathar, Solomon was supported by Zadok, Benaiah and Nathan (1 7–8). There are scholars who contend that the real origin of the struggle was the conflict between the Judahites from Hebron and the Jebusites from Jerusalem[18]. But it rather seems to have been simply the rivalry between Haggith, Adonijah's mother, and Bathsheba, Solomon's. Possibly, Bathsheba was of Jebusite stock[19], but there is

---

[16] R. de Vaux assumes that the term *šegal* (Ps 45 10) was the Israelite equivalent of the Judaean *gᵉḇîrā* (Les institutions, I 182 [ET 118f.]). B. Landsberger maintains that the term *šegal* came into Hebrew as a loanword from Akkadian *ša ēkalli* in the ninth or the eighth century B. C. and took the place of the *gᵉḇîrā* under the Assyrian influence (Akkadisch-hebräische Wortgleichungen, in: Baumgartner Festschrift, 1967, 198ff.).

[17] The Hittite queen had an independent position called *tawananna* for life, see A. Goetze, Kleinasien, 1957², 92ff.; O. R. Gurney, The Hittites, 1961³, 66f.; A. Kammenhuber, Die Arier im Vorderen Orient, 1968, 30. 42 n. 100. About the position of the queen in Ugarit, see Rainey, A Social Structure of Ugarit, 1966, 38f. (Hebrew). In the Assyrian court the principal lady called *ša ēkalli*, see Landsberger, in: Baumgartner Festschrift, 198ff. About the queen's active role in Mari, see P. Artzi & A. Malamat, The Correspondence of Šibtu, Queen of Mari, in *ARM* X, Or NS 40 (1971), 75–89.

[18] Ahlström, Der Prophet Nathan und der Tempelbau, VT 11 (1961), 113–127; H. Haag, Gad und Nathan, in: Galling Festschrift, 1970, 135–143.

[19] See S. Yeivin, The Beginning of the Davidids (1944/45), in: Studies in the History of Israel and His Country, 1959/60, 198ff. (Hebrew); idem, in: EncBib, II 1954, 379f. (Hebrew).

no evidence of the Jebusite or Jerusalemite provenance of Solomon's other supporters[20]. Nor can we discern any ideological difference between the two parties. It was rivalry, it appears, which gathered the courtiers round the two focal points. Obviously, Zadok was Abiathar's rival in religious matters, Benaiah and Joab were contestants in military affairs (cf. I Kings 2 35). At the critical moment, Bathsheba said to David: "Otherwise it will come to pass, when my lord the king sleeps with his fathers, that I and my son Solomon will be counted offenders" (1 21). Her words betray that the challenger was Solomon and his party. While Joab and Abiathar had followed David since the days of his wandering in the wilderness (I Sam 22 1. 20 26 6; cf. I Kings 2 26), and Haggith came to David's harem during his reign at Hebron (II Sam 3 4 I Chron 3 2), all the main supporters of Solomon – Zadok, Benaiah, Nathan and Bathsheba – appeared for the first time after David moved to Jerusalem (II Sam 7 2 8 17. 18 11 3). The conflict seems to have had its roots in the newcomers' challenge of the old authority. In the issue, Solomon and his party only succeeded in undoing Adonijah's original superiority by exploitation of David's preference for Bathsheba; the end came with Solomon's accession (I Kings 1 38–40) and the purge of Adonijah and his adherents (2 13–34).

By contrast, an ideological confrontation was involved in the fight for the succession from Abijah to Joash[21]. Although not the first-born, Abijah was designated as successor by Rehoboam under Maacah's influence (II Chron 11 21–22). There must have been a clash between Maacah-Abijah and Mahalath, another wife of Rehoboam, and her sons (11 18–20). But Rehoboam settled the matter peacefully (11 23). After Abijah's short reign, Maacah remained as the Great Lady under Asa (I Kings 15 10), but when he carried out the religious reform in his fifteenth regnal year (II Chron 15 10), Asa, whose authority had grown stronger than hers by that time, deprived her of the rank (I Kings 15 13 II Chron 15 16). For his reform, Asa had the backing of the prophet Azariah and the people of Judah, Benjamin and others (II Chron 15 1–15). Plainly, Maacah's demotion resulted from a counter-attack by the people of Judah against foreign influences at court, which had been brought in by the first three generations of Great Ladies – Bathsheba, the wife of Uriah the Hittite (II Sam 11 3), Naamah the Ammonite woman (I Kings 14 21) and Maacah, the daughter of Abishalom (15 2.

---

[20] According to the "Jebusite hypothesis", Zadok was originally a Jebusite priest of El Elyon, see above pp. 138–139. n. 117; cf. also C. E. Hauer, Who was Zadok?, JBL 82 (1963), 89–94.

[21] See T. Ishida, "The People of the Land" and the Political Crises in Judah, Annual of the Japanese Biblical Institute 1 (1975), 23–38.

10)[22]. Possibly, Mahalath took the part of this opposition movement, since she was a pure Judahite woman, kin to the House of David on her father's side and to the House of Jesse, David's father, on her mother's (II Chron 11 18)[23].

In his last years, however, Asa was compelled to make a treaty with Benhadad, king of Damascus, to defend his kingdom from the invasion of Baasha, king of Israel (I Kings 15 17–20). This foreign policy was criticized by the nationalists who had supported his religious reform (II Chron 16 7–10). But Jehoshaphat, his son, pursued the two-pronged policy: on the one hand, he was loyal to the national tradition in domestic affairs, so that he gained strong support (II Chron 17 1–9 19 3–20 33)[24]; on the other, he made a treaty with the House of Omri (I Kings 22 45 II Chron 18 1; cf. II Chron 20 35–37), and married his son Jehoram to Athaliah, Omri's daughter[25], to set a seal on the treaty. This foreign policy had devastating consequences for the House of David in succeeding generations[26].

Jehoshaphat was also criticized by the nationalists (II Chron 19 2), with whom his younger sons seemed to be connected[27]. But he designated as heir-apparent Jehoram, the first-born, who was a stubborn anti-nationalist (II Kings 8 18 II Chron 21 6). It seems that Jehoram's suppression of his brothers (II Chron 21 1–4) was in the context of a nationalist revolt which broke out after Jehoshaphat's death. As a result of his victory over the opposition party, Jehoram, together with his wife Athaliah, could establish the regime in full co-operation with the House of Omri, and, despite his defeat in battle (II Chron 21 8–10. 16–17) and his unpopularity (21 19–20), it was not shaken. When he died, the "inhabitants of Jerusalem" took the initiative to enthrone Ahaziah, the son of Jehoram and Athaliah (22 1). It appears that these "inhabi-

---

[22] For the three generations of the foreign queen-mother, see Albright, Archaeology and the Religion of Israel, 157f.; Malamat, Aspects of the Foreign Policies of David and Solomon, JNES 22 (1963), 8ff.

[23] According to MT, Abihail is the second wife of Rehoboam, but v. 19–20 seem to indicate that she is Mahalath's mother, see I. Eph'al, in: EncBib, IV 1962, 801 (Hebrew).

[24] Cf. Mazar, in: EncBib, III 1958, 565ff. (Hebrew).

[25] According to one tradition (II Kings 8 26 II Chron 22 2), Athaliah was Omri's daughter, while according to the other (II Kings 8 18 II Chron 21 6), she was Ahab's. From chronological studies it must be concluded that she was Omri's daughter, see J. Begrich, Athalja, die Tochter Omris, ZAW 53 (1935), 78–79; H. J. Katzenstein, Who were the Parents of Athaliah?, IEJ 5 (1955), 194–197. About the implication of "Athaliah, the daughter of Ahab", see Ishida, The House of Ahab, IEJ 25 (1975), 135–137.

[26] Cf. H. L. Ginsberg, The Omrid-Davidid Alliance and its Consequences, in: Fourth World Congress of Jewish Studies, I 1967, 91–93.

[27] Cf. Tadmor, in: EncBib, III 539ff. (Hebrew).

tants of Jerusalem" represented the supporters of the Jehoram-Athaliah regime against the nationalists, called the "people of the land", with whom we will deal presently. Ahaziah was a faithful follower of his parents (II Kings 8 27 II Chron 22 3) and a loyal ally of the House of Omri (II Kings 8 29 II Chron 22 6). As such, he was involved in the Yahwist revolution led by Jehu in the Northern Kingdom and lost his life (II Kings 9 27 II Chron 22 9).

As for Athaliah's usurpation and her overthrow, H. Reviv[28] has argued that Joash was actually placed in the custody of Jehosheba at her instance, and that she became queen-regent but never usurped the throne. In his opinion, the present text is distorted by hatred against the foreign queen. It is likely, indeed, that Athaliah's massacre of the royal family was not as wholesale as biblical source claims[29]. It is more probable that she put to death only those who might pretend to the throne as rivals of the infant Joash, her own grandson. Her regime was also lenient enough to allow the temple of Yahweh to enjoy a sort of extra-territoriality; she must have made some compromise with the priesthood of Yahweh in Jerusalem. Nonetheless, if she had not suppressed the nationalists, her regime would have been overthrown once the dynasty of Omri fell. Jehu deprived her at one blow of all her supporters – Ahaziah, her son, and his kinsmen, as well as the House of Omri, her family. It is certain that this Yahwist revolution in the Northern Kingdom profoundly affected the political situation in Judah. Yet even under these unfavourable circumstances Athaliah continued to rule for six years, evidence of her tight grip on Judah, which could be secured only by seizing the sceptre. In fact, Jehoiada eventually hatched a plot against her in a claim of the House of David to the throne (II Chron 23 3). All in all, there is no reason to doubt that she usurped the throne[30].

As the anti-nationalist suppression grew harsher, the "people of the land" appeared for the first time as an important factor determining the royal succession in Judah. Many studies have been devoted to the problem of *ʿăm haʾaræṣ*, the "people of the land". Although the opinions of scholars still remain widely diversified[31], we can summarize more or less generally approved conclusions as follows:

a) The expression "people of the land" is used sometimes in reference to any autochthonous inhabitants (Gen 23 12–13 42 6 Num 14

---

[28] On the Days of Athaliah and Joash, Beth Mikra 47 (1970/71), 541ff. (Hebrew).

[29] Cf. Ginsberg, in: Fourth World Congress of Jewish Studies, I 91f.; Reviv, Beth Mikra 47, 542f. (Hebrew).

[30] Cf. Molin, ThZ 10, 164.

[31] For the summary of various opinions on *ʿăm haʾaræṣ*, see S. Talmon, in: EncBib, VI 1971, 239ff. (Hebrew).

9; cf. Ex 5 5), but it has a special implication in the Books of II Kings, Jeremiah, Ezekiel and II Chronicles. Not only is it associated exclusively with the people of Judah but it is also synonymous with them[32].
b) The "people of the land" do not include the kings, his servants, the priests and the prophets (cf. Jer 1 18 34 19 37 2 Ez 22 25–29), namely, those bound up with the royal administration[33].
c) The "land" in this expression is used in contrast to the "city", that is, Jerusalem (II Kings 11 20 II Chron 23 21)[34].
d) The people of the Northern Kingdom are never called the "people of the land"[35].

According to R. de Vaux[36], the last mentioned fact is accidental. It seems, however, that it shows the difference of structure betwen the two kingdoms. The Northern Kingdom included various populations and regions which were too dissimilar to be called the "land" all together in contrast to the capital city, while the kingdom of Judah consisted of the "city" and the "land", Jerusalem and Judah. Although it also included Benjamin and other elements apart from the tribe of Judah, these minorities did not prevent the "land" from being called "Judah". As we have demonstrated (see above pp. 65–66), the people of Judah, who made up the great majority of the population of the kingdom, was brought into existence when David came up to Hebron and was made king over the "house of Judah" (II Sam 2 1–4). This is the origin of the special relationship of mutual dependence between the House of David and the people of Judah. Though the nexus weakened at one time under David, he succeeded in restoring good relations at the expense of the northern tribes by settling the difficult situation after the revolt of Absalom (see above p. 70). Their unanimous support of Rehoboam when the northern tribes broke away (I Kings 12 20) shows that the royalist tradition towards the House of David was firmly implanted among the people of Judah until that moment. Their charac-

---

[32] E. Würthwein, Der *'amm ha'arez* im Alten Testament, 1936, 8ff.; de Vaux, Les institutions, I 112 (ET 71).

[33] R. de Vaux, Les institutions, I 111 (ET 71); idem, Le sens de l'expression "Peuple du pays" dans l'Ancien Testament et le rôle politique du peuple en Israël, RA 58 (1964), 168; Tadmor, "The People" and the Kingship in Ancient Israel: The Role of Political Institutions in the Biblical Period, JWH 11 (1968), 67.

[34] Würthwein, Der *'amm ha'arez*, 25; Alt, Das Königtum in den Reichen Israel und Juda (1951), in: Kleine Schriften, II 1953, 127 (ET The Monarchy in the Kingdoms of Israel and Judah, in: Essays on Old Testament History and Religion, 1966, 252); de Vaux, Les institutions, I 112 (ET 71). A different view is advanced by G. Buccellati, Cities and Nations of Ancient Syria, 1967, 224ff.

[35] R. de Vaux, RA 58, 168; Talmon, The Judaean *'Am Ha'areṣ* in Historical Perspective, in: Fourth World Congress of Jewish Studies, I 71.

[36] RA 58, 168.

teristic features were conservative as well as nationalistic. As such, they favoured Asa's religious reform (II Chron 15 8–15). Jehoshaphat cultivated their nationalism (17 7–9) and strengthened their ties to the House of David (19 4–11). But when they were suppressed under Jehoram-Athaliah, they emerged as a political factor called the "people of the land" in contrast to the "inhabitants of Jerusalem" during the revolt against Athaliah.

According to the currently prevailing view, the "Judaean people of the land" were "*Vollbürgerschaft* of Judah", that is, the "whole body of citizens of Judah"[37]. The expression stands for neither a party nor a social class[38]. They were governed by Jotham, regent of Azariah (II Kings 15 5), made their offerings alongside those of Ahaz at the temple of Jerusalem (16 15), were taxed by Jehoiakim (23 35) and mustered in times of war (25 19). There was disparity in wealth among them: the "people of the land" who owned slaves (Jer 34 19) and oppressed the poor (Ez 22 29) on the one side, and the "poorest people of the land" (II Kings 24 14; cf. Jer 40 7) on the other. Basically, we accept this view. But it seems that the role of the "people of the land" in the political sphere, especially where problems of succession are concerned, has not yet been sufficiently elucidated. Let us examine each instance of succession in times of crisis, from the overthrow of Athaliah onwards:
a) Joash: the "people of the land" participated in the revolt against Athaliah under the leadership of Jehoiada the priest, and attended the enthronement of the king (II Kings 11 II Chron 23).
b) Amaziah: after Joash, his father, was murdered by his servants (II Kings 12 21–22 II Chron 24 25), he "reigned in his stead" (II Kings 12 22 II Chron 24 27).
c) Azariah: "all the people of Judah" chose him and made him king (II Kings 14 21 II Chron 26 1).
d) Josiah: the "people of the land" slew the rebels who murdered

---

[37] L. Rost, Die Bezeichnungen für Land und Volk im Alten Testament (1934), in: Das kleine Credo und andere Studien zum Alten Testament, 1965, 92; Würthwein, Der *'amm ha'arez*, 14; de Vaux, Les institutions, I 112 (ET 71); idem, RA 58, 167. Against this view, E. W. Nicholson maintains that this expression is not a technical term, but "it is used in a very general manner varying in meaning from context to context" (The Meaning of the Expression *'ăm ha'ar æṣ* in the Old Testament, JSS 10 [1965], 59–66). On the other hand, Talmon is of the opinion that the "people of the land" of Judah were a body of Judaeans in Jerusalem who were loyal to the Davidic dynasty (in: Fourth World Congress of Jewish Studies, I 71–76); idem, in: EncBib, VI 241f. (Hebrew).

[38] See de Vaux, Les institutions, I 112 (ET 71); J. L. McKenzie, "The People of the Land" in the Old Testament, in: Akten des vierundzwanzigsten Internationalen Orientalisten-Kongresses, München 1957, 1959, 206ff.

Amon, his father, and made him king (II Kings 21 23–24 II Chron 33 24–25).

e) Jehoahaz: when Josiah, his father, was killed at Megiddo, the "people of the land" chose him and made him king (II Kings 23 30 II Chron 36 1).

Of these five kings, it is striking that Amaziah succeeded in the normal way, namely, without the intervention of the people. A. Malamat[39] has suggested that Amaziah was already adult, while the others were still minors at their accession. But Jehoahaz was twenty-three years old when he ascended the throne (II Kings 23 31 II Chron 36 2). Therefore, Malamat[40] regards Jehoahaz's case as exceptional on the basis of his assumption that a *coup d'état* had been carried out by the "people of the land". Building on this suggestion, we may assume that the people intervened as a successor had not yet been designated at the time of the king's death. It is very likely that Joash had designated Amaziah as crown prince before he was assassinated at the age of forty-seven, Amaziah being already then twenty-five years old. Joash naturally had no designation, although he was the only surviving son of Ahaziah. Nor is it surprising that Amon was murdered before he could designate Josiah as his successor, for they were twenty-two and eight years old, respectively, at that time. As for the transfer of the throne from Amaziah to Azariah, it can be assumed that Azariah was enthroned when Amaziah was taken captive by Jehoash king of Israel (II Kings 14 13 II Chron 25 23); they were then thirty-eight and sixteen years old, respectively[41]. We may guess that an ambitious young king such as Amaziah was not yet prepared to transfer the throne to his son. Besides, the term "to take" (*wăyyiqᵉḥû*) (II Kings 14 21 II Chron 26 1) implies that the people "chose" Azariah from among the princes, which also underlines that there was no designation. Similarly, the people "chose" Jehoahaz (II Kings 23 30 II Chron 36 1)[42]. Although his two sons were already grown-up – Jehoiakim was twenty-five and Jehoahaz

---

[39] The Last Kings of Judah and the Fall of Jerusalem, IEJ 18 (1968), 140 n. 6.

[40] Ibid. 139f.; idem, The Twilight of Judah: in the Egyptian-Babylonian Maelstrom, SVT 28 (1975), 126.

[41] See J. Lewy, Die Chronologie der Könige von Israel und Juda, 1927, 12ff.; H. Frumstein (Tadmor), in: EncBib, I 1950, 439 (Hebrew); Thiele, The Mysterious Numbers, 84; idem, Coregencies and Overlapping Reigns among the Hebrew Kings, JBL 93 (1974), 192.

[42] Abner also "took" Ishbaal to make him king (II Sam 2 8). Since Ishbaal was the only surviving son of Saul (cf. I Chron 8 33 and I Sam 31 2), the term לקח does not mean here Abner's choice of him from among the other princes. Nevertheless, did not Abner choose him as king? The meaning "select" or "choose" for this term is found also in Yahweh's election of David (II Sam 7 8 I Chron 17 7), cf. K. Seybold, Das davidische Königtum im Zeugnis der Propheten, 1972, 30.

twenty-three, it appears that Josiah had not yet decided whom to designate as his successor when he was killed in his thirty-ninth year. Apart from his relative youth, it seems that political antagonism at court held up his decision. We shall discuss this below.

For the four kings in whose enthronement the people intervened, the situation at Azariah's succession was quite different from that of the others. As we have mentioned, he was made king to occupy a throne left empty by the reigning king who had been defeated and captured by Jehoash of Israel. His enthronement was vital, if Judah was to hold on to its independence against the threat of the external enemy. It is inferable that "all the people of Judah" who made him king embraced every man who engaged in politics and war, and not only the ordinary citizens but also the royal officials, soldiers and courtiers. We are driven to the conclusion, against the prevailing view[43], that "all the people of Judah" who enthroned Azariah were not identical with the "people of the land", for the latter excluded the royal staff. Moreover, the nature of the crisis at Azariah's enthronement was different from what it was in other instances. Joash ascended the throne as a result of the revolt against the regime of Athaliah. The counter-revolution made Josiah king[44]. Jehoahaz was enthroned through a sort of *coup d'état* which upset normal succession by primogeniture. That is to say, Azariah was crowned to cope with an external crisis, the others won kingship by tiding over domestic crises with the help of the "people of the land".

Many scholars regarded Athaliah's overthrow as a "national revolution" because of the part taken by the "people of the land" in the

---

[43] Würthwein, Der *ʿamm haʾarez*, 15; de Vaux, Les institutions, I 112 (ET 71); idem, RA 58, 169; Tadmor, JWH 11, 66. According to Talmon, the expressions *ʿăm haʾaræṣ* and *ʿam yᵉhûḏā* are two different abbreviations of the same full designation of a political body: *ʿăm haʾaræṣ liḇnê yᵉhûḏā* (in: Fourth World Congress of Jewish Studies, I 74).

[44] The nature of the revolt against Amon and the counter-revolution achieved by the "people of the land" is not clear enough. Malamat once argued that Amon was assassinated by an anti-Assyrian party (The Historical Background of the Assassination of Amon, King of Judah, IEJ 3 [1953], 26–29); cf. J. Bright, A History of Israel, 1972², 315. But it is difficult to assume that the "people of the land", who were the main supporters of Josiah's anti-Assyrian policy, opposed the anti-Assyrian conspirators. Recently, Malamat has suggested that the "people of the land" must be regarded as an anti-Egyptian faction opposing a pro-Egyptian party which was responsible for Amon's murder (Josiah's Bid for Armageddon. The Background of the Judaean-Egyptian Encounter in 609 B. C., JANES 5 [1973], 271); idem, SVT 28, 126. It seems to me that Amon's murder resulted from the political conflict at the court but the "people of the land" belonged neither to the pro-Assyrian party nor to the pro-Egyptian faction, see my article, Annual of the Japanese Biblical Institute 1, 34ff.

revolt[45]. Generally, they also find a contrast between the "people of the land" and the "city" in II Kings 11 20: "So all the people of the land rejoiced; and the city was quiet after Athaliah had been slain with the sword at the king's house" (cf. II Chron 23 21)[46]. However, the "people of the land" took neither the initiative nor the leadership in the revolt. The leader of it was Jehoiada the priest and the main power lay in the hands of the royal mercenaries[47]. Evidently, both belonged to the "city". It seems, therefore, that the sentence *wᵉhaʿîr šaqaṭā* implies only that "the city Jerusalem became peaceful"[48]. Athaliah's overthrow was a court revolution carried out with popular support. In fact, if the "people of the land" had played the leading role in the revolt against her, they could also have intervened in the political unrest caused by regicide after regicide in the following generations[49]. But they made no contribution at all to those conflicts between the royal authority and the priesthood[50]. It appears that of the "people of the land" who shared in Athaliah's overthrow actually only a small fraction came from the "land". But the whole situation was dissimilar at the enthronements of Josiah and Jehoahaz. The "people of the land" were the dominant political power in Judah then. Although we have no intention of entering into a discussion of the relationship between the "people of the land" and Josiah's reform[51], we must concede that the

---

45 Würthwein, Der *ʿamm haʾarez*, 23ff.; de Vaux, Les institutions, I 112 (ET 71); Alt, Das Königtum, in: Kleine Schriften, II 127 (ET 252).

46 See above p. 161 n. 34.

47 It has been suggested that II Kings 11 is resolved into two sources: a priestly source (v. 1–12. 18b–20) and a popular one (v. 13–18a), see J. A. Montgomery & H. S. Gehman, The Books of Kings, 1951, 417f.; J. Gray, I & II Kings, 1970², 566ff.; cf. also Würthwein, Der *ʿamm haʾarez*, 23. According to the two-source theory, the role played by the "people of the land" is more stressed in the second source. Against this view, W. Rudolph argues for the unity of the chapter, but regards all the mentions of *ʿăm haʾaræṣ* before v. 20 as secondary (Die Einheitlichkeit der Erzählung vom Sturz der Athalja [2 Kön. 11], in: Bertholet Festschrift, 1950, 473–478). Recently, M. Liverani has suggested that II Kings 11 was originally political propaganda like the inscription of Idrimi, whose purpose is to legitimize the second *coup d'état* by a son of a usurped king (L'histoire de Joas, VT 24 [1974], 438–453).

48 Cf. Buccellati, Cities and Nations, 168f.

49 Both Joash and Amaziah were murdered by the conspirators (II Kings 12 21–22 14 19 II Chron 24 25–26 25 27).

50 Cf. de Vaux, Les institutions, II 239f. (ET 377). We may assume, however, that Amaziah's assassination resulted from his unsuccessful attempt to take the throne back from Azariah, his regent. In fact, we never hear about the punishment of the conspirators against Amaziah, as we do about Amaziah killing the rebels against Joash (II Kings 14 5–6 II Chron 25 3–4), see Frumstein (Tadmor), in: EncBib, I 439 (Hebrew).

51 See G. von Rad, Deuteronomiumstudien (1947), in: Gesammelte Studien, II 1973,

"people of the land" in Josiah's time had decisive authority to designate the king.

The foregoing survey on the "people of the land" may be summarized as follows:

a) The origin of the "people of the land" can be traced back to David's establishment of the kingdom of Judah with the co-operation of the people of Judah.

b) The "people of the land" first appeared at the time of the revolt against Athaliah as a political factor opposed to the "inhabitants of Jerusalem". In actuality, they were a small number of activists from the land of Judah.

c) Only in the time of Josiah had they the power to choose the king from amongst the princes of the House of David.

d) In the broad sense of the term, the "people of the land" were the whole body of citizens of the land of Judah. But the term is not always synonymous with the "people of Judah", who sometimes include not only the "people of the land" of Judah but also the inhabitants of the city of Jerusalem, while the former never includes the royal officials in Jerusalem. This corresponds exactly to the geographical concept of Judah, which is used in both ways, including Jerusalem as well as excluding it[52].

In the Northern Kingdom, the people's intervention in enthronements took place only when a new dynasty was founded (I Kings 12 20 16 16 II Kings 9 13). Apart from dynastic changes with which we will duly deal, we have some information on the election of a successor in the framework of dynastic succession, though it was not carried out. After murdering Joram of Israel at Jezreel, Jehu sent a letter to the rulers of the city of Samaria, that is, to the official in charge of the palace and the official in charge of the city, to the elders and to the guardians of the sons of Ahab (II Kings 10 1 LXX. 5) as follows:

> "Now then, as soon as this letter comes to you, seeing your master's sons with you . . . select the best and fittest of your master's sons and set him on his father's throne, and fight for your master's House!" (10 2–3).

The recipients were the royal administrators and the nobles of Samaria. Here we have a case when a successor had not yet been designated at

---

143ff. (ET Studies in Deuteronomy, 1953, 60ff.); J. A. Soggin, Der judäische *'am hā'āræṣ* und das Königtum in Juda, VT 13 (1963), 187–195; M. Sekine, Beobachtungen zu der josianischen Reform, VT 22 (1972), 367f.

[52] Because of its prominence, Jerusalem is mentioned frequently side by side with Judah (II Kings 23 1. 2. 5). In this case, Jerusalem and Judah are two different areas. But in the words of the kings of Damascus and Samaria: "Let us go up against Judah" (Is 7 6), Jerusalem is clearly included in Judah (cf. II Kings 16 5).

the time of king's unforeseen death. The situation is similar to that of Azariah's elevation to the throne, when his father was defeated and taken captive. Since the House of David was still supported by "all the people of Judah", Azariah could ascend the throne. But the House of Omri had already lost control over the kingdom with the exception of Samaria, when Jehu's challenging communication arrived. Under these circumstances, the ruling class in Samaria possessed the authority to designate the successor to the throne. They could have chosen a prince as their king (10 5), but, by obeying Jehu's order to send the heads of the sons of Omri's House, they testified that they held the power of life and death over the royal family (10 7).

Likewise, when Saul's monarchy collapsed after the king and the crown prince had died in battle together, the throne stood vacant, and, because of the swift Philistine conquest, the people of Israel fell into total confusion (cf. I Sam 31 7). It is understandable, then, that Abner, commander of Saul's army, should take the initiative to crown Ishbaal, son of Saul, as the successor (II Sam 2 8–9). It was not Abner's arbitrary experiment, as A. Alt[53] maintains, but the common procedure for designating a successor when the throne was empty without heir designated.

When a kingdom lost its independence through a foreign invasion, the succession to the throne was completely dependent on the will of the conqueror, who sometimes expelled the reigning dynasty and enthroned its rival. This is the case at the change of regime from Pekah to Hoshea (II Kings 15 30). Although the situation is not clear in the biblical source, we can learn about it from an annalistic text of Tiglath-Pileser III, king of Assyria (744–727):

> ^kur^*Bīt-Ḫu-um-ri-a* [. . .] *el-lut* ^lú^[*ṣabē*^ḫi.a^-*šu pu*]-*ḫur nišē*^meš^-*šu* [. . .*a-na*] *māt Aš+šur ú-ra-a* ^[m]^*Pa-qa-ḫa šarra-* ⌜*šú*⌝ - ⌜*nu*⌝ [. . .] -*du*-⌜x⌝-⌜x⌝-*ma* ^m^*A-ú-si-ʾi* [*a-na šarru-ti i*]-*na muḫḫi-šú-nu áš-kun*
>
> "The land of Beth-Omri (i. e. Israel) . . . [his troops,] all of his people, . . . I carried off to Assyria. Pekah, their king, I smote(?) and I installed Hoshea [king] over them."[54] (Quoted from H. Tadmor, The Inscriptions of Tiglath-Pileser III, King of Assyria, [in preparation]).

The House of David once experienced a like crisis, when Rezin, king of Damascus, and Pekah of Israel wanted to set up the son of Tabeel as king of Judah instead of Ahaz (Is 7 6; cf. II Kings 16 5). Presumably, the name Tabeel is related to ^kur^*Ṭa-ab-i-la-a-a+a*, situat-

---

[53] Die Staatenbildung der Israeliten in Palästina (1930), in: Kleine Schriften, II 1953, 30ff. (ET The Formation of Israelite State in Palestine, in: Essays, 202ff.); cf. Noth, Geschichte, 169 (ET 183).

[54] IIIR 10, 2 15–18; cf. ANET 284.

ed east of the Jordan[55]; since Pekah ascended the throne with the assistance of the Gileadites (II Kings 15 25), the fair deduction is that the son of Tabeel came from the same region[56]. But there is no convincing evidence for the assumption that he was kin to the House of David[57]; rather it seems that he was chosen as its rival. In any case, the attempt came to nothing because of Assyrian intervention (II Kings 16 7–9; cf. Is 7 7–9).

Occasionally the conqueror was satisfied with the appointment of a rival prince of the royal family in the place of the hostile king. This sort of decision was made when the conqueror thought that he would be able to exploit the reigning dynasty[58]. In a kingdom such as Judah, where the House of David had firmly established its rule over four hundred years, it was not advantageous for a foreign conqueror to destroy it, if he wanted to rule Judah as a vassal kingdom, for political stability in Judah could hardly be attained without the House of David. Thus, both the Egyptian and the Babylonian conquerors chose their puppet kings from among the princes of the House of David in the last days of the kingdom.

From indirect evidence, we can see that there was a conflict between two factions at Josiah's court[59]. As we have suggested, it seemed to make Josiah undecided about the designation of his successor. The factions were divided by opposing political opinions as well as

---

[55] H. W. F. Saggs, The Nimrud Letters, 1952, Part II, Iraq 17 (1955), 131 no. XIV (ND. 2773) 5.

[56] Cf. Albright, The Son of Tabeel (Isaiah 7, 6), BASOR 140 (1955), 34–35; Mazar, The Tobiads, IEJ 7 (1957), 232ff.; M. Ottosson, Gilead, 1969, 235f.; B. Oded, The Historical Background of the Syro-Ephraimite War Re-Considered, CBQ 34 (1972), 161ff. S. Mittmann suggests the identification of ^{kur}D/Ṭa-ab/p-i-la-a+a with eṭ-Ṭafīle to the southeast of the southern end of the Dead Sea, but rejects its relation to Tabeel (Das südliche Ostjordanland im Lichte eines neuassyrischen Keilschriftbriefes aus Nimrud, ZDPV 89 [1973], 17f.). According to A. Vanel, Tabeel was Tubail, king of Tyre, whose name is mentioned as ^{m}Tu-ba-ìlu ^{uru}Ṣur-a+[a] in a newly discovered stele of Tiglath-Pileser III (Ṭâbe'él en Is. VII 6 et le roi Tubail de Tyr, SVT 26 [1974], 17–24); see L. D. Levine, Two Neo-Assyrian Stelae from Iran, 1972, 18 II 6. But Levine points out that such an identification is untenable, since the name Tubail seems a form of Ethbaal (ibid. 23); cf. M. Weippert, Menahem von Israel und seine Zeitgenossen in einer Steleninschrift des assyrischen Königs Tiglathpileser III. aus dem Iran, ZDPV 89 (1973), 47.

[57] Against Albright, BASOR 140, 35; Mazar, IEJ 7, 236; Oded, CBQ 34, 161.

[58] As an example, we can mention Sargon II's intervention in the change of kings at Ashdod, see ARAB II § 30; cf. Tadmor, The Campaigns of Sargon II of Assur: A Chronological-Historical Study, JCS 12 (1958), 80; idem, Philistia under Assyrian Rule, BA 29 (1966), 94.

[59] Cf. Malamat, IEJ 18, 139f.; idem, SVT 28, 125ff.

by the rivalry of two ladies of the harem, Zebidah and Hamutal[60]. Zebidah's son Eliakim (i. e. Jehoiakim) (II Kings 23 36) was the leader of the pro-Egyptian and anti-Babylonian faction, Hamutal's son Jehoahaz (23 31) was supported by the anti-Egyptian and pro-Babylonian party. When Josiah was killed in battle at Megiddo by Neco, king of Egypt, the "people of the land" set up Jehoahaz, setting aside the principle of primogeniture (23 30 II Chron 36 1). But Judah succumbed to Neco after three months. "And Pharaoh Neco made Eliakim the son of Josiah king in the place of Josiah his father, and changed his name to Jehoiakim. But he took Jehoahaz away; and he came to Egypt, and died there" (II Kings 23 34; cf. II Chron 36 3–4). However, when Nebuchadnezzar conquered Jerusalem eleven years later, Jehoiachin, the son of Jehoiakim, was taken captive to Babylon (II Kings 24 12 II Chron 36 10), and "the king of Babylon made Mattaniah, Jehoiachin's uncle, king in his stead, and changed his name to Zedekiah" (II Kings 24 17; cf. II Chron 36 10). Zedekiah was another son of Hamutal (II Kings 24 18)[61]. The same event is reported in the Babylonian chronicle for Nebuchadnezzar's seventh year:

> "In the seventh year, the month of Kislev, the king of Akkad mustered his troops, marched to the Hatti-land, and encamped against the city of Judah and on the second day of the month of Adar he seized the city and captured the king. He appointed there a king of his own choice (*šarra ša libbišu ina libbi ipteqid*)."[62]

From the foregoing study it has emerged that the designation of the successor to the throne in Judah and Israel was determined by a variety of factors. According to the fundamental rule, the reigning king designated his first-born or eldest surviving son, but, on occasion, appointed a younger son under the influence of the mother. When the king died without designating his heir, the successor was determined by such elements as a commander of the army like Abner, a chief priest like Jehoiada, the "inhabitants of Jerusalem", the ruling class of Samaria, the "people of the land" of Judah, or the "people of Judah",

---

[60] In his lecture in May 1974, Malamat suggested that Jehoahaz received backing from the "people of the land" because of not only his anti-Egyptian stance but his maternal lineage as well, for his mother Hamutal, the daughter of Jeremiah of Libnah (II Kings 23 31 24 18), was of the Judaean rural nobility which comprised the "people of the land", as the name of the town of her origin indicates; on the other hand, Rumah, from where Zebidah came (II Kings 23 36), was a Galilean town, with which the "people of the land" of Judah had nothing to do; see SVT 28, 126; a similar opinion is advanced by Ihromi, Die Königinmutter und der *ʿAmm Haʾarez* im Reich Juda, VT 24 (1974), 421–429.

[61] Cf. Malamat, IEJ 18, 144f.; idem, SVT 28, 126.

[62] D. J. Wiseman, Chronicles of Chaldaean Kings (626–556 B. C.) in the British Museum, 1961, 72f. (B. M. 21946) rev. 11–13; cf. ANET 564.

comprising the inhabitants of Jerusalem and the people of the land. Moreover, foreign conquerors could depose one king and install another as they pleased. So we can conclude that whoever possessed the strongest power at the time of designation could determine the succession.

The institution of co-regency is attested in Egypt and in Assyria. Its purpose was to avoid ideological and political chaos during the interregnum and to ease the dynastic succession[63]. In Judah, we have assumed six co-regencies: David and Solomon, Asa and Jehoshaphat, Jehoshaphat and Jehoram, Amaziah and Azariah, Azariah and Jotham, and Azariah and Ahaz (see above p. 153). R. de Vaux[64] is sceptical, except in the cases of David and Solomon and of Azariah and Jotham. It is true, as he maintains, that the co-regencies in Judah and Israel have been postulated mainly "to harmonize the discordant data of biblical chronology". All the same, it is undoubted that some co-regencies reflect considerations of dynastic stability. It seems that the institution was at times a device to confirm the reigning king's designation of his successor. Solomon ascended the throne during David's lifetime (I Kings 1 32–40), according to de Vaux[65], because David was too old to rule. But David would not have ordered Zadok, Nathan and Benaiah to anoint Solomon as king forthwith (1 32–34) unless Adonijah had made an attempt to seize the throne. When the report on Solomon's accession reached Adonijah and his supporters, they realized that they had lost the day (1 41–50). Therefore, the purpose of Solomon's co-regency was to confirm David's designation of him and its announcement. It is no less likely that Jehoshaphat wanted to confirm his designation of Jehoram by a co-regency, since Jehoram's kingship was not established without resistance (see above p. 159). But the nature of the co-regency of Amaziah and Azariah was entirely different. If our assumption is correct, Azariah was enthroned when the people of Judah enforced a kind of retirement on Amaziah, who had failed utterly in foreign politics. Azariah, in his turn, had to abdicate in the midst of his reign because of leprosy, and Jotham reigned in his stead (II Kings 15 5; cf. II Chron 26 16–21)[66]. As de Vaux[67] has pointed out, the term co-regency seems inaccurate in those last two cases.

---

[63] Cf. Frankfort, Kingship and the Gods, 101f. 243f.

[64] Les institutions, I 157 (ET 101).

[65] Ibid. 157 (ET 101).

[66] Montgomery assumes that *šop̱eṭ æṯ ʿăm haʾaræṣ* was a title for regency (The Books of Kings 448).

[67] Les institutions, I 157 (ET 101).

B. THE CHANGES OF DYNASTIES IN THE NORTHERN KINGDOM

Between the reigns of Jeroboam ben Nebat and Hoshea ben Elah, the throne of the Northern Kingdom of Israel was seized by usurpers nine times within two centuries. Among them, only Omri and Jehu succeeded in founding relatively stable dynasties, which embraced four and five kings, respectively, but the House of Jeroboam as well as the Houses of Baasha and Menahem retained the kingship for scarcely two generations, while Zimri, Shallum, Pekah and Hoshea could not bequeath the throne even to their immediate offspring. Zimri's reign lasted for only a week (I Kings 16 15), Shallum's for a month (II Kings 15 13).

A. Alt[68] has attempted to find an explanation for this difficulty of establishing a stable dynasty in the Northern Kingdom. According to his thesis, the principle of dynastic succession was not acknowledged as licit by the people of Israel, especially during the first century of the kingdom, since the monarchy was based on "charismatic leadership", which endowed a person not by descent, but by Yahweh's personal designation and popular acclamation. While the thesis has been widely accepted[69], both T. C. G. Thornton[70] and G. Buccellati[71] have argued against it. Their argument can be summarized as follows. The alleged "charismatic kings", both Jeroboam and Baasha, were succeeded by their sons. The Deuteronomic redactor regarded their succession as legitimate but stigmatized usurpations as "conspiracy". Moreover, the very notion of dynasty is expressed by the term "House", like the House of Jeroboam, the House of Baasha. Usurpers always liquidated the previous dynasty, which clearly shows their recognition of the dynastic principle. Basically we accept this criticism of Alt's thesis. However, we believe that the remarkable dynastic shakiness of the Northern Kingdom deserves a reinvestigation of its causes.

As one of the striking features common to the circumstances of dynastic changes in the Northern Kingdom, we can mention the military failures of the reigning dynasty:

a) Jeroboam I suffered much from Shishak's invasion (cf. I Kings 14 25–26 II Chron 12 1–12)[72]. After that, he was routed by Abijah of Judah

---

[68] Die Staatenbildung, in: Kleine Schriften, II 17f. 22f. 31ff. (ET 189f. 194f. 203f.); idem, Das Königtum, in: Kleine Schriften, II 116ff. (ET 241ff.).

[69] For instance, Noth, Geschichte, 209ff. (ET 228ff.); de Vaux, Les institutions, I 142f. 149ff. (ET 91f. 96ff.); J. A. Soggin, Das Königtum in Israel, 1967, 98f.; Bright, A History, 234ff.

[70] Charismatic Kingship in Israel and Judah, JThS NS 14 (1963), 1–11.

[71] Cities and Nations 200ff.

[72] Although the biblical sources do not mention Shishak's campaign against the

and lost part of his southern territory (II Chron 13 2b–20). Then, Nadab, his son, succeeded him, but the House of Jeroboam was overthrown by Baasha immediately afterwards (I Kings 15 27)[73].

b) Baasha was successful in war at the beginning, but was eventually overcome by both Asa of Judah and Benhadad of Damascus (15 16–22)[74]. Elah, his son, ascended the throne, but was soon murdered by Zimri (16 8–10).

c) Jehoram failed to suppress the Moabite revolt (II Kings 3 4–27)[75]. When he was convalescing from the wound inflicted upon him in battle at Ramoth-gilead against Hazael of Damascus, Jehu revolted and overthrew the House of Omri (II Kings 8 29–9 26).

d) Menahem was compelled to send a crippling tribute to Tiglath-Pileser III, king of Assyria (15 19–20)[76]. Pekahiah, his son, could not reign longer than two years before he was assassinated by Pekah (15 23. 25).

e) Pekah failed to conquer Jerusalem (16 5 Is 7 1–9). When Tiglath-Pileser III invaded his country, Hoshea overthrew Pekah (II Kings 15 29–30)[77].

Apart from Zimri and Shallum, who could not consolidate their rule at all, Zechariah, the last king of the Jehu dynasty, seemingly makes an exception. Jeroboam II, his predecessor, was undoubtedly one of the most successful kings of the Northern Kingdom. We have no information on his disappointment in military affairs. Nor have we any

---

Northern Kingdom, his Karnak inscription shows that his main target was not Judah but Israel, see ANET 242f.; Mazar, The Campaign of Pharaoh Shishak to Palestine, SVT 4 (1957), 57–66; Y. Aharoni, The Land of the Bible, 1966, 283ff.

[73] Tadmor points out that Jeroboam's military failure and the political-administrative difficulties in the kingdom led to Baasha's revolt (in: EncBib, III 1958, 774 [Hebrew]).

[74] Cf. M. F. Unger, Israel and the Aramaeans of Damascus, 1957, 57ff.; Mazar, The Wars of Israel with Aram, in: The Military History of the Land of Israel in Biblical Times, ed. J. Liver, 1965, 209 (Hebrew).

[75] According to the biblical source, Mesha's revolt broke out "after the death of Ahab" (II Kings 1 1 3 5). But from the Moabite inscription (KAI § 181 7–8), we can assume that he actually revolted in the last days of Ahab, see A. H. van Zyl, The Moabites, 1960, 139; Mazar, in: EncBib, IV 1962, 921f. (Hebrew); J. Liver, The Wars of Mesha, King of Moab, PEQ 99 (1967), 20.

[76] The tribute of Menahem is mentioned in the inscriptions of Tiglath-Pileser III, see P. Rost, Die Keilschrifttexte Tiglat-Pilesers III, 1893, 26 151; ANET 283; Levine, Two Neo-Assyrian Stelae from Iran, 18 II 5. But the whole situation is not clear enough, see Tadmor, Azriyau of Yaudi, in: Scripta Hierosolymitana, VIII 1961, 251ff.; Levine, Menahem and Tiglath-Pileser: A New Synchronism, BASOR 206 (1972), 40–42; M. Weippert, ZDPV 89, 45 n. 76. 46f.

[77] See above p. 167.

evidence of Zechariah's reverse in battle. Still, we may assume that the authority of the Jehu dynasty had already began to wane in the last years of Jeroboam's long and prosperous span, though we have no direct proof[78]. Perhaps we may compare the situation with that of the last years of Solomon's reign: although the climax of the United Kingdom was marked in the middle of his rule (I Kings 5 1)[79], the political conditions which he left were so bad that Rehoboam, his successor, could no longer prevent the defection of the northern tribes (12 16–24).

It is noteworthy that usurpation took place most frequently in the second regnal year of a king whose predecessor had experienced a grievous defeat in battle. The cases in point are Jeroboam-Nadab, Baasha-Elah, Menahem-Pekahiah and probably Saul-Ishbaal (II Sam 2 10)[80]. A. Alt[81] has maintained that this two-year reign "represents nothing more than the interval" between the death of a legitimate king and the emergence of a charismatic leader. It seems, however, that this was the best opportunity for a usurpation. The military impotence of the reigning king inspired a prospective usurper with ambitions to rule in his stead, but it was difficult for him to carry out his design at once, for a king who had reigned lengthily exercised firm control over his dominion. A new king was inexperienced, and had to make a great effort to consolidate his authority during his first years. For instance, Solomon purged all his opponents on the morrow of his accession, and thereby "the kingdom was established in the hand of Solomon" (I Kings 2 46; cf. 2 12). Therefore, a man who aimed at seizing the throne had to execute his plan before the new king could stabilize his governance of a kingdom enfeebled by the military failure of his predecessor. This is the implication of the two-year reigns of Nadab, Elah, Pekahiah and Ishbaal. Zechariah also falls into this category: he succeeded Jeroboam II but was assassinated six months later (II Kings 15 8). The

---

[78] Cf. M. Vogelstein, Jeroboam II: The Rise and Fall of his Empire, 1945, 12; Tadmor, in: Scripta Hierosolymitana, VIII 248; Ottosson, Gilead, 234. Against this view, M. Haran argues that Jeroboam died at the peak of his power and Menahem inherited his empire (The Rise and Decline of the Empire of Jeroboam ben Joash, VT 17 [1967], 280. 284f.).

[79] Cf. Malamat, JNES 22, 17.

[80] By comparison with David's regnal years in Hebron (II Sam 2 11 5 5), Ishbaal's reign is too short. Many scholars assume, therefore, that the text is corrupted, see S. R. Driver, Notes on the Hebrew Text and the Topography of the Books of Samuel, 1913², 242; H. W. Hertzberg, Die Samuelbücher, 1960², 204f. (ET I & II Samuel, 1964, 250); K.-D. Schunck, Benjamin, 1963, 122f.; but see also Noth, ÜSt, 25 n. 1; Mazar, David's Reign in Hebron and the Conquest of Jerusalem, in: Silver Festschrift, 1963, 242ff.

[81] Das Königtum, in: Kleine Schriften, II 121 (ET 246).

actual length of a two-year reign might well be only a few months, straddling two consecutive calendar years.

The safe conclusion is that the military frustration of the reigning dynasty was one of the direct causes of dynastic changes in the Northern Kingdom. In this connection, we may note that almost all of the usurpers were military men[82]: Zimri was the commander of half the chariots of the kingdom (I Kings 16 9); Omri and Jehu were the commanders of the army (16 16 and II Kings 9 5); Pekah was the king's aide-de-camp (*šalîš*)[83]; Baasha was also most probably a soldier, as otherwise he could hardly have attacked the king in the military camp (I Kings 15 27). Evidently, it was easy for these generals to mobilize power and carry out a *coup d'état*. Moreover, they could justify the usurpation from the ideological point of view. If the reigning king fails to fulfil his duty as war-leader of the nation, which is one of the most important royal tasks (cf. I Sam 8 20), is it not warranted for someone who is his superior to him in military affairs to lay claim to the throne? In fact, usurpations frequently took place in times of war (I Kings 15 27 16 15–16 II Kings 9 1–13 15 29–30): with the king occupied with external enemies, the usurper could take advantage of his unpreparedness, like Baasha, Zimri and Jehu did; at the same time, he could instantly show his prowess in battle, like Omri.

There is some evidence for the suggestion that dynastic instability in the Northern Kingdom was due to rivalry between tribes. Jeroboam I, founder of the Northern Kingdom, was an Ephraimite (I Kings 11 26). His dynasty was overthrown by Baasha "of the house of Issachar" (15 27). Although there is no decisive testimony, it appears that Omri also came from the tribe of Issachar[84]. First, the House of Omri had its estate and a second palace in Jezreel (21 1ff. II Kings 8 29 9 15ff.), a town of Issachar (Josh 19 18)[85]. Secondly, we can assume that there was a tribal affinity between Shemer, from whom Omri bought the hill of Samaria for his new capital (I Kings 16 24), and Shimron a son of

---

82 Cf. Tadmor, JWH 11, 62ff.

83 About *šalîš*, see de Vaux, Les institutions, I 187f. (ET 122); H. Donner, Der „Freund des Königs", ZAW 73 (1961), 275ff.; H. J. Cook, Pekah, VT 14 (1964), 125f.

84 Cf. W. Herrmann, Issakar, FuF 37 (1963), 24; Mazar, in: EncBib, VI 1971, 304 (Hebrew). But Noth assumes that Omri originated from foreign mercenaries, since the name Omri and Ahab are, in his opinion, not Israelite but Arabic (Die israelitischen Personennamen, 1928, 63. 222 n. 7; idem, Geschichte, 210 n. 1 [ET 230 n. 1]). His argument seems unconvincing, see Herrmann, FuF 37, 24.

85 A. T. Olmstead assumes that Omri was a native of Jezreel (History of Palestine and Syria, 1931, 368). According to B. D. Napier, not Samaria but Jezreel was the main residence of Ahab's family (The Omrides of Jezreel, VT 9 [1959], 370ff.).

Issachar (I Chron 7 1)[86]. If our assumption as to the tribal origin of the House of Omri is accepted, we may reconstruct a power struggle for the throne between Ephraim and Issachar in the first century of the kingdom.

As soon as Zimri's usurpation became known, all Israel, that is, the troops who were encamped against Gibbethon under the command of Omri, installed Omri as king of Israel (I Kings 16 16). Omri's quick reaction shows that he had sound reasons for being unable to accept Zimri's kingship, and his campaign against Zimri looks like an act to avenge Elah, son of Baasha. Although we cannot prove that Omri was related by blood to the House of Baasha[87], it is possible to assume that he took revenge on its behalf because of a common tribal origin. If so, Zimri was not a man of Issachar[88].

Omri defeated Zimri. But half of the people of Israel did not accept his kingship and followed Tibni, son of Ginath (16 21). If we identify Ginath with Gina in the El-Amarna letter[89] and with biblical Beth-haggan (II Kings 9 27), Tibni was a man of Manasseh[90]. But this is not certain, for Ginath might be the name of Tibni's father[91]. In any case, we can hardly exclude the premiss that the Northern Kingdom was divided by tribal rivalry into two groups. It is likely that Tibni was not a man of Issachar either. Now, if we suppose that Zimri and Tibni were Ephraimites, the struggle between the House of Jeroboam and of Baasha, between the House of Baasha and Zimri, between Zimri and Omri, and between Omri and Tibni could be explained as a chain of tribal feuds between Ephraim and Issachar. Unfortunately, the evidence at our disposal is too slender to prove that decisively.

We do not know to which tribe the House of Jehu belonged. Obviously, he was inspired by the resistance movement against the House of Omri headed by Elijah and Elisha. Elijah came from Tishbe in Gilead (I Kings 17 1). Abelmeholah, Elisha's home town (19 16), is generally located in northern Gilead, too[92]. It is permissible to think, therefore, that the Gileadite involvement in the power struggles in the

---

86 Cf. Mazar, in: EncBib, VI 304 (Hebrew).

87 W. Herrmann assumes that there was a blood-tie between Baasha and Omri (FuF 37, 24).

88 According to W. Herrmann, Zimri was a Canaanite, since the chariot fighters seemed to be Canaanites at that time (FuF 37, 24). But Solomon's chariot commanders were Israelites (I Kings 9 22). There is no reason to assume that Zimri was non-Israelite.

89 EA § 250 17. 21.

90 Cf. Gray, I & II Kings, 365f.

91 Cf. S. E. Loewenstamm, in: EncBib, II 1954, 483f. (Hebrew).

92 See Loewenstamm, in: EncBib, I 1950, 38f. (Hebrew); B. Oded, Israelite Transjordan during the Period of the Monarchy, Diss. Jerusalem, 1968, 19f. (Hebrew); Ottosson, Gilead, 217.

Northern Kingdom had its origin in the inception of the Jehu dynasty. Elisha's relation to Joash, the third king of that dynasty, as the authority over the king (II Kings 13 14–19; cf. 5 1–27 6 8–7 20) shows that the Gileadites had a fairly powerful influence over the dynasty. Shallum's taking over of the throne from the House of Jehu can thus be considered as the culmination of the Gileadite influence, since Shallum was from Jabesh, as Elijah was (15 10). But his one month's reign was terminated by Menahem, son of Gadi (15 14), whose surname *bœn gaḏî* is sometimes regarded as an indication of his Gileadite descent[93]. It appears, however, that he was a man of Manasseh, because Tirzah, whence he went up to Samaria (II Kings 15 14. 16), was a town within the boundary of Manasseh (Num 26 33 27 1 Josh 17 3)[94]. From his assault on Tappuah (II Kings 15 16 LXX) we may infer the Ephraimite opposition to his rise (cf. Josh 17 8)[95]. In any case, Pekahiah, son of Menahem, was murdered by Pekah, who was assisted by fifty Gileadites (II Kings 15 25). Some scholars maintain that Pekah had reigned over Gilead independently since the fall of the House of Jehu[96]. Irrespective of this suggestion, we can discern a power struggle between the Gileadites and the men of Manasseh in the changes of dynasties from Shallum to the House of Menahem and from the House of Menahem to Pekah. If so, we might assume that Hoshea's usurpation of the kingdom from Pekah was a counter-attack from the west side of the Jordan, though his tribal origin is entirely uncertain (cf. 15 30). Admittedly, it is extremely difficult to clarify thoroughly the circumstances of these dynastic changes, owing to the paucity of evidence, but the fragmentary information available would indicate that the rivalry between the Gileadites and the tribes west of the Jordan flared a good deal in the struggles for the throne from the fall of the Jehu dynasty till the end of the kingdom[97].

We cannot overlook, however, that the antagonism between the ruling class and the people sometimes triggered off revolts against the reigning dynasty. In fact, the kingdom of Jeroboam I was founded by the popular assembly of the northern tribes, which rejected the rule of the House of David when Rehoboam refused the people's demand for

---

[93] See Liver, in: EncBib, V 1968, 30f. (Hebrew).

[94] Cf. Gray, I & II Kings, 622.

[95] Cf. ibid. 622f. But Haran argues that Menahem carried out a campaign against Thapsacus on the Euphrates, as it is stated in MT (VT 17, 284ff.).

[96] Vogelstein, Jeroboam II, 6 n. 13; Cook, VT 14, 121ff.; Thiele, The Mysterious Numbers, 124ff.; idem, Pekah to Hezekiah, VT 16 (1966), 86ff.; cf. Oded, in: EncBib, VI 537f. (Hebrew).

[97] J. B. Curtis maintains that the tribes east of the Jordan were of crucial significance throughout the period of the monarchy (East is East . . ., JBL 80 [1961], 355–363).

an alleviation of the heavy taxes and *corvée* imposed by Solomon (I Kings 12 1–20)[98]. The primary cause of the revolt was, clearly, the people's resentment against the House of David, which exploited the northern tribes so burdensomely. But, judging from the role played by Ahijah the Shilonite (11 29–39), we may conclude that some antagonism in religious matters was also involved. It seems that Jeroboam's cultic reform, directed against Jerusalem (12 26–33), was actually one of the major tasks which his supporters expected him to carry out when he became king. But the later Judaean historiographer distorted the reform as the foundation of the syncretistic religion[99]. This separatist movement from the House of David headed by Jeroboam became the prototype of uprisings in the Northern Kingdom, in which the people's demands of the ruling dynasty for social justice and cultic reform proved to be ultimate agent of the dynastic change.

The downfall of the House of Omri was the consequence of this sort of antagonism. According to the biblical source, the cause of the revolt was the denial of social justice by Ahab and Jezebel (I Kings 21 1–24 II Kings 9 26) and their suppression of Yahwism (I Kings 18 4. 13. 18 21 25–26 II Kings 9 22). It is a point of interest that this dynasty is never called the "House of Omri" but always the "House of Ahab" in biblical sources (II Kings 8 18 9 7 10 10 21 13 Mic 6 16 II Chron 21 6 22 3, etc.), though Omri was its founder (I Kings 16 16. 22). Undoubtedly, the "House of Omri" was the official name, as the name Bīt-Humri in Assyrian sources indicates [100]. It seems that the use of the name "House of Ahab" reflects the tendentiousness of the source, expressing the tenet of those who regarded Ahab as responsible for injustice and apostasy[101]. Similarly, the Jehu dynasty was called the "House of

[98] From MT it is not clear whether Jeroboam played the role of the leader of the assembly (I Kings 12 2. 3. 12) or the assembly invited him after negotiations were broken off (12 20). Scholars generally, with the help of LXX, regard the second story as historical, see Montgomery & Gehman, The Books of Kings, 248f.; Malamat, Organs of Statecraft in the Israelite Monarchy (1965), in: BAR 3, 1970, 167; J. Debus, Die Sünde Jerobeams, 1967, 19ff.; H. Seebass, Zur Königserhebung Jerobeams I, VT 17 (1967), 325–333. Noth, Könige, I 1968, 268ff.; Gray, I & II Kings, 299f.

[99] See above p. 117 n. 190; cf. also Debus, Die Sünde Jerobeams, 37ff. But E. Danelius maintains that Jeroboam introduced the Egyptian cult of Hatḥor (The Sins of Jeroboam ben Nabat, JQR 58 [1967/68], 95–114. 204–223).

[100] S. Parpola, Neo-Assyrian Toponyms, 1970, 82f.; cf. also above p. 124.

[101] Cf. J. M. Miller, The Fall of the House of Ahab, VT 17 (1967), 318; in his opinion, this fact shows that "the author of the account of Jehu's rebellion was a northerner who was well aware that Omri had ascended the throne by legitimate means" but "Ahab and his sons were guilty of ruling without charismatic credentials" (ibid. 321). In our opinion, however, this phenomenon has nothing to do with the ideology of the

Jeroboam" by the prophet Amos (7 9), when he condemned Jeroboam II, but the "House of Jehu" in Hosea's denunciation of Jehu's bloodshed at Jezreel (1 4). We may conclude that, in prophetic condemnations, the dynasty was sometimes called not by the name of the founder but by the name of the king who was regarded as responsible for the transgression denounced.

As for the downfall of the House of Jeroboam and the Baasha dynasty, we have only stereotyped indictments of their syncretism by prophets (I Kings 14 7–11 16 1–4), generally regarded as Deuteronomistic[102]. We may assume, however, that this sort of charge was always levelled against the reigning dynasty by its opponents. In other words, it could be utilized for the legitimation of the new dynasty, whenever the usurpation was successfully carried out. We may learn about this situation from the words of Hosea: "They made kings, but not through me. They set up princes, but without my knowledge" (8 4); "I have given you kings in my anger, and I have taken them away in my wrath" (13 11). Needless to say, Hosea meant exactly the opposite of what the propagandists of usurpers said. The usurpers in the last decades of the Northern Kingdom are condemned here for their opportunistic manipulation of Yahweh's backing to legitimize themselves[103]. So we may take it that Yahweh's rejection of the previous dynasty and his election of the new one were always claimed by every usurper. This is nothing but the ideology of the so-called "charismatic monarchy". Was the charismatic monarchy exercised, then, in the Northern Kingdom, as Alt maintained? First, it should be pointed out that this ideology cannot be regarded as the specific tradition of the northern tribes, since we find it in the "defence of David" (see above pp. 56ff.). In other words, it was the standard assertion of whoever seized the throne from the previous dynasty. But this self-justification could be converted into a persuasive ideology when the new dynasty succeeded in proving its validity by an enduring existence. If our argument is right, the ideology of the charismatic monarchy could be established, ironically enough,

---

"charismatic monarchy", see my article, The House of Ahab, IEJ 25 (1975), 135–137.

[102] Gray analyses 14 1–18 into a local prophetic tradition (v. 1–6. 12. 17) and its expansion to the prophecy of the doom by the Deuteronomist (I & II Kings 333f.). Noth regards this section as a whole as a Deuteronomistic modification of a prophetic story (Könige, I 310ff.). As for 16 1–4, both Gray (360) and Noth (345) find in them a direct dependence on Ahijah's denunciation against Jeroboam (14 7–11).

[103] There is a view that the term *mælæḵ* in the Book of Hosea designates a deity but not a human king, see H. Cazelles, The Problem of Kingship in Osee 8:4, CBQ 11 (1949), 14–25; but we can hardly doubt that the historical situation is reflected in Hosea's words about the kings of Israel, see H. W. Wolff, Dodekapropheton, I 1961, xix.

only in Judah, not in Israel. In reality, an ideology of charismatic monarchy, such as Alt suggested, was prevalent neither in Judah nor in Israel. There is no evidence of any "charismatic king" who regarded his son's successsion as illegitimate from the ideological point of view. Moreover, so far as the biblical sources are concerned, neither Nadab nor Elah was responsible for the downfall of his dynasty. It was because of the transgression of their fathers, Jeroboam I and Baasha, whom Alt regarded as the charismatic kings that their dynasties were doomed[104]. It follows that we must dissent from the view that frequent dynastic changes in the Northern Kingdom were caused by an ideology of the charismatic monarchy which categorically rejected the dynastic principle.

How, then, did the Omrides and the House of Jehu succeed in establishing relatively stable dynasties? According to A. Alt[105], the dualism between Samaria and Jezreel, which served as capitals of the Canaanites and the Israelites, respectively, provided the Omrides with a solid foundation. In his view, Samaria was built as a city-state on the Canaanite pattern, where the dynastic monarchy was established, while from Jezreel the Omrides ruled over Israel, where the charismatic monarchy prevailed. Then, Canaanites and Israelites were united under the personal union of the king of the House of Omri. This thesis has been criticized as too inferential[106]. In any case, we can scarcely admit the view that the dynastic monarchy in Israel was Omri's innovation. It seems that the durability of the Omrides was due mainly to his victory over Tibni after a five-year civil war (I Kings 16 21–22). The situation reminds us of David's accession to the throne of Israel when Ishbaal was assassinated, after "a long war between the House of Saul and the House of David" (II Sam 3 1). Although David was finally offered the crown by the people of Israel, the ex-supporters of the House of Saul, that peaceful agreement was brought about only after he overcame Ishbaal (4 1). In a kingdom where tribal rivalry was rife, it is not surprising that a king who crushed the opposing power at the beginning of his rule could establish a more stable rule than one elected by the people's assembly, like Jeroboam (I Kings 12 20), or one who ascended the throne only by annihilating the previous royal family, like Baasha (15 29).

---

[104] According to Miller, the Deuteronomist is responsible for this description; since he was a Judaean, "he took dynastic kingship for granted" and ignored the ideal of charismatic kingship (VT 17, 320f.); cf. above pp. 177f. n. 101.

[105] Der Stadtstaat Samaria (1954), in: Kleine Schriften, III 1959, 258–302; cf. idem, Das Königtum, in: Kleine Schriften, II 123f. (ET 248f.).

[106] G. E. Wright, JNES 15 (1956), 124f.; de Vaux, RB 63 (1956), 101–106; idem, Les institutions, I 142 (ET 92); Buccellati, Cities and Nations, 181ff.; Bright, A History, 240 n. 50.

Jehu, no less, undertook a large-scale liquidation of the opposing power during the revolt. He exterminated not only all the members of the House of Omri, the royal court and officialdom (II Kings 10 11. 17; cf. I Kings 21 21–22), but also all the worshippers of Baal (II Kings 10 18–27). In this respect, the Jehu dynasty started out in the same way as the Omrides, but the political conditions after the establishment of the two dynasties were completely different. While Omri stabilized his rule by successful international policies, Jehu, who enfeebled the kingdom by his excessive bloodshed, was compelled to pay onerous tribute to Shalmaneser III of Assyria[107]. Moreover, he was defeated by Hazael of Damascus and lost much territory (II Kings 10 32–33). If the rule that the king's failure in battle generated the dynastic change, as we have demonstrated, had functioned normally, Jehu's dynasty would have been overthrown in the time of Jehoahaz, his successor. But the House of Jehu established the longest-lived dynasty in Israel and passed the throne to more than four kings. We must explain this exceptional phenomenon. First, the House of Jehu enjoyed the strong support of the prophetic circle headed by Elisha (II Kings 9 1–10 13 14–19); this certainly contributed to its dynastic establishment[108]. Secondly, in a sense, the Jehu dynasty was more successful in diplomacy, paradoxically enough, than were the Omrides. The pro-Phoenician policy of the Omrides brought about economic prosperity and political stability, but in the end resulted in calamity. On the other hand, from Assyrian sources we learn that both Jehu and Joash paid tribute to the Assyrian kings[109], a pro-Assyrian policy which seems to have strengthened the hand of the dynasty without provoking popular resistance. This was exactly what Menahem had intended but could not translate into reality (II Kings 15 19). Thirdly, we must heed the relations of the Jehu dynasty to the House of Hazael in Damascus. During the period of Assyrian absence from Syria-Palestine, Hazael defeated the House of

---

[107] ARAB I § 590. § 672; ANET 280f.

[108] Cf. M. Sekine, Literatursoziologische Beobachtungen zu den Elisaerzählungen, Annual of the Japanese Biblical Institute 1 (1975), 58f. Some scholars find in the narratives of Elijah and Elisha apologetic motives for the revolution of Jehu, see J. B. Knott, The Jehu Dynasty: An Assessment based upon Ancient Near Eastern Literature and Archaeology, Diss. Emory University, 1971, 21ff.; H. Seebass, Der Fall Naboth in 1 Reg. XXI, VT 24 (1974), 474–488.

[109] Joash's tribute to Adad-Nirari III is mentioned in a newly discovered stele from Tell al-Rimah, see S. Page, A Stela of Adad-Nirari III and Nergal-Ereš from Tell al Rimah, Iraq 30 (1968), 142 8. For the name ^{m}Ia-ʾa-su ^{kur}Sa-me-ri-na-a+a, see Malamat, On the Akkadian Transcription of the Name of King Joash, BASOR 204 (1971), 37–39. About the Syria-Palestine campaign of Adad-Nirari III, see ANET 281f.; A. R. Millard & H. Tadmor, Adad-Nirari III in Syria, Iraq 35 (1973), 57–64; Tadmor, The Historical Inscriptions of Adad-Nirari III, Iraq 35 (1973), 141–150.

Jehu in revenge for its betrayal to Assyria; it seems that both Jehu and Jehoahaz were subdued by Hazael so completely that they became his vassals (cf. 13 7)[110]. If the Jehu dynasty made a vassal-treaty with the House of Hazael, we may assume that, ironically indeed, the dynasty was protected from internal opposition by the kings of Damascus. Vassal-treaties generally included the overlord's guarantee of the throne and of the succession of members of the vassal's family[111].

So we see that the dynastic instability of the Northern Kingdom was due to the following three problems: a) the reigning dynasty's failure in military affairs; b) the rivalry between the tribes; c) the antagonism between the ruling dynasty and the people. But comparison between Judah and Israel makes it clear that tribal rivalry was the decisive factor. The Davidic kings, too, were not only defeated in battle and had to send tribute to foreign kings (I Kings 14 25–26 15 17 II Kings 8 21 12 19 14 11–14 16 6–8 23 29), but were also criticized for their infidelity to Yahweh (I Kings 11 9–13 15 3 II Kings 8 27 16 2–4 21 2–16 23 37 24 9. 19). Yet no one contested the royal throne against the House of David save Athaliah, a foreign queen, who was compelled to seize it to save her own regime (see above p. 160). But tribal rivalry did not exist in Judah. The homogeneity of the people of Judah was expressed by the term "land" in the "people of the land".

A further comparison shows that no dynasty of Israel could establish a royal-dynastic ideology such as the covenant of David. It is true that we can deduce from Ahijah's prophecy to Jeroboam (I Kings 11 38), as well as from Yahweh's promise to Jehu (II Kings 15 12), that every royal dynasty of Israel also received a divine promise of dynastic stability. But tribal rivalry overthrew dynasties one after the other, before any one of them could succeed in proving the authenticity of the prophecy. A mystical union of the royal dynasty with the capital city, such as that existing between the House of David and Jerusalem, was also lacking in the Northern Kingdom. Jeroboam established royal sanctuaries at Bethel and at Dan, the southern and northern tips of the kingdom (I Kings 12 26–33)[112]. Thereafter, the two sanctuaries stood as

---

110 Cf. A. Jepsen, Israel und Damaskus, AfO 14 (1941), 167f.; Unger, Israel and the Aramaeans of Damascus, 79; Malamat, The Aramaeans, in: Peoples of Old Testament Times, ed. D. J. Wiseman, 1973, 145.

111 About the overlord's protection of his vassal in the vassal treaties, see D. J. McCarthy, Treaty and Covenant, 1963, 33f.; F. C. Fensham, Clauses of Protection in Hittite Vassal-Treaties and the Old Testament, VT 13 (1963), 133–143. We can find the clause of the overlord's protection also in the Aramaic treaties from Sefire in the eighth century B. C., see KAI § 222 B 23–25. § 223 B 4–7; J. A. Fitzmyer, The Aramaic Inscriptions of Sefîre, 1967, 16f. 80f.

112 Y. Aharoni maintains that these temples were built, like shrines at Arad, Beersheba or Gilgal in Judah, as "an indispensable institution at the royal administrative and

"the king's sanctuary and a temple of the kingdom" (Am 7 13) until the end of the kingdom (cf. Judg 18 30 II Kings 17 28). By contrast, the capital city moved four times in the first half-century of the kingdom, from Shechem, Penuel (I Kings 12 25), and Tirzah (14 17 15 33) to Samaria (16 24). These frequent moves reflect the unstable political conditions caused by external enemies as well as by internal conflicts[113]. But the kings of Israel never attempted to found another Jerusalem, where both the political and the religious centres were situated. It is likely that the well-established ancient religious traditions eschewed involvement in political affairs, though the royal sanctuaries were clearly under the king's control (cf. I Kings 12 32–33 Am 7 10–13). This fact also testifies to the schismatic tendency which prevented any royal house from establishing a stable dynasty in the Northern Kingdom.

We must conclude, however, that there was no fundamental difference between Israel and Judah respecting the principle of succession to the throne[114].

---

military centres dominating the borders" (Arad: Its Inscriptions and Temple, BA 31 [1968], 28f.); cf. K.-D. Schunck, Zentralheiligtum, Grenzheiligtum und „Höhenheiligtum" in Israel, Numen 18 (1971), 136.

[113] N. Allan assumes that Jeroboam moved from Shechem because of the Levites, who were loyal to the House of David (Jeroboam and Shechem, VT 24 [1974], 353–356).

[114] Cf. K. Galling, Die israelitische Staatsverfassung in ihrer vorderorientalischen Umwelt, 1929, 18ff.

Chapter 8: Conclusions

Our study has demonstrated that the dynastic succession always functioned as a basic principle in every monarchy in Israel as well as in the ancient Near East. Our inquiry into the source materials has found evidence against the views that a monarchy was elective in some parts of the ancient Near East and that the monarchy of Israel was originally not hereditary but "charismatic". In other words, we have confirmed that monarchy was a political institution based on the dynastic principle, both in Israel and in the neighbouring countries. In respect of basic structure, therefore, the Israelite monarchy and the monarchies of the neighbouring countries resembled each other in many ways. This is not surprising, because the Israelites established their monarchy to "be like all the nations" (I Sam 8 5. 20).

On the other hand, we have pointed to a unique development of the monarchy in Israel. To begin with, the first monarchy was not founded without resistance. Only after the anti-monarchical argument had been overcome was Saul's monarchy established as an attempt to tide over the Philistine crisis by the unification of Israel under a monarchical regime. But, once accepted, the monarchy remained the sole system of government in Israel until foreign Powers destroyed it. Although the people participated actively in politics from time to time, the monarchy, as a political system, never became a target of criticism, let alone the dynastic principle. When they rejected the rule of the House of David, the northern tribes established one of their own. It seems that the anti-monarchical argument had been silenced by the time of David and Solomon (cf. II Sam 7 11 I Chron 17 10)[1], and was never resumed. Accordingly, we cannot accept the view that the anti-monarchical arguments in the biblical sources either stemmed from or were revived by those who suffered from the monarchy in its late period, such as the prophet Hosea or the Deuteronomist[2].

---

[1] According to J. Dus, II Sam 7 10–11a were royalist propaganda of David against the regime of *šop̱eṭîm*, which was, in his opinion, republican (Die ,,Sufeten" Israels, ArOr 31 [1963], 450); a different view on these verses is held by N. Poulssen, König und Tempel im Glaubenszeugnis des Alten Testamentes, 1967, 45ff.

[2] Against J. Wellhausen, Prolegomena zur Geschichte Israels, 1905^{6}, 264ff. (ET Prolegomena to the History of Ancient Israel, 1885, 254ff.); A. Lods, Histoire de la littérature hébraïque et juive, 1950, 317ff.; C. F. Whitley, The Sources of the Gideon

We are now in a position to reconsider the implications of the episode, where the hereditary rulership was offered to Gideon by the men of Israel, with which our study began. Regardless of the historical evaluation of the episode, it seems correct to look upon it as secondary in the Gideon cycle[3]. From the thematic point of view, it does not belong to Gideon's heroic deeds but is associated with Abimelech's kingship in Judg 9[4]. We do not know exactly whether Gideon actually established a monarchy[5]. But it is clear that he bequeathed a sort of ruling authority to his sons (9 2). The fact that Abimelech set up his kingship by slaying all the sons of Gideon but one (9 5) shows that a struggle went on for the succession to a hereditary authority. It is true that Abimelech relied heavily upon the Shechemites to establish his kingship (9 1–6). But his kingship was not founded without Gideon's authority, which he usurped. Therefore, we can consider it as a continuation of Gideon's rulership, despite a wide deviation. But when the tradition of Israel stigmatized Abimelech and his kingship as a cursed person and regime (9 56–57), a difficulty arose. No one could dispute the fact that Gideon-Jerubbaal was one of the greatest deliverers whom Yahweh sent (I Sam 12 11). How, then, was it possible to conceive the accursed kingship of Abimelech as a continuation of Gideon's rulership? It had to be proved that Gideon was not responsible for it. Thus, it becomes likely that the episode of Gideon's refusal of the hereditary

---

Stories, VT 7 (1957), 161f. M. Noth attributes the so-called anti-monarchical passages to the Deuteronomist (ÜSt 54ff.), but at the same time admits that the anti-monarchical ideology did exist in Israel before the rise of the monarchy (Geschichte Israels, 1954², 152f. 159f. [ET The History of Israel, 1960², 164f. 172f.]). About the assessment of various views on the anti-monarchical ideology in Israel, see K.-H. Bernhardt, Das Problem der altorientalischen Königsideologie im Alten Testament, 1961, 114ff.; cf. also W. H. Schmidt, Kritik am Königtum, in: G. von Rad Festschrift, 1971, 440–461 – in his opinion, Hosea's criticism must be regarded as a fundamental rejection of the monarchy (ibid. 450f.).

[3] See W. Beyerlin, Geschichte und heilsgeschichtliche Tradition im Alten Testament. Ein Beitrag zur Traditionsgeschichte von Richter VI-VIII, VT 13 (1963), 19ff.; B. Lindars, Gideon and Kingship, JThS NS 16 (1965), 321ff. But W. Richter regards these passages as a literary component of chapters 6 to 9 (Traditionsgeschichtliche Untersuchungen zum Richterbuch, 1963, 235f.).

[4] Lindars maintains that "the equation of Gideon and Jerubbaal is the result of the fusion of separate traditions, and that the offer of kingship in 8:22 belongs to the Jerubbaal strand" (JThS NS 16, 315); cf. H. Haag, Gideon-Jerubbaal-Abimelek, ZAW 79 (1967), 305–314.

[5] H. Davies suggests that Gideon actually accepted the offer of kingship, though his acceptance is "couched in the form of a pious refusal" (Judges VIII 22–23, VT 13 [1963], 151–157). A. Malamat also holds that Gideon exercised kingly rule *de facto* (The Period of the Judges, in: WHJP, III 1971, 148).

rulership was composed to deny completely any contribution on his part to Abimelech's sway.

When was the episode composed? Some scholars attribute it to the Deuteronomist[6], others find in it a reflection of the Israelite outlook in Gideon's time[7]. It offers two clues to a solution of the problem. The first is the nature of the rulership offered to Gideon. Although the term rule (משל) is carefully substituted for the term reign (מלך), it is very likely that the rulership nevertheless implied a kingship. The authority of the deliverer-*šop̱eṭîm* was never transferred to their descendants, while the kingship was always transmitted hereditarily. The second is the theocracy on which Gideon's refusal was based. According to his view, a hereditary rulership, that is, a monarchy, would encroach upon the kingship of Yahweh over Israel. It is true that Jotham's fable (Judg 9 8–15) seems to indicate that the anti-monarchical view prevailed in Gideon's day. But a careful examination shows that it is not aimed at monarchy in general but at Abimelech's kingship[8]. On the other hand, Gideon's answer is the categorical refusal of a monarchy. This idea, it seems, stemmed only from the anti-monarchical circles, which quarrelled with the royalists about the legitimacy of a monarchy in the traditions of Israel on the eve of the formation of Saul's kingdom. Moreover, Gideon's view of Yahweh's kingship is precisely identical with Samuel's opinion (see above p. 39). It appears, therefore, that both clues suggest that the episode originated in the time of Samuel.

By making a covenant with Yahweh, David accepted Yahweh as the tutelary God of the dynasty. Since this implies a suzerain-vassal relationship, as R. de Vaux[9] has pointed out, the theology of Yahweh's kingship was incorporated without further ado into the royal-dynastic ideology of the House of David. The anti-monarchical ideology was no longer a matter of grave concern under David and Solomon. Instead, the House of David, because of its Judaean origin, had to make an immense effort to legitimize its dynastic rule over Israel. This Davidic legitimation became the source of the important development of such ideologies as the covenant of David and the joint election of his House

---

[6] See above pp. 183–184 n 2.

[7] M. Buber, Königtum Gottes, 1956[3], 3ff. (ET Kingship of God, 1967, 59ff.); Noth, Geschichte, 153 (ET 165); Bernhardt, Das Problem der altorientalischen Königsideologie, 146f.; Y. Kaufmann, The Book of the Judges, 1962, 44f. 48f. 188f. (Hebrew); J. A. Soggin, Das Königtum in Israel, 1967, 17ff.; Malamat, in: WHJP, III 147; J. Bright, A History of Israel, 1972[2], 173. 175.

[8] Cf. E. H. Maly, The Jotham Fable – Anti-Monarchical?, CBQ 22 (1960), 299–305.

[9] Le roi d'Israël, vassal de Yahvé (1964), in: Bible et Orient, 1967, 287–302 (ET The King of Israel, Vassal of Yahweh, in: The Bible and Ancient Near East, 1972, 152–166).

and of Jerusalem. This development served not only as the ideological foundation of the dynastic establishment of the House of David but eventually as the foundation of the great synthesis of the ancient traditions of Israel in the exilic and the post-exilic periods.

Indices

I. TEXTS

A. Biblical Texts

1. The Hebrew Bible (MT)

II Samuel

I Kings

II Kings

II Chronicles

B. Non-Biblical Texts

1. Akkadian Texts

II. WORDS AND TERMS

III. AUTHORS

IV. GENERAL INDEX